Cook It RIGHT!

The Comprehensive Source for Substitutions, Equivalents and Cooking Tips

BARBARA NOWAK

Chicago Public Library

Sandcastle Publishing

Cook It Right: Copyright © 1995 by Barbara Nowak
Book Cover Design by Renee Rolle-Whatley
Book Cover Photograph by Christi Collier
Food Styling by Bonnie Jossen Cummings
Cooking Equipment pictured in cover photo, courtesy of Williams-Sonoma

This publication is designed to provide accurate and authoritative information with regard to the subject covered. Although the information has been researched and tested, the author assumes no responsibility for errors, inaccuracies, omissions or any other inconsistencies herein. It is sold with the understanding that the author is providing educational material and is not rendering other professional advice. Therefore, Barbara Nowak, as author, will not accept liability for the consequences of placing into action any of the strategies or methods described in Cook It Right!, which action you take at your own risk. The food additive/substitute industry is always updating its recommendations, policies and procedures. Therefore, the author and her representatives do not guarantee the accuracy of the information contained within Cook It Right! whatsoever.

Publisher's Cataloging in Publication
(Prepared by Quality Books Inc.)

Nowak, Barbara
  Cook It Right! the comprehensive source for substitutions, equivalents and cooking tips / Barbara Nowak.
      p. cm.
      Includes bibliographical references and index.
      ISBN 0-9627756-8-1

   1. Ingredient substitutions (Cookery) 2. Cookery I. Title.

TX652.N68 1994   641.5   93-86735
                                        QB194-511

Printed and bound in the United States of America

97 96 95 94   10 9 8 7 6 5 4 3 2 1

DEDICATION

*To
Paul,
with love*

⚔︎

ACKNOWLEDGEMENTS

To my parents, Tiny and Adolph Wichman,
who taught me to appreciate inventive and adventurous home cooking.

To my sister, Beverly Wichman Stewart,
who proofread the continually changing manuscript, with only an occasional glass of champagne as compensation.

To Judy McKenna,
who designed the computer program which made this book's unique format possible.

To Christi Collier,
who created the cover photographs and provided insight and encouragement.

To Rick Rittner, owner of Seafood Emporium in Woodland Hills, California,
who provided invaluable assistance on the subject of seafood.

To Carolyn Thacker,
whose experience as a cooking educator greatly improved my manuscript.

To my wonderful mother-in-law, Mary Nowak,
and to Chris Reulbach, Janet Sallee, Stephanie Wagner and Sandy Howard,
great cooks among my family and friends
who provided cooking tips for the book.

To Renee Rolle-Whatley and Gary Whatley of Sandcastle Publishing,
for making it all happen.

And to Sheba and Duke,
who were my constant companions and occasional distractions during the writing of this book.

CONTENTS

FOREWORD

Those of us who write about food are often asked tons of questions concerning our specialty. Our readers want to know what it is, where it comes from and what can they do with it once they take it home from the supermarket. Some questions we can answer, some we can't.

We in America are lucky. We have a cornucopia of wonderful fruits, vegetables, meats, spices and seasonings at our fingertips that we can bring to our tables. Unfortunately, many times it is difficult to find basic food information that is needed to use these ingredients in the best manner possible. Even if you've got shelves full of cookbooks as I do, basic information is sometimes hard to come by.

Since many of today's cooks do not have mothers or grandmothers to turn to, I am happy they now have Barbara Nowak and *Cook It Right!*

This book is both a learning tool and a delightful source of useful information that makes the cook's job a lot more fun and much less confusing. Barbara tells you everything you need to know, from A to Z, about our food supply. She covers the entire food chain, starting with Abalone and ending with Zucchini, with everything in between from Colewort (Kale) to Turbot.

Cook It Right! takes the guesswork out of preparing fresh fruit, vegetables and meats. You'll never again have to estimate how many pounds of broccoli it takes to feed a family of four or what you can substitute in a recipe if you run short of say, cream cheese.

With so much to do and so little time to do it, don't waste time and money when you cook. Make *Cook It Right!* your kitchen how-to handbook.

—Beverly Zelenka
Former Food Editor, *The Tennessean*

PREFACE

It wasn't until I got married that cooking became more than a passing thought. For a short time, Paul and I tried to live on love and his tuna casserole. But even for two young, nutrition-unconscious people, there was a limit to the amount of cheese food product we could eat.

Like most home cooks, I learned my way around the kitchen by following recipes. Because my attempts were by trial and error, there were times when even my best efforts ended in disaster. I reached the conclusion that recipes, in spite of their great promise upon first reading, don't always provide a clear path to successful results.

Cook It Right! came about because I needed a cooking compass to guide me through certain recipes. For example, the first time I made a recipe for chicken enchiladas that called for 5 cups of cooked chicken, I didn't have a clue about how much raw chicken to buy. Each time I came up with an answer (either by personal experimentation or by research) to a quandary like that, I wrote it down on an index card and filed it in a shoe box. Admittedly, this was no high-tech solution, but my card catalog helped me out hundreds of times.

All the time I was collecting information, I thought about turning it into a book. I figured that if this accumulated data was useful to me, surely other cooks could benefit from it as well.

Eventually, I got down to the task of writing. My plan was to conduct additional research and kitchen testing, develop a visual format that would make information retrieval easy, put everything on computer and complete the manuscript in four to six months. Looking back, I know it's true that ignorance is bliss. Two years later, I was still investigating new food products and techniques and updating existing entries.

Cook It Right! will be an ongoing project because food technology advances every day. But the point came when I had to end the book, turn off the computer and move on to the next stage. Now that *Cook It Right!* is in print, I believe you'll find it a valuable reference tool. And I sincerely hope that this book will also add to your daily enjoyment of cooking.

—**Barbara Nowak**

HOW TO USE THIS BOOK

Before using this book, please note the following:

All temperatures are in degrees Fahrenheit, unless otherwise indicated.

Entries are arranged alphabetically by *word*, rather than by letter. For example, bran and bran flour precede brandy; and corn grits and corn syrup appear before corn-flakes.

The information in this book is presented in column form. The first column lists the food or ingredient. If the food is also known by another name, the alternative name is presented in parentheses. Each alternative name also appears in the alphabetical listing and is cross-referenced to the primary name.

The second and third columns provide yield and equivalent information. They refer to different forms and measures of the same ingredient.

The remaining columns are shaded in green and provide the substitution information. The first shaded column tells the purpose of the substitution. For example, the substitution for flour will depend on whether it is to be used for thickening, baking, yeast bread or for combating wheat allergies.

The next two shaded columns describe possible substitute ingredients and the amounts of these substitutes you should use. Occasionally, the recommended substitutions require specific cooking instructions or explanations. In those cases, a foot-note number appears next to the substitution. The last shaded column, instructions for substituting, provides the footnoted information.

Cooking and preparation tips appear in boxed areas immediately to the side or below the food or ingredient.

Finally, we've included pages for the letters "U" and "X" because the world of food ingredients spans the globe. If you have ingredients which should be listed in these two sections, we've left you a place to record them. Then please, write to me at Sandcastle Publishing and let me know. I'm always interested in new ingredients, their equivalents and tasty substitutions.

INGREDIENT	YIELD		SUBSTITUTION			
	Amount Market Form	Yield Equivalent	For Purpose of	Amount	Substitution	Instructions
Abalone See also Fish/Shellfish	In 7" shell 6 - 8 oz.	4 servings 1 serving	All Recipes	8 oz.	8 oz. squid (1)	(1) The taste and texture are similar.
Cooking and Preparation Hints * Abalone needs to be tenderized before cooking by pounding with a mallet. * Abalone needs only brief cooking. Overcooking will make it tough.						
Acorn Squash See Squash						
Agar (Agar-Agar)	1 t. powder	1 T flakes	Gelling	2 t. powder 2 t. powder	1 T (1 envelope) gelatin granules (1) 2 - 3 T Irish moss (2)	(1) The setting properties of gelatin are not as strong as agar; about 50% more gelatin is required to achieve comparable results. (2) Irish moss should be rinsed and soaked for 10 minutes before using. Avoid using Irish moss as a substitute when an acid (lemon juice, vinegar) is called for in the recipe because the mixture will thin in the presence of an acid.
Cooking and Preparation Hints * Use 1 t. powdered agar for every 1 c. of liquid to be gelled. Soften the agar first in 1/4 c. of cold liquid, then add 3/4 c. of hot liquid to dissolve. If it is not dissolved, it will not set.				* Agar is also available in stick form. It must be simmered in liquid about 10 minutes to dissolve. 1 1/2 sticks will thicken 4 c. liquid to a pudding-like consistency.		
Alcohol See Spirits See also Wine, Beer						
All Purpose Flour See Flour						
Allspice (Jamaica Pepper) See also Herbs/Spices	6 whole berries	1/4 - 1/2 t. ground	Seasoning	1 t. ground	1/2 t. ground cinnamon + 1/8 t. ground cloves	
Cooking and Preparation Hints * Allspice complements such foods as ham, seafood, sweet potatoes, winter squash, sweet pickles and relishes, cakes, cookies, fruit pies, mincemeat and plum pudding.						
Almond See also Nuts	1 lb. in shell 1 lb. shelled 1 lb. shelled 1 lb. shelled 7/8 c. whole 1 lb. slivered 4 oz. slivered 1 lb. sliced 3 oz. sliced	1 1/4 c. shelled 3 c. whole 3 1/3 c. chopped 3 1/2 c. ground 1 c. ground 4 c. 1 c. 5 1/3 c. 1 c.	All Recipes	1 lb. shelled	1 lb. macadamia nuts shelled	(1) The macadamia is a similar, delicately flavored nut and can be easier to use because there is no skin to remove.
Cooking and Preparation Hints * Almonds should be toasted before you use them in a recipe. Toasting gives them a more intense flavor and crunchier texture. Small quantities cook faster than large quantities. Almonds will continue to brown after they've been removed from the oven, so take them out of the oven before they are completely done.				* To make almond meal, grind whole blanched almonds in a food processor or blender until finely ground. Be careful not to overprocess or the result will be almond butter. Sift out any large pieces left in the mixture. * Shelled almonds will keep for several months. To ensure freshness, store them in a sealed container in the refrigerator or freezer.		
Almond Butter	16 oz. jar	2 c.	All Recipes	1 c.	1 c. other nut butter (1)	(1) Other nut butters available include cashew, macadamia, pistachio and, of course, peanut.

INGREDIENT	YIELD			SUBSTITUTION		
	Amount Market Form	Yield Equivalent	For Purpose of	Amount	Substitution	Instructions
Almond Meal See Almond						
Almond Milk			All Recipes	3/4 c.	1 1/2 T blanched, ground almonds + 3/4 c. water + 1 t. honey (1)	(1) Blend all ingredients. The milk will last in the refrigerator for 3 to 4 days.
Almond Paste	7 oz. tube	7/8 c.	All Recipes	1 1/3 c.	1 3/4 c. ground blanched almonds + 1 1/2 c. powdered sugar + 1 egg white + 1 t. almond flavoring + 1/4 t. salt (1)	(1) Combine all ingredients and work into a stiff paste.
				Almond paste has a more distinct almond flavor. Marzipan is sweeter and smoother and can be made by combining 2 c. almond paste, 1 c. powdered sugar and 2 T corn syrup.		

Cooking and Preparation Hints
* If almond paste hardens and becomes difficult to work with, it can be softened by heating in the microwave for 2 to 3 seconds.
* Almond paste and marzipan are not interchangeable.

INGREDIENT	YIELD			SUBSTITUTION		
Anchovy (Sardelle)	2 oz. can 2 oz. can	7 - 10 fillets 3 T mashed	Seasoning	1 t. mashed	1 t. anchovy paste (1)	(1) Commercial anchovy paste contains added vinegar, spices and water and has a milder flavor than plain anchovies.

Cooking and Preparation Hints
* To remove some of the saltiness from anchovies, soak them in cool water for 10 minutes and pat dry.

INGREDIENT	YIELD			SUBSTITUTION		
Anise (Aniseed) See also Herbs/Spices			Seasoning	1 1/2 t. seeds	1 t. anise extract	

Cooking and Preparation Hints
* Crushing the seeds before adding them to a recipe will release their full flavor.
* Anise complements such foods as poultry, game, spicy meat dishes, pickles, cookies, breads and coffee cakes.

INGREDIENT	YIELD			SUBSTITUTION		
Apple See also Fruit	1 lb. fresh 1 lb. fresh 1 lb. fresh 1 medium 1 medium 1 medium 4 lb. fresh 2 lb. fresh 4 lb. fresh	2 large 3 medium 3 c. cored, sliced 1 c. cored, sliced 3/4 c. chopped 1/2 c. mashed 4 c. applesauce Filling for 9" pie 1 lb. dried	Salads Pies/Sauces	1 lb. Delicious 1 lb. Delicious 1 lb. Delicious 1 lb. Delicious 1 lb. Delicious 1 lb. Delicious 1 lb. Newton Pippin 1 lb. Newton Pippin	1 lb. Golden Delicious (1) 1 lb. McIntosh 1 lb. Stayman 1 lb. Jonathan 1 lb. Winesap 1 lb. Fuji 1 lb. Gravenstein (2) 1 lb. Greening (2)	(1) Golden Delicious apples tend not to turn brown when sliced. (2) The varieties that are best suited for pies and sauces are tart and slightly acid.

Cooking and Preparation Hints
* Apples soften 10 times faster at room temperature than when refrigerated. Refrigerate as soon as possible in a plastic bag and away from other strong-smelling foods, such as onions, to prevent transferring flavors.
* Apples that are overripe or those that have been stored improperly are plagued by mealiness and aren't good for baking or eating.
* To keep slices from turning brown, cover them with water mixed with a small amount of lemon juice or ascorbic acid. Drain and pat dry before using.

INGREDIENT	YIELD			SUBSTITUTION		
	Amount Market Form	Yield Equivalent	For Purpose of	Amount	Substitution	Instructions
Apple continued	**Cooking and Preparation Hints (continued)** * If a recipe calls for soaking dried apples, cover the apples with boiling water and soak until tender. To avoid wasting the natural sugars that are lost during soaking, use the soaking water for a liquid called for in the recipe. * Very crisp apples can be frozen whole, but their uses are limited to cooked dishes — and they last only a short period of time. To use them, do not thaw. Run cold water over them, peel, slice and use at once. Or core them and bake them whole. * To freeze apple slices, first put the slices into cold water mixed with some lemon juice or ascorbic acid. Then blanch for 2 minutes, drain and pat dry.				The slices can then be packed dry, unsweetened, or sprinkled with sugar (1/2 c. sugar per qt. of fruit). Alternatively, the apple slices can be frozen in a 40% syrup pack. Dissolve 3 c. sugar in 4 c. water and refrigerate. Add 1/2 t. ascorbic acid. Add 1/2 to 2/3 c. syrup per pt. of fruit. * Frozen apple slices will keep from 12 to 16 months. * For uncooked desserts, apples frozen in a syrup pack are preferred. However, slices frozen with sugar are easier to separate when thawing. * Frozen apple slices can be thawed in a covered container at room temperature for 2 to 3 hours or in the microwave at the defrost/low setting for 8 minutes per 1 lb. of fruit.
			Pies/Sauces	1 lb. Newton Pippin 1 lb. Newton Pippin 1 lb. Newton Pippin 1 lb. Newton Pippin	1 lb. Grimes Golden (2) 1 lb. Jonathan (2) 1 lb. Granny Smith (2) 1 lb. Fuji (2)	(3) The varieties best suited for baking are firm-fleshed and hold their shapes well.
			Baking	1 lb. Rome Beauty 1 lb. Rome Beauty 1 lb. Rome Beauty 1 lb. Rome Beauty 1 lb. Rome Beauty 1 lb. Rome Beauty 1 lb. Golden Delicious	1 lb. Winesap (3) 1 lb. Greening (3) 1 lb. Newton Pippin (3) 1 lb. Stayman (3) 1 lb. Granny Smith (3) 1 lb. York (3) 1 lb. Winesap	
			Applesauce	1 lb. Golden Delicious	1 lb. Newton Pippin	
Apple Juice			All Recipes	1 c.	1 c. apple cider (1)	(1) Apple cider is not pasteurized or heated and hermetically sealed, as is apple juice. Hard cider has attained some degree of alcohol fermentation.
	Cooking and Preparation Hints * Freeze individual boxes of apple juice for lunch boxes. The juice will thaw by lunch time		and, meanwhile, will keep the other food cool. * Frozen apple juice makes a naturally sweet juice pop for snacks or dessert.			
Apple Pie Spice See also Herbs/Spices			Seasoning	1 t.	1/2 t. ground cinnamon + 1/4 t. ground nutmeg + 1/8 t. ground allspice + 1/8 t. ground cardamom	
Applesauce	16 oz. jar	2 c.		**Cooking and Preparation Hints** * Before freezing homemade applesauce, add 1/2 t. ascorbic acid for every 1 c. of sugar used in the applesauce recipe. * Applesauce can be used in place of fats in many baked goods. See Fats.		

INGREDIENT	YIELD		SUBSTITUTION		
	Amount Market Form	Yield Equivalent	For Purpose of	Amount	Substitution	Instructions

Apricot (See also Fruit)

Amount Market Form	Yield Equivalent
1 lb. fresh	8 - 12 apricots
1 lb. fresh	3 c. sliced
6 lb. fresh	1 lb. dried
16 oz. can	2 c. drained
6 oz. dried	1 c.
6 oz. dried	2 c. cooked

Cooking and Preparation Hints
* To hasten ripening of fresh apricots, store them in a closed paper bag at room temperature.
* To peel fresh apricots, put them in boiling water for 20 seconds. Cool them quickly in cold water, and the skin will come off easily.
* When chopping dried apricots in the food processor, toss them with a little of the flour called for in the recipe to prevent sticking.
* To prevent sticking when chopping dried apricots with a knife or kitchen scissors, oil the blades or dip them in flour frequently.
* When using dried apricots in baked goods, toss them with flour to keep them from settling to the bottom of the batter or dough during baking.
* Dried apricots will keep unopened at room temperature for 2 to 5 months. Opened packages will keep

Instructions:
for 2 weeks. For longer storage, keep opened fruit in an airtight container in the refrigerator.
* Fresh apricots can be frozen peeled or unpeeled. For peeled, just cut in half and remove pits. For unpeeled, blanch for 30 seconds to prevent skin from toughening. Chill in cold water, halve and pit. From there, halves can be frozen unsweetened in a water solution containing 2 t. lemon juice or 1/2 t. ascorbic acid per qt. of water. Or they can be juice-packed in vitamin C-enriched unsweetened apple juice. For pies and cooked desserts, a dry sugar pack is preferred. Mix 1/2 c. sugar and 1/4 t. ascorbic acid for each qt. of apricots. Alternatively, apricots can be frozen in a 40% syrup pack. Dissolve 3 c. sugar and 3/4 t. ascorbic acid in 4 c. water and refrigerate. Add 1/2 to 2/3 c. syrup per pt. of fruit. Frozen apricots will keep 12 to 16 months.

Arrowroot

For Purpose of	Amount	Substitution
Thickening	1 T	1 T cornstarch (1)
	1 T	2 T all purpose flour (2)
	1 T	2 t. kudzu (3)

Instructions:
(1) Cornstarch has slightly less thickening power than arrowroot, so you may have to use a little more.
(2) Flour-thickened sauces will be cloudy compared to those thickened with arrowroot. Also, while arrowroot is added at the end of preparation, flour must be added sooner and cooked longer. Flour does not work well as a thickener in the presence of acidic fruits such as strawberries, cranberries and tart cherries.
(3) To use, crush kudzu into a powder and dissolve in a small amount of cold liquid. Add to the liquid to be thickened and bring to a high heat stirring constantly.

Cooking and Preparation Hints
* Arrowroot produces thickened sauces that are transparent with a delicate texture — excellent for fruit sauces and fruit tarts. Because arrowroot thickens below the boiling point, it is also suited for egg sauces and other sauces that should not boil.
* Use arrowroot as a thickener only when the sauce will be served within 10 minutes of preparation. Arrowroot has no holding power and can't be reheated successfully.
* Arrowroot should be dissolved in a cold liquid before being heated or added to a hot mixture.
* Arrowroot attains its maximum thickening between 158° and 176°. Higher temperatures or extended heating will cause thinning. Thinning will also occur because of excessive stirring.
* In contrast to other starches, arrowroot is flavorless and does not have to be cooked at length to remove the raw taste.
* Use about 1 T arrowroot per 1 c. of liquid to produce a medium-thick sauce.

Artichoke (Globe Artichoke) — See also Jerusalem Artichoke, Vegetables

Amount Market Form	Yield Equivalent
2 - 3 oz. fresh	1 small (baby)
8 - 10 oz. fresh	1 medium
15 - 20 oz. fresh	1 large
6 large	1 1/2 c. pulp
15 oz. can hearts	1/4 c. drained
15 oz. can hearts	1 c. diced

Cooking and Preparation Hints
* If your artichokes are not as fresh as they should be, you can sweeten them a bit and help retain their color by adding a pinch of sugar and 1/4 t. salt to each 1 c. of cooking liquid.
* Don't use cast iron or aluminum pots to cook artichokes or anything but stainless steel knives. They will turn your artichokes black.
* To keep artichokes from darkening when cooked, place them in a large pot of cold water, add 1 T

Instructions:
vinegar or lemon juice for each 1 qt. of water and let stand 1 hour before cooking.
* Cooking artichokes in broth instead of water will add flavor.
* Don't freeze uncooked artichokes. They will turn brown, and the taste and texture will suffer.
* To freeze whole artichokes, pull off coarse outer leaves and cut off 1" from tops and stems. Wash. Blanch 8 to 10 minutes, adding 1 T ascorbic acid or 1/2 c. lemon juice to each 2 qts. of water. Chill and

INGREDIENT	YIELD		SUBSTITUTION			
	Amount Market Form	Yield Equivalent	For Purpose of	Amount	Substitution	Instructions

Artichoke continued

Cooking and Preparation Hints (continued)
pack in pairs in freezer bags. To use, put frozen artichokes into boiling water, return to a boil and cook for 12 to 15 minutes.
* To freeze hearts, cut to edible pale leaves. Blanch 2 to 5 minutes, adding 1 T ascorbic acid or 1/2 c. lemon juice to each 2 qts. of water. Chill and pack in freezer bags.
* To freeze artichoke bottoms, cook trimmed whole artichokes about 20 min-

utes until tender. Cool in ice water, pull off all leaves and discard the choke. Trim bottoms and pat dry. Wrap individually in plastic wrap and pack in freezer bags. Thaw bottoms covered in the refrigerator for 4 to 5 hours or at room temperature for 2 hours. Alternatively, artichoke bottoms can be stuffed and baked frozen.
* Frozen artichokes will keep 10 to 12 months.

INGREDIENT	Amount Market Form	Yield Equivalent	For Purpose of	Amount	Substitution	Instructions
Arugula	1/2 oz. fresh	1/2 c.				
Ascorbic Acid (Vitamin C)	1/8 t. powder/crystals 1/4 t. powder/crystals 1/2 t. powder/crystals 1 t. powder/crystals	375 mg tablet 750 mg tablet 1500 mg tablet 3000 mg tablet	Antidarkening	1/4 t. powder	1 t. lemon juice (1)	(1) Other citrus juices such as lime, orange or grapefruit may be used as well. However, juices tend to impart their own flavor in many cases because the quantity needed is so large.

Ascorbic Acid — Cooking and Preparation Hints
* Ascorbic acid tablets must be crushed and dissolved in a small amount of water before use. They may be more difficult to dissolve than the powder and crystalline forms.
* Syrups and other liquids made with the tablet form of ascorbic acid may be cloudy as a result of the filler substances used in tablets.

INGREDIENT	Amount Market Form	Yield Equivalent	For Purpose of	Amount	Substitution	Instructions
Asparagus See also Vegetables	1 lb. fresh 1 lb. fresh 1 1/2 - 2 lb. fresh 15 oz. can 15 oz. can 10 oz. frozen, cut	16 - 20 spears 3 c. 1" pieces 4 servings 12 - 18 spears 1 3/4 c. pieces 2 c. pieces				

Asparagus — Cooking and Preparation Hints
* To revive wilted asparagus, cut an X in the butt end of each spear and stand them in a container of water for about an hour.
* Peeling asparagus offers several advantages:
  (1) More of the asparagus can be used because, by peeling, the entire stalk is tender.
  (2) Peeled asparagus cooks more quickly.
  (3) Peeled asparagus stays greener and fresher when cooked.
* The best way to cook asparagus spears is to stand them on their ends in a covered pot in a couple inches of water. Cook for about 7 minutes — a minute or two more for fatter stalks, a minute or two less for thinner stalks.
* When microwaving asparagus, uncover the container the moment the asparagus is done or the spears will continue to cook and become mushy.
* Herbs and spices that complement asparagus include nutmeg, mustard seed, dry mustard, sesame seed, tarragon and black pepper.
* The best way to store asparagus is standing upright in a plastic bag with the cut ends on a damp towel. Do not close the bag tightly because too much humidity will hasten spoilage.
* To freeze asparagus, sort spears according to thickness. Wash. Trim stalk ends. Blanch 2 minutes for small spears, 3 minutes for medium and 4 minutes for large. Dry. Cover a baking sheet with plastic wrap and lay the spears on the sheet in a single layer. Cover with more plastic wrap and freeze until firm. Pack spears in freezer bags. To cook frozen asparagus, cook it in boiling water for 5 to 7 minutes.
* Frozen asparagus will last from 6 to 8 months.

| **Aubergine** See Eggplant | | | | | | |

A-5

INGREDIENT	YIELD			SUBSTITUTION			
	Amount Market Form	Yield Equivalent	For Purpose of	Amount	Substitution		Instructions
Avocado	1 lb.	2 medium					
	1 lb.	2 1/2 c. chopped					
	1 medium	1 - 1 1/4 c. chop'd					
	1 medium	3/4 c. mashed					
	10 oz. frozen mashed	1 1/4 c. defrosted					

Cooking and Preparation Hints

* It is not true that you can speed up the ripening of an avocado in the microwave. The best way to ripen it is by placing it in a paper bag with a banana or banana peel. The peel gives off a natural gas that will hasten ripening.
* The easiest way to remove the pit from an avocado is to slice the avocado in half lengthwise and separate the halves. Insert the blade (not the point) of a large knife into the pit and twist the knife. The pit should come out easily.
* It is not true that placing an avocado pit into mashed avocado will prevent discoloration. You can postpone discoloration of cut avocados a couple of ways:
(1) By dropping avocado pieces into cold water, draining, and placing in a covered bowl. This will be effective for several hours.
(2) By sprinkling slices with lemon or lime juice.
* Avocados should not be heated because they develop a bitter taste. When using avocados in a hot entree, it's better to have the avocados at room temperature and add them at the end of the recipe preparation.
* For the best flavor, avocados should be served at room temperature.
* Avocados should not be frozen whole because they become watery. The best way to freeze them is mashed with added lemon juice or ascorbic acid. Frozen avocado will last up to 2 months.

INGREDIENT	YIELD		SUBSTITUTION			
	Amount Market Form	Yield Equivalent	For Purpose of	Amount	Substitution	Instructions
Bacon	1 lb. 1 lb. 1 lb. 1 lb. 1 lb. 1 regular strip 1/4 lb. back bacon	35 thin strips 16-20 regular strips 12-16 thick strips 1 c. bacon fat 1 1/2 c. fried chop'd 1 T fried, chopped 1 c. cracklings	All Recipes	1 oz. 1 oz. 1 strip fried, chop'd 1 strip fried, chop'd	1 oz. Canadian bacon 1 oz. ham 1 T commercial bacon bits 1 T artificial bacon bits	extend that time by a couple of weeks if you pre-cook the bacon until it is not quite done. Then wrap it in paper towels and freezer wrap. * Some recipes benefit from removing the salt and smoky taste from the bacon. To do so, blanch it for 5 to 8 minutes, drain, refresh in cold water and dry in paper towels.

Cooking and Preparation Hints
* An unopened package of bacon should last in the refrigerator for a week beyond its printed last date of sale. An opened package will maintain its quality when refrigerated for up to 1 week.
* Bacon does not freeze well because the salt in the bacon causes the fat to turn rancid. Store bacon in the freezer no more than 3 to 4 weeks. You can

INGREDIENT	YIELD		SUBSTITUTION			
Baker's Cheese See also Cheese			All Recipes	8 oz. 8 oz. 8 oz. 8 oz. 8 oz.	8 oz. dry cottage cheese 8 oz. cream'd cottge cheese, drain'd 8 oz. hoop cheese 8 oz. pot cheese 8 oz. farmer cheese (1)	(1) Farmer cheese is drier than baker's cheese.
Baking Powder			All Recipes	1 t. 1 t.	1/4 t. baking soda + 1/2 t. cream of tartar 1/4 t. baking soda + 1/2 c. acidic liquid (1)	(1) You can use acidic liquids such as sour milk, molasses or vinegar. When making this substitu-tion, reduce the amount of total liquid called for in the recipe by 1/2 c. (2) Double-acting baking powder should be used in recipes that call for baking powder.
			Replacing single-acting powder	1 t. single-acting powder	2/3 t. double-acting baking powder (2)	

Cooking and Preparation Hints
* The shelf life for baking powder is 6 to 18 months. To check for effectiveness, dissolve 1/2 t. baking powder in 1/4 c. hot water. If the water bubbles, it's still fresh.
* The amount of baking powder should be reduced for high-altitude baking. At 3,000 ft. above sea level, reduce baking powder 1/8 t. for every t.

called for in the recipe; at 5,000 ft. reduce baking powder 1/8 to 1/4 t. for every t. called for; and at 7,000 ft. reduce by 1/4 t. for each t. called for.
* In spite of the fact that baking powder increases the volume of cakes, too much will do just the opposite and make the cake fall.
A rule-of-thumb is 1 t. baking powder for every 1 c. of flour used in the recipe.

INGREDIENT	YIELD		SUBSTITUTION			
Baking Soda (Sodium Bicarbonate)			All Recipes/ Reducing Sodium	1 t.	1 t. potassium bicarbonate	

Cooking and Preparation Hints
* Baking soda is added to recipes to react with acid ingredients such as sour cream, buttermilk, yogurt, vinegar, molasses, honey or lemon juice to pro-duce carbon dioxide.

Without the baking soda or without enough, a cake will fall and taste doughy. As a rule-of-thumb, use about 1/4 t. of baking soda per 1 c. of flour.
* Baking soda should be added to the dry ingredients in a recipe rather

A B C D E F G H I J K L M N O P Q R S T U V W X Y Z

INGREDIENT	YIELD Amount Market Form	YIELD Yield Equivalent	For Purpose of	SUBSTITUTION Amount	SUBSTITUTION Substitution	Instructions
Baking Soda continued	**Cooking and Preparation Hints (continued)** than to the liquid to prevent the immediate loss of carbon dioxide that results when baking soda and any liquid are mixed.				* The reaction between baking soda and the acid called for in the recipe occurs very quickly. Be sure to bake the batter immediately after mixing.	
Banana See also Fruit	1 lb. fresh 1 lb. fresh 1 lb. fresh 1 lb. dried	3 medium 2 1/2 c. sliced 1 1/2 - 2 c. mashed 4 1/2 c. slices	Flavoring	2 medium	1/2 - 1 t. banana extract (1)	(1) This amount can enhance the flavor of fresh bananas used in a recipe (such as banana bread) or can flavor a dish where no bananas are used (such as custard).
			Cooking and Preparation Hints * To freeze, simply peel and wrap each whole banana in foil or plastic wrap. When thawed, it will be softer and darker than a fresh banana. Mash or puree as			needed. * To freeze mashed bananas, add a little lemon juice or 1/4 t. ascorbic acid for each c. of bananas. They will keep in the freezer for several months.
Barbecue Sauce	18 oz. bottle	1 3/4 c.	All Recipes	2 c. bottled	2 c. tomato sauce + 1/4 c. red wine vinegar + 1/4 c. chopped onion + 1/4 c. brown sugar + 1 clove garlic + 2 t. Worcestershire sauce + 1 t. dry mustard + 1/2 t. chili powder + 1/2 t. salt (1)	(1) Mix all ingredients and simmer 20 minutes.
Barley See also Grains	1 lb. pearl barley 1 c. pearl barley 1 c. pearl barley	2 c. uncooked 3 1/2 c. cooked 6 servings	**Cooking and Preparation Hints** * Herbs and spices that complement barley include cinnamon, parsley, thyme, marjoram and garlic. * When cooking barley, use 2 times as much liquid as grain. * When using in soup, add about 1 1/2 c. of cooked barley for every 2 qt. of soup.			
Barley Flour See Flour						
Basil See also Herbs/Spices	1/2 oz. fresh leaves 1 T chopped fresh	1 c. chopped 1 t. dried	**Cooking and Preparation Hints** * Heat turns fresh basil black. It's best to add basil to warm foods at the last minute. * Basil attains its strongest flavor when in blossom. This is the best time to add it to oils or vinegars. * Use younger basil leaves for pestos. * Basil complements such foods as poultry, egg dishes,			tomato sauces, tomatoes, artichokes, eggplant, spinach and zucchini. * Fresh basil can be frozen for up to 1 year. Remove the leaves from the stems, put them in boiling water for 2 seconds, then rinse in cold water. Pat dry and put the leaves in plastic freezer bags.

INGREDIENT	YIELD			SUBSTITUTION		
	Amount Market Form	Yield Equivalent	For Purpose of	Amount	Substitution	Instructions
Bass, Freshwater See also Fish/Shellfish, Sea Bass, Striped Bass			All Recipes	1 lb. 1 lb.	1 lb. freshwater perch 1 lb. tilapia	

Cooking and Preparation Hints
* Herbs and spices that complement freshwater bass include parsley, black pepper, bay leaf, tarragon, dill weed, chives and basil.
* Freshwater bass can be frozen for 7 to 9 months.

Bay Leaf See also Herbs/Spices	1 whole dried 1 whole dried	1/4 t. cracked 1/8 - 1/4 t. ground				before serving.

As a rule-of-thumb, use about 1/6 of a dried bay leaf (or 1/3 of a fresh leaf) to season 1 qt. of soup, stock or stew.
* Whole bay leaves should be removed from food before serving.
* Bay leaf complements such foods as poultry, game, beef, lamb, veal, ham, crab, shrimp, soups, stews, artichokes, cabbage, carrots, onions, potatoes, green beans, eggplant, tomatoes and marinades.

Cooking and Preparation Hints

Bean Curd See Tofu						
Bean Sprout See Sprout						
Beans, Dried See also Individual listings	1 lb. large 1 lb. large 1 c. large 1 lb. small 1 lb. small 1 c. small 3 c. cooked	2 1/2 c. uncooked 6 1/4 c. cooked 2 1/2 c. cooked 2 c. uncooked 6 c. cooked 3 c. cooked 6 servings	All Recipes	1 c. dried	1 c. dried of most other varieties (1)	(1) Most varieties of dried beans can be used interchangeably in recipes. They have differing tastes but similar cooking qualities.

Cooking and Preparation Hints
* Dried beans can be stored in the cupboard for up to 1 year. After that, they lose their flavor, become hard and take longer to cook.
* The alternative method to soaking beans overnight is to boil hard in a large amount of water for 3 to 5 minutes, then let the beans stand in the water for 1 hour.
* Because older beans take longer to cook, new and old beans should not be mixed.
* Dried beans will cook faster without the addition of salt to the cooking water.
* You can always add salt during the last 10 minutes of cooking.
* To shorten cooking time, add acids such as tomatoes or vinegar to beans only after they have softened.
* Sometimes, very hard water will lengthen the cooking time for beans.

In this case, add 1/8 t. baking soda for each 1 c. of beans.
* To prevent beans from splitting while cooking, the water should be just barely simmering. Also, letting the beans cool in the cooking water will keep them from splitting.
* If you marinate beans for 2 hours before cooking, you don't have to flavor them during cooking.
* By using a pressure cooker, you can cut cooking time for beans. However, don't cook more than 1 lb. of beans at a time because they can froth up and block the safety valve. You can reduce the foaming by adding 1 to 2 t. oil to the cooking water.
* The "discomforting" effect of beans can be substantially reduced by the following: Boil beans for 10 minutes using 5 times the amount of water to beans; soak them 8 to 10 hours; discard soaking water and prepare according to the recipe.

A B C D E F G H I J K L M N O P Q R S T U V W X Y Z

| INGREDIENT | YIELD | | | Amount | SUBSTITUTION | |
	Amount Market Form	Yield Equivalent	For Purpose of		Substitution	Instructions
Beau Monde Seasoning			Seasoning	3/4 t.	1/2 t. onion powder + 1/4 t. celery salt	
	Cooking and Preparation Hints		* Use 1/2 to 1 t. for a dish serving 4 people.			
Beef See also Meat	1 lb. raw	2 c. ground	Pot Roast	3 lb. pot roast	3 lb. top round roast	(1) For best results cook ahead, then reheat before carving.
	4 oz. raw	3 oz. cooked		3 lb. pot roast	3 lb. bottom round roast	
	5 oz. dried	24 slices		3 lb. pot roast	3 lb. chuck roast	
	5 oz. dried	2 c. shredded		3 lb. pot roast	3 lb. eye of round roast (1)	
	1 lb. flank steak	4 servings		3 lb. pot roast	3 lb. brisket (1)	
	1 lb. porterhouse steak	2 1/2 servings	All Recipes	1 lb. ground beef	1 lb. ground pork	
	1 lb. ribeye steak	3 servings		1 lb. ground beef	1 lb. ground veal	
	1 lb. round steak (full cut)	3 servings		1 lb. ground beef	1 lb. ground lamb	
	1 lb. brisket	3 servings		1 lb. ground beef	1 lb. ground turkey (2)	(2) When substituting ground turkey, use slightly more seasoning than called for in the recipe to enhance the turkey's milder flavor. Also, the different moisture content of ground turkey can affect recipes; if the ground turkey appears soft, decrease the liquid in the recipe by 1 to 2 T.
	1 lb. short ribs	1 1/2 - 2 1/2 servings				
	1 lb. sirloin steak	3 servings				
	1 lb. T-bone steak	2 servings				
	1 lb. tenderloin	3 servings				
	1 lb. boneless top loin steak	3 servings				
	1 lb. eye of rnd roast	4 servings				
	1 lb. rib roast	2 servings				
	1 lb. boneless rump rst	4 servings				
	1 lb. chuck pot roast	2 1/2 servings				

Cooking and Preparation Hints

* Cuts from the less-used muscles along the back of the animal (the rib and loin sections) are more tender than cuts from the active muscles such as shoulder (chuck), flank and round.
* Ground beef is usually labeled with the fat content — which cannot exceed 30%. If labeled "lean" or "extra lean," the fat content can't exceed 22.5%. If there is no lean-to-fat ratio on the package, use the following as a guideline: ground round is the leanest; ground sirloin has more fat; and ground chuck has the most fat.
* For a juicier hamburger, add cold water to the beef before grilling. Add 1/2 c. of water to 1 lb. of meat.
* Instead of pan-frying meatballs, bake them on a jelly-roll pan at 350° to 375°. They take less attention and maintain their shape just as well.
* For a nutritional change of pace, use oat bran or wheat bran in place of

bread crumbs as a filling for meatloaf. Add 1/2 c. bran for 2 lb. of ground beef.
* Herbs and spices that complement beef include black pepper, thyme, oregano, marjoram, bay leaf, garlic, onion powder, chili powder, parsley, cumin, red pepper, rosemary, dry mustard, ginger and curry.
* When you defrost ground beef in the microwave, stop at the point where the meat still has ice crystals but can be broken up with a fork. This way, the meat retains its natural juices.
* The recommended storage time for beef in the refrigerator is: 3 to 4 days for roasts and steaks; 1 to 2 days for ground; and 3 to 4 days for leftover cooked beef.
* Beef can be stored in the freezer for: 6 to 12 months for roasts and steaks; 3 to 4 months for ground; 6 to 8 months for cubes or pieces; and 2 to 3 months for leftover cooked beef.

INGREDIENT	YIELD		SUBSTITUTION			
	Amount Market Form	Yield Equivalent	For Purpose of	Amount	Substitution	Instructions
Beef Stock See Stock						
Beer See also Spirits			All Recipes	1 c. 1 c.	1 c. nonalcoholic beer (1) 1 c. broth	(1) Nonalcoholic beer is a better substitute for regular beer than a light beer because both nonalcoholic and regular beer contain starches, the solid part of the beer which will provide better flavor. With light beer the flavor boils off faster.
	Cooking and Preparation Hints * When cooking with beer, choose one with a distinctive flavor. Cooking with mass-marketed commercial beers will have the same effect as cooking with water.				* The longer you cook a dish made with beer, the less intense the beer flavor will be. However, the essential taste will remain; if you choose a bitter-tasting beer, the bitterness will remain.	
Beet (Garden Beet) See also Vegetables	2 lb. fresh with tops 2 lb. fresh with tops 1 lb. fresh w/o tops 1 lb. fresh w/o tops 1 lb. fresh w/o tops 16 oz. can whole 8 oz. can sliced	3 medium 3 oz. trim'd greens 2 c. sliced 2 c. chopped 3-4 servings 2 c. 1 c.	**Cooking and Preparation Hints** * When preparing fresh beets, do not peel or cut them before cooking and cut the greens above the root. This will help to keep their color from bleeding out. * Adding vinegar to the water in which beets are boiled will help the beets retain their color as well as eliminate the cooking odor. * Herbs and spices that complement beets include garlic, cloves, allspice, bay leaf, chives, dill weed, thyme and grated orange peel. * When the leaves and bulbs are attached, the leaves sap root moisture and nutrients from the		bulbs. For that reason, remove the leaves and store the leaves and bulbs separately in plastic bags. They can be refrigerated up to 1 week. * To freeze beets, trim tops leaving 1/2" of stems. Scrub and wash and cook until tender (about 35 to 45 minutes). Peel. Leave whole or cut as desired. Chill and pack. They can be frozen for up to 10 months. * Beets can stain your fingers and your cutting board. To clean your hands, wet them then rub with salt. Wash with soap and water. For your cutting board, wipe it with a little bleach.	
Beet Greens See also Greens, Cooking	1 lb. fresh, trimmed 1 lb. fresh, trimmed	4 c. cooked 4 servings	**Cooking and Preparation Hints** * The tough stems and ribs of mature greens should be removed and discarded.		* Before freezing, remove tough stems and imperfect leaves. Blanch for 1 1/2 to 2 minutes. Chill and pack.	
Belgian Endive (Witloof) See also Vegetables	1 head 2 heads	12 - 18 leaves 1 serving cooked	**Cooking and Preparation Hints** * After cutting, rinse the Belgian endive in cold water to prevent the cut edges from turning dark.			
Bell Pepper (Sweet Pepper) See also Vegetables	1 large 15 oz. roasted 15 oz. roasted	1 c. chopped 2 c. drained 1 3/4 c. chopped	All Recipes	1 c. chopped 1 c. chopped 1 1/2 lb. fresh 3 T chopped 1 T dried, rehydrated	1 c. chopped mild Anaheim chili (1) 1 c. chopped Poblano chili 4 oz. dried flakes (2) 1 T dried flakes (2) 2 T chopped pimiento	(1) The result will be slightly hotter. (2) Rehydrate before using.
	Cooking and Preparation Hints * To make raw green peppers more digestible, core and seed them, and blanch for 1 minute. Put immediately into cold water to stop the cooking				process to maintain their raw quality. * With the exception of the purple variety, bell peppers of all colors can be substituted for each other. The purple peppers turn a khaki	

INGREDIENT	YIELD		FOR PURPOSE OF	SUBSTITUTION		
	Amount Market Form	Yield Equivalent		Amount	Substitution	Instructions

Bell Pepper continued

Cooking and Preparation Hints (continued)
color when heated.
* Herbs and spices that complement bell peppers include basil and oregano.
* Don't store bell peppers next to ethylene-producing fruits and vegetables such as apples, pears, cantaloupe and tomatoes. They will hasten ripening and reduce storage life.
* To freeze bell peppers, first core and seed them. You can leave the peppers whole or slice or chop them. Pack them in small containers and freeze. They will keep for 8 to 12 months.

Beurre Manié

	Yield Equivalent	For Purpose of	Substitution	Instructions
1 T	1 T butter + 1 T flour			* Do not boil. * Add 1 T beurre manié for each 1 c. of liquid to achieve a thin consistency. Add 2 T beurre manié per 1 c. of liquid for a medium to thick consistency. * Beurre manié can be frozen in balls to have on hand for last minute thickening purposes.

Cooking and Preparation Hints
* Beurre manié (equal parts butter and flour kneaded into a paste) is especially good for thickening sauces at the end of the cooking process and for rescuing sauces that have not thickened properly.
* Do not use it for sauces with long cooking times.
* Stir beurre manié into sauce over low heat.

Biscuit Mix

For Purpose of	Amount	Substitution	Instructions
All Recipes	9 c.	8 c. sifted flour + 1/4 c. baking powder + 4 t. salt + 1 c. shortening (1)	(1) Sift the dry ingredients together, then cut in the shortening until it is the consistency of coarse cornmeal. The mixture should be stored covered tightly in the refrigerator. To make biscuits, add 2/3 to 3/4 c. milk for each 2 c. biscuit mixture.

Cooking and Preparation Hints
* Do not overmix biscuit dough or the biscuits will be tough.

Black Bean
(Turtle Bean)
See also Beans, Dried

Amount Market Form	Yield Equivalent
1 lb. dried	2 c. uncooked
1 c. dried	3 c. cooked
16 oz. can	2 c. with liquid
16 oz. can	1 1/2 c. drained
3 c. cooked	6 servings

Black-Eyed Pea
(Cowpea)
See also Beans, Dried

Amount Market Form	Yield Equivalent
1 lb. fresh shelled	2 1/3 c.
1 lb. dried	2 1/2 c. uncooked
1 lb. dried	6 1/2 c. cooked
1 c. dried	2 1/2 c. cooked
15 1/2 oz. can	1 1/2 c. drained
10 oz. frozen	1 1/2 c. cooked

Cooking and Preparation Hints
* To freeze fresh black-eyed peas, shell and sort by size. Discard any immature or tough peas. Blanch 1 to 2 minutes, chill and pack. They can be stored for up to 12 months.

Blackberry
See also Fruit

Amount Market Form	Yield Equivalent	For Purpose of	Amount	Substitution
1 pt. fresh	3/4 lb.	All Recipes	1 c.	1 c. boysenberries
1 pt. fresh	1 3/4 c.		1 c.	1 c. dewberries
1 pt. fresh	3 servings		1 c.	1 c. loganberries
17 oz. can	2 c.		1 c.	1 c. youngberries
16 oz. frozen	2 c.			

Cooking and Preparation Hints
* To keep these highly perishable berries at their prime in the refrigerator, spread them in a single layer on a jelly-roll pan lined with paper towels. Store them in the refrigerator uncovered.
* Blackberries can be frozen unsweetened. Quick-freeze them on a tray for 2 hours, then transfer to airtight plastic storage bags. They will last for up to 6 months. They can also be frozen in a dry sugar pack (3/4 c. sugar per 1 qt. berries) or in a 40% to 50% syrup pack. Dissolve 3 to 4 3/4 c. sugar in 4 c. water and refrigerate. Add 1/2 to 2/3 c. syrup for each pt. of berries. Blackberries in syrup can be frozen for up to 16 months.

INGREDIENT	YIELD			SUBSTITUTION		
	Amount Market Form	Yield Equivalent	For Purpose of	Amount	Substitution	Instructions
Blackfish See Tautog						
Blue Cheese See also Cheese	4 oz.	1 c. crumbled	All Recipes	8 oz. 8 oz. 8 oz.	Roquefort cheese Gorgonzola cheese Stilton cheese (1)	(1) Stilton has undertones of cheddar.

Cooking and Preparation Hints
* To keep blue cheese from crumbling while cutting, try using a heavy thread, dental floss or wire.
* Before refrigerating blue cheese, wrap it in a damp cloth. The cloth replaces moisture that is lost and, at the same time, allows some air to reach the cheese.
  Cover the cheese with a cheese dome if you have one. If your blue cheese is underripe, let it sit at room temperature for 1 to 2 days before refrigerating.

INGREDIENT	YIELD			SUBSTITUTION		
Blueberry See also Fruit	1 pt. fresh 1 pt. fresh 1 pt. fresh 14 oz. can 10 oz. frozen	3/4 lb. 1 3/4 - 2 c. 3 servings 1 1/2 c. 1 1/2 c.				

Cooking and Preparation Hints
* If you plan to use blueberries in a batter and want to prevent excessive streaking of color, toss them first with a little flour. Using frozen (unthawed) berries will also help.
* When using blueberries in a mixture with other fruit, add the blueberries last to prevent coloring the other fruit.
* For pancakes and waffles, add the blueberries after the batter has been poured onto the griddle. This will improve the appearance and make it easier to turn them over. If you use frozen blueberries, you may have to increase the cooking time some-what to insure that the berries are heated through.
* Blueberries can change color when cooked. When cooked with an acid (such as lemon juice or vinegar), they will turn reddish. When cooked in a basic environment (such as a batter with too much baking soda), the berries will turn a greenish blue.
* To freeze fresh blueberries, arrange them in a single layer on a cookie sheet and freeze. When frozen, transfer them to a plastic bag or freezer container. The secret to successful freezing is to have the blueberries completely dry before freezing.

INGREDIENT	YIELD			SUBSTITUTION		
Bluefish See also Fish/Shellfish			All Recipes	1 lb. 1 lb. 1 lb. 1 lb. 1 lb. 1 lb.	mackerel king mackerel jack mackerel bonito skipjack tuna wahoo	

Cooking and Preparation Hints
* It's best to prepare bluefish fresh because its flavor is dramatically diminished by freezing.
* The dark midline portion of the bluefish can be removed for a milder flavor.
* Removing the skin of the bluefish can also achieve a milder flavor. If you plan to grill the skinned fish, use a double layer of heavy duty aluminum foil on the grill to prevent the skinned fish from sticking to the grill.
* Herbs and spices that complement bluefish include tarragon, garlic, pepper, oregano, dill weed, bay leaf and fennel seed.

INGREDIENT	YIELD			SUBSTITUTION		Instructions
	Amount Market Form	Yield Equivalent	For Purpose of	Amount	Substitution	
Bok Choy (Chinese Cabbage) See also Vegetables	2 lb. whole, fresh	1 1/2 c. cooked leaves				
Borecole See Kale						
Bouillon See Broth						
Boysenberry See also Fruit	1 pt. fresh	3/4 lb.	All Recipes	1 c.	1 c. blackberries	
	1 pt. fresh	1 3/4 c.		1 c.	1 c. dewberries	
	1 pt. fresh	3 servings		1 c.	1 c. loganberries	
	17 oz. can	2 c.		1 c.	1 c. youngberries	

Cooking and Preparation Hints
* Boysenberries can be frozen unsweetened for up to 6 months. Quick-freeze on a tray for 2 hours, then transfer to freezer storage bags. They can also be frozen in a dry sugar pack (3/4 c. sugar per qt. of berries) or in a 40% to 50% syrup pack. Dissolve 3 to 4 3/4 c. sugar in 4 c. water and refrigerate. Add 1/2 to 2/3 c. syrup for each pt. of berries. Boysenberries in syrup can be frozen for up to 16 months.

INGREDIENT	YIELD			SUBSTITUTION		Instructions
	Amount Market Form	Yield Equivalent	For Purpose of	Amount	Substitution	
Brains See also Meat	1 lb. raw	5 3-oz. servings, cooked				
Bran See also Grains	16 oz.	8 1/2 c. flakes				

Cooking and Preparation Hints
* Store bran in a sealed container in the freezer to prevent it from turning rancid.

INGREDIENT	YIELD			SUBSTITUTION		Instructions
	Amount Market Form	Yield Equivalent	For Purpose of	Amount	Substitution	
Bran Flour See Flour						
Brandy See also Spirits			Flavoring	5 T	1 T brandy extract	

Cooking and Preparation Hints
* Brandy must first be warmed before igniting for flambé dishes. Heat the brandy over low heat, then put a lighted match just above the surface to ignite the fumes.

INGREDIENT	YIELD			SUBSTITUTION		Instructions
	Amount Market Form	Yield Equivalent	For Purpose of	Amount	Substitution	
Brazil Nut See also Nuts	2 lb. in shell	1 lb. shelled				
	2 lb. in shell	3 c. shell'd & chop'd				
	1 oz. in shell	3 large nuts				
	1 lb. shelled	3 c. chopped				
	1 oz. shelled	6 large nuts				

Cooking and Preparation Hints
* To make brazil nuts easier to crack, freeze them for several hours or overnight. The shells will become brittle enough to be cracked easily.

INGREDIENT	YIELD		SUBSTITUTION			
	Amount Market Form	Yield Equivalent	For Purpose of	Amount	Substitution	Instructions
Bread See also Quick Bread	1 lb. loaf 1 lb. loaf 1 slice 1 slice	18 - 20 slices 12 c. toasted croutons 1/2 c. soft bread crumbs 1/4 c. dry bread crumbs	All Recipes/Non-Wheat	1 slice 1 pkg. bread/roll mix	1 slice gluten-free bread 1 pkg. gluten-free bread/roll mix	
Bread Crumbs	8 oz. prepared dry	2 c.	All Recipes Coatings	1 c. 1 c. 1 c. 1 c. 1 c. 1 c.	1 c. cracker crumbs 1 c. crushed cornflakes 1 c. crushed potato chips 1 c. crushed corn chips 1 c. ground oats 1 c. matzo meal	

Cooking and Preparation Hints

* Using milk instead of water in bread recipes produces a softer crumb. To prevent it from being too soft, try first heating and cooling the milk before mixing with the other ingredients.
* Using buttermilk, cream, sour cream or yogurt will promote tenderness in bread recipes.
* Fruit and vegetable juices in bread recipes may cause a dry result. Try adding some fat for tenderness, but too much fat in a bread recipe will produce a heavy loaf.
* Try using potato water (water that potatoes have been boiled in) as the liquid in your bread recipe. It will enhance softness and will help the loaf stay fresh.
* Kneading activates the gluten in bread dough and is responsible for its rising. Too little kneading will cause the bread not to rise as high as it should. Overkneading may cause large holes in the bread but is still preferable to inadequate kneading.
* You can hasten the rising process for bread in the microwave. Boil 3 c. of water. Place the dough in a large bowl in the microwave oven next to the container of water. Heat on high for 30 seconds, then let them sit in the oven with the door closed for 20 minutes. Repeat as necessary until the dough has doubled in size.
* A quick test for whether a yeast dough has "doubled" is to press 2 fingers into the middle of the dough. If the indentations remain in the dough after you remove your fingers, the dough has doubled.
* If you're using a bread machine: (1) Don't use rapid rise yeast; (2) Cool any ingredients that have been preheated to prevent

killing the yeast; (3) Cut butter into small pieces to insure proper blending; and (4) Remove the bread from the pan as soon as it is done to keep the crust from becoming soggy.
* To put a sheen on the crust of your homemade bread, remove it from the oven when it's almost done, brush the top with white distilled vinegar or cider vinegar, and return it to the oven until done.
* Bread dough freezes well before baking. After kneading, shape the dough and place it in a baking dish. Cover and freeze. When the dough is frozen, remove it from the dish, put it into a plastic bag and return it to the freezer. When you're ready to bake the bread, remove it from the freezer and put it into a buttered baking dish. Let it thaw and rise in a warm place until doubled (approximately 5 hours for a large loaf of bread).
* Freshly baked bread also freezes well. Cool the loaf completely on a wire rack. Put it into the freezer, unwrapped, until it's frozen. Remove from the freezer, double wrap in plastic wrap or aluminum foil and return to the freezer for up to 2 months. When you're ready to use it, thaw the bread, remove the wrapping, then heat it at 350° for 5 to 10 minutes until just warm. If you want a soft crust, wrap in aluminum foil while heating. For a crisper crust, heat uncovered.
* If you're freezing a sliced loaf of bread and don't plan on using the entire loaf at once, make smaller packages of 2 to 8 slices, depending on the size of your family. It's easier to defrost and keeps the remainder of the loaf fresh longer. Frozen bread slices do not have to be thawed before toasting.

INGREDIENT	YIELD			SUBSTITUTION		
	Amount Market Form	Yield Equivalent	For Purpose of	Amount	Substitution	Instructions

Bread Crumbs continued

Cooking and Preparation Hints
* Use soft bread crumbs as a binder for such dishes as meatloaf and meatballs. Fine dry bread crumbs are better for coating meat, chicken and fish for frying or baking.
* To make soft bread crumbs, process 2- to 4-day-old bread in a food processor or blender. If the bread is too fresh, the crumbs will have a gummy consistency.
* To make dry bread crumbs, put bread slices in a 250⁰ oven for several minutes to crisp. Then put into food processor or blender until the appropriate texture is achieved. An alternative to the processor is to put the dried bread into a bag and crush with a rolling pin.
* For buttered soft crumbs, toss 1 c. crumbs with 1/4 to 1/3 c. melted butter. For buttered dry crumbs, sauté 1 c. crumbs in 3 T butter until golden.
* When using cheese as a topping for casseroles or vegetables, add 1 T bread crumbs for every 3 T of grated cheese to keep the cheese from becoming tough and stringy.

Bread Flour
See Flour

Bread Stuffing
See Stuffing Mix

Brie Cheese — All Recipes — 8 oz. — 8 oz. Camembert (1) — (1) Camembert has a more pungent aroma than brie and a somewhat stronger flavor.
See also Cheese

Broad Bean
See Fava Bean

Broccoli
See also Vegetables

Amount Market Form	Yield Equivalent
1 lb. fresh	2 medium heads
1 lb. fresh	9 oz. trimmed
1 lb. fresh	2 1/4 c. chop'd, cook'd
1 lb. fresh	4 servings
10 oz. frozen	2 1/2 c. chop'd, cook'd

Cooking and Preparation Hints
* To insure tender stalks, peel them before cooking.
* Broccoli will stay greener when cooking if you periodically lift the top off the pot so that some of the steam escapes.
* Drop 2 or 3 cloves into the cooking water before steaming to prevent cooking odor.
* Herbs and spices that complement broccoli include black pepper, red pepper, garlic, oregano, dill weed and rosemary.
* To freeze broccoli, wash, trim and peel the stalks. Split lengthwise and make X-cuts in the stem ends. Blanch for 3 minutes. Chill and pack the broccoli in a freezer container, leaving no headspace. It can be frozen for up to 12 months.

Broth
See also Stock

Amount Market Form	Yield Equivalent	For Purpose of	Amount	Substitution
10 3/4 oz. can cond'ns'd	2 3/4 c. prep'd liquid	All Recipes	1 c.	1 c. water left from cooked vegetables
1 cube	1 c. prep'd liquid		1 c.	1 c. water
1 t. granules	1 c. prep'd liquid			+ 1 T soy sauce
1 envelope powder	3/4 c. prep'd liquid		1 c.	1 c. consommé
2 t. concentr. liquid	1 c. prep'd liquid			
3/4 t. soup base pste	1 c. prep'd liquid			
1 T soup base paste	1 qt. prep'd liquid			

Cooking and Preparation Hints
* Broth is easily clarified by pouring it through a coffee filter fitted into a funnel.

INGREDIENT	YIELD		SUBSTITUTION			
	Amount Market Form	Yield Equivalent	For Purpose of	Amount	Substitution	Instructions
Brown Rice See Rice						
Brown Sugar See Sugar						
Brussels Sprout See also Vegetables	1 lb. fresh 1 lb. fresh 10 oz. frozen 10 oz. frozen	4 c. cooked 3 - 4 servings 18 - 24 sprouts 2 c. cooked				* Brussels sprouts can be refrigerated for up to 2 days. Store them unwashed in a paper bag with a few holes in it. * To freeze, trim sprouts and make an X-cut in the stem ends. Blanch 3 minutes for small sprouts, 4 minutes for medium and 5 minutes for large. Chill and pack, leaving no headspace. They can be frozen for up to 12 months.

Cooking and Preparation Hints
* To prepare for cooking, cut a thin slice from the stem, and cut an X in the stem end to reduce cooking time.
* Put a shelled walnut into the pot to prevent a cabbagy smell from cooking.
* Herbs and spices that complement Brussels sprouts include black pepper, dry mustard, basil, chives, dill weed, parsley, rosemary and thyme.

INGREDIENT	YIELD		SUBSTITUTION			
Buckwheat See also Kasha, Grains	1 c. groats	2 1/2 c. cooked				

Cooking and Preparation Hints
* Unroasted, crushed buckwheat kernels are called buckwheat groats. When they are roasted, they are called kasha.

INGREDIENT	YIELD		SUBSTITUTION			
Buckwheat Flour See Flour						
Bulgur (Bulghur Wheat) See also Grains	1 lb. dry 1 c. dry	2 1/2 c. uncooked 2 3/4 c. cooked	All Recipes	1 c.	1 c. cracked wheat (1)	(1) Bulgur has been partially cooked and has a more toasted flavor than cracked wheat.

Cooking and Preparation Hints
* Store bulgur in a sealed container in the freezer to prevent it from turning rancid.
* If you're adding bulgur to bread dough, the finely ground can be added as is; however, the coarsely ground or whole bulgur should first be soaked in hot water.
* Herbs and spices that complement bulgur include black pepper, oregano, marjoram, thyme, garlic and parsley.

INGREDIENT	YIELD		SUBSTITUTION			
Butter See also Fats	1 lb. 1 lb. 1 stick 1/4 stick 8 T	4 sticks 2 c. 1/2 c. 2 T 6 T clarified	Stove Top Cooking Baking	1 c. 1 c. 1 c. 1 c. 1 c. 3/4 c. 1 c. unsalted 1 c.	margarine soy-based margarine (1) soft margarine (2) 1/3 c. whipped butter (3) oil clarified poultry fat salted butter (4) vegetable shortening (5)	(1) Products will lack a buttery taste. However, you can use butter flavorings to compensate. (2) A slight flavor difference will result because soft margarine has a high liquid oil content. (3) Whipped butter has had its volume increased by adding air or inert gas. (4) When unsalted butter is specified, it is usually considered important to the results. Unsalted butter has a richer flavor due to its higher percentage of cream to water. If substituting salted butter, decrease the amount of additional salt called for in the recipe. (5) Shortening is 100% fat while butter is 80%-85% fat (and the rest is water). However, when comparing shortening and butter volume for volume, the air in the shortening compensates for the

Cooking and Preparation Hints
* Butter is salted to extend its shelf life. It will keep in the refrigerator for 3 to 4 weeks or in the freezer for 5 to 6 months in its original waxed carton and overwrapped with aluminum foil or freezer wrap. To extend the shelf life of unsalted butter, freeze it. It will maintain its quality for 6 to 8 weeks or longer.
* Clarified butter is called for in recipes because it can be heated to a higher temperature for frying and sautéing. To clarify butter, heat unsalted butter over medium heat until melted. Skim off the foam. Pour off the yellow clarified liquid, leaving behind the milk solids (the part of the butter that burns easily). Clarified butter will keep in the refrig-

B-12

INGREDIENT	YIELD			SUBSTITUTION		
	Amount Market Form	Yield Equivalent	For Purpose of	Amount	Substitution	Instructions
Butter continued						water in the butter. If you substitute weight for weight, use 15%-20% less shortening.

Cooking and Preparation Hints (continued)
erator for 2 to 3 weeks, or it can be frozen.
* Clarifying butter can be taken a step further by simmering it until the milk solids turn brown. The remaining butter is called ghee, and it can withstand even higher temperatures than clarified butter. Ghee will also keep longer; it can be refrigerated for up to 6 months and frozen for up to 1 year.

* Another method (besides clarifying) that allows butter to be heated to a higher temperature without burning is adding 1 T oil for every 2 T of butter.
* When an old recipe calls for butter "the size of a walnut," use 2 T butter.
* For cooking vegetables with a butter flavor, add 1/4 t. butter flavor extract to the cooking water.

For Purpose of	Amount	Substitution	Instructions
Baking	1 c.	1/2 c. butter + 1/2 c. shortening (6) 1 c. margarine	(6) While butter contributes flavor to baked goods, shortening produces a higher and more tender product. This substitution will provide the taste and texture advantages of both.
	1 c. melted	1 c. soft margarine (7)	(7) Soft margarine is not recommended for recipes that require the shortening to remain firm, such as for hard cookie doughs, pastry shells and puff pastry.
	1 c. unsalted	1 c. salted butter (4)	
	1 c.	7/8 c. lard (8)	(8) Lard is 100% fat while butter is only 80%-85% fat.
	1 c.	7/8 c. oil (9)	(9) Oil is not the best substitute for baking. Oil is 100% fat compared to butter's 80%-85% fat content. This precise substitution is important for baking. Other cooking and frying methods do not require such preciseness.
Flavoring/Reducing Fat	2 t.	1/2 t. Butter Buds ® Sprinkles	
	2 t.	1 Tliquified Butter Buds® Mix (10)	(10) Mix 1 t. Butter Buds ® Mix with 1 T liquid.
	2 T	1/8 t. butter flavor extract (11)	(11) This amount is recommended for recipes that do not require cooking. If the dish will be cooked or baked, increase the amount of extract to 2 t. so that it will retain the flavor strength equivalent to 2 T butter.
Spread/Reducing Fat	1 T	1 T light butter (12)	(12) Light butter is 40% butterfat compared to 80% for butter. Margarine is 80% vegetable fat.
	1 T	1 T nonfat margarine	
Baking/Reducing Fat	1 c.	8 t. (1 envelope) Butter Buds® Mix + 1/2 c. liquid	
		+ 1/2 c. butter (13)	(13) For cookie recipes, eliminate the liquid and decrease the flour by 25%.
	1 c.	2 T Butter Buds® Sprinkles (14)	(14) For best results when using the Sprinkles, slightly decrease the amount of flour in the recipe. Do not use the Sprinkles for pie crusts.
Greasing Pans	1 T	1 T vegetable shortening (15)	(15) Shortening is better than butter for dishes such as meringues or mixtures that contain sticky fruit.
	1 T	1 second nonstick cooking spray	
Greasing/Flouring Cake Pans	1 T	Cake pan coating spray as needed	

INGREDIENT	YIELD		For Purpose of	Amount	SUBSTITUTION	
	Amount Market Form	Yield Equivalent			Substitution	Instructions
Butter Bean See Lima Bean						
Buttercup Squash See Squash						
Buttermilk			Baking	1 c. 1 c. 1 c. 1 c.	1 c. milk + 1 T vinegar or lemon juice (1) 1 c. milk + 1 3/4 t. cream of tartar 1 c. yogurt 1 c. water + 3 T powdered cultured butter- milk (2)	(1) Let stand for about 10 minutes before adding to other ingredients. (2) The powder can be reconstituted before adding to other ingredients. Or you can add the powder to the other dry ingredients and add the water separately.

Cooking and Preparation Hints

* Buttermilk will keep in the refrigerator for about 2 weeks and in the freezer for about 3 months. To use frozen buttermilk, thaw it in the refrigerator overnight and stir to thoroughly mix the separated liquids and solids. Thawed buttermilk is better for baking than drinking.
* Buttermilk, because of its acidity, reacts with baking soda to promote the leavening process. As a result, light and fluffy breads and cakes are produced. Buttermilk also promotes browning of baked goods.
* Powdered buttermilk can be stored in the refrigerator at least a year.
* Commercially produced buttermilk usually has salt added to it (about twice the level of sodium as regular milk). Be sure to read the label if you are on a sodium-restricted diet.

INGREDIENT	YIELD		SUBSTITUTION			
	Amount Market Form	Yield Equivalent	For Purpose of	Amount	Substitution	Instructions
Cabbage See also Vegetables	1 lb. fresh	1 small head				
	1 lb. fresh	3 1/2 - 4 1/2 c. shredd				
	1 lb. fresh	2 c. cooked				
	1 lb. fresh	9 - 10 servings raw				
	1 lb. fresh	4 servings cooked				

Cooking and Preparation Hints
* Cabbage develops a strong odor and flavor when it is over-cooked. To prevent this, cook it quickly only until it is tender-crisp. To reduce the smell of boiled cabbage, add a little vinegar to the cooking water. To soften the taste and texture, you can blanch it or salt it before further cooking.
* To preserve the bright color of red cabbage when cooking, add an acid ingredient such as lemon juice, vinegar, red wine or apples.
* Herbs and spices that complement cabbage include garlic, caraway seed, black pepper, thyme, celery seed, dill weed, mint, mustard seed, nutmeg, savory and tarragon.
* Cabbage will stay crisp for at least 2 weeks refrigerated in a plastic bag.
* Cabbage should be blanched for 3 to 4 minutes before freezing.

INGREDIENT	Amount Market Form	Yield Equivalent	For Purpose of	Amount	Substitution	Instructions
Cabbage Turnip See Kohlrabi						
Caciocavallo Cheese See also Cheese			All Recipes	1 oz.	1 oz. provolone cheese	
Cactus Pear (Prickly Pear) See also Fruit	16 oz. jar, chopped	2 c. drained				

Cooking and Preparation Hints
* Ripen firm cactus pears at room temperature until they soften. Once they are ripe, you can refrigerate them for up to 1 week.
* Diced cactus pears will thicken soups and stews, as okra does.

INGREDIENT	Amount Market Form	Yield Equivalent	For Purpose of	Amount	Substitution	Instructions
Cajun Spice Powder			All Recipes	7 T	2 T paprika + 1 T ground red pepper + 1 T black pepper + 1 T celery salt + 1 T ground thyme + 1 T garlic powder	
Cake	2-layer cake mix	4 - 6 c. batter	Box Cake Mixes	1 c. water	1 c. milk (1)	(1) The cake will have a firmer texture.
	2-layer cake mix	2 8" round layers		1 c. water	1/2 c. water + 1/2 c. sour cream (2)	(2) This will enhance the flavor and add moisture to the cake.
	2-layer cake mix	10" round layer		1 c. oil	1 c. shortening	
	2-layer cake mix	9"x13"x2" sheet cake	Box Cake Mixes/Non-Wheat	2-layer cake mix	2-layer gluten-free cake mix	
	2-layer cake mix	1 character pan cake				

Cooking and Preparation Hints
* It's not usually a good idea to increase or decrease cake recipes. However, if you do, don't increase the amount of salt proportionately.
* Overbeating breaks down the cake structure, causing low volume and shrinkage during cooling.
* A rule-of-thumb for greasing cake pans is 1/2 to 1 T fat per pan. Do not use salted butter because it tends to make the cake stick to the pan.
* Bake your cake immediately after mixing, and position the pan in the middle (both vertically and horizontally) of the oven. If you have 2 pans on the same rack, allow at least 1" between pans. If you're using 2 racks, position the pans so that one is not directly over the other.

INGREDIENT	YIELD		For Purpose of	Amount	SUBSTITUTION	
	Amount Market Form	Yield Equivalent			Substitution	Instructions

Cake continued

Cooking and Preparation Hints (continued)

* To make sure your cake rises to a good height, try one of the following: (1) Add 2 t. meringue powder to your batter. (2) Lower the oven temperature 25° and bake the cake for 5 minutes longer. (3) Wrap a wet terry cloth around the cake pan. The cloth should be double thickness and the same height as the pan. Just pin the cloth together and bake.

* In low-fat baking, you can use fresh fruit purees to substitute for fat. Since the tenderizing effect of the fat is gone, however, you have to compensate by being careful not to overmix or overbake the cakes. Cakes made with fruit purees tend to get moister as they stand, rather than drier. See Fats.

* Adjustments to cake recipes need to be made for baking at high altitudes. At 3,000 ft. above sea level reduce baking powder 1/8 t. for each 1 t. called for, reduce sugar 1 T for each 1 c. called for, and increase the liquid by 1 to 2 T for each 1 c. called for; at 5,000 ft. reduce baking powder 1/8 to 1/4 t. per t. called for, reduce sugar 2 T for each c. called for, and add 2 to 3 T liquid for each c. called for; at 7,000 ft. reduce baking powder 1/4 t. for each t. called for, reduce sugar 2 to 3 T for each c. called for, and increase liquid by 3 to 4 T for each c. called for. For cake mixes the leavening cannot be reduced; so to help strengthen the cell walls of the cake, you can add a little flour, an egg yolk and some liquid.

* If you want a level cake for decorating purposes and yours comes out of the oven with a hump, you don't have to cut off the top. While the cake is still warm and in the pan, put a dry cloth over the cake; then place a board on top and press until the cake is level.

* Cakes should be cooled for 10 minutes (15 minutes for cakes more than 14" in diameter) in their pans on a cake rack before removing them from the pans. If cooled for less time, the cake is still warm and tender and will

break apart too easily. Beyond that time the greasing agent will harden and cause the cake to stick to the pan. If the cake does stick, return it to a 250° oven for a few minutes.

* Before you remove the cake from the pan, spray your wire cooling rack with nonstick spray to keep the cake from sticking to the rack.

* An angel food cake needs to be cooled completely before it is removed from the pan and should be cooled inverted and suspended. Otherwise, your cake is likely to be soggy. To achieve this with a regular tube pan, invert the pan and fit the tube onto the neck of a wine bottle or the spout of a funnel.

* The easiest way to cut an iced cake is to dip the knife into cold water between slices. For an ice cream cake, dip the knife into hot water between slices. For cheesecake, you can facilitate cutting by using dental floss, wire or sturdy thread.

* Unfrosted cakes can be frozen for up to 3 months wrapped in heavy-duty foil. They can be thawed, wrapped, at room temperature in 1 to 2 hours or in a 275° oven for 20 to 25 minutes.

* Some spices and flavorings don't freeze well. Cloves, for example, get stronger when frozen; so reduce the amount you add to the batter if you intend to freeze the cake. Also, be sure to use pure vanilla instead of the artificial flavoring because artificial vanilla will turn bitter during freezer storage.

* To freeze an iced cake without disturbing the icing, cut a cardboard circle 1" larger than the cake and cover it with foil. Place the cake on the cardboard, put the cardboard on a baking sheet and freeze until the cake is firm. You can then wrap the cake for storage. A frosted 2-layer cake will thaw at room temperature in 1 to 2 hours. Cupcakes will thaw in 30 minutes.

Cake Flour
See Flour

| **Camembert Cheese** See also Cheese | | | All Recipes | 8 oz. | 8 oz. Brie (1) | (1) Brie has a milder aroma and flavor. |

| **Cannellini Bean** (Tuscan Bean) See also Beans, Dried | | | All Recipes | 1 c. cooked
1 c. cooked
1 c. cooked
1 c. cooked
1 c. cooked
1 c. cooked | 1 c. cooked white beans
1 c. cooked great northern beans
1 c. cooked white kidney beans
1 c. cooked navy beans
1 c. cooked pea beans
1 c. cooked marrow beans | |

Ingredient	Amount Market Form	Yield Equivalent	For Purpose of	Amount	Substitution	Instructions
Cantaloupe See also Melon, Fruit	3 lb. whole	5 c. cubed	**Cooking and Preparation Hints** * To select a mature, ripe cantaloupe look for a slight indentation at the stem end; thick, well-raised netting; and yellow (not green) color. A ripe cantaloupe will yield slightly to pres-		sure on the blossom end and will have a pleasant cantaloupe aroma. * Store unripe cantaloupe at room temperature. Ripe cantaloupe should be refrigerated in a plastic bag to prevent its absorbing the odors of other food.	
Caper		**Cooking and Preparation Hints** * If you use capers that have been packed in salt, rinse them before using to remove the saltiness.	All Recipes	1 T	1 T pickled nasturtium seeds	
Caraway Seed See also Herbs/Spices		**Cooking and Preparation Hints** * Caraway seeds should not be subjected to prolonged heating because they will develop a bitter taste. It's best to add	All Recipes	1 t.	1 t. fennel seeds them to cooked foods at the end of cooking. * Caraway seeds complement such foods as cheese, breads, cakes, meats, cabbage, carrots, green beans and potatoes.	
Cardamom See also Herbs/Spices	1 pod 10 seeds	17 - 20 seeds 1/2 t. ground	**Cooking and Preparation Hints** * Cardamom is available in the pod or ground. The whole cardamom offers a fuller flavor than the ground. The seeds can be removed from the pod and ground, or the whole pod can be	Seasoning	1 t. ground	1 t. ground cinnamon ground. * Cardamom complements foods such as pastries, cookies, spicy meat dishes, fruit, coffee and punches.	
Carob Powder		**Cooking and Preparation Hints** * Store carob powder in the refrigerator because it does not contain a preserva-	All Recipes	1 T	1 T cocoa powder	
			five. * If carob powder hardens, you can put it through a sifter or food processor.			
Carrageenan See Irish Moss						
Carrot See also Vegetables	1 lb. fresh, w/o tops 1 lb. fresh, w/o tops 1 lb. fresh, w/o tops 1 lb. fresh, w/o tops 16 oz. can 16 oz. frozen	4 medium 2 1/2 - 3 c. sliced 2 1/2 c. shredded 2 - 2 1/2 c. cook'd 2 c. 2 1/2 c.	**Cooking and Preparation Hints** * If you buy carrots with the green tops, remove the tops immediately. They rob the roots of moisture and vitamins. * Store carrots in a plastic bag in the refrigerator. They will keep for several months. Store them away from apples, which emit ethylene gas, causing carrots to develop a bitter taste. * If carrots have become limp, you can restore their		crispness by soaking them in a bowl of ice water. * To make carrot curls, cut long strips of carrot with a vegetable peeler. Coil the strips and secure them with a toothpick. Refrigerate them in ice water for at least 30 minutes, then drain and remove the toothpicks. *Herbs and spices that complement carrots include ginger, dry mustard, dill weed, chives, black pepper, allspice, bay leaf, caraway seed, fennel,	

A B C D E F G H I J K L M N O P Q R S T U V W X Y Z

INGREDIENT	Amount Market Form	Yield Equivalent	For Purpose of	Amount	Substitution	Instructions
Carrot continued						

Cooking and Preparation Hints (continued)
mace, marjoram, mint, nutmeg, thyme, basil and parsley.
* Carrots should be blanched before freezing. Blanch whole carrots for 5 minutes and slices for 2 minutes. They will keep for up to 12 months.

INGREDIENT	Amount Market Form	Yield Equivalent	For Purpose of	Amount	Substitution	Instructions
Cashew See also Nuts	1 oz. shelled 6 1/4 oz. can	14 large - 18 medium 1 1/3 c.				

Cooking and Preparation Hints
* Cashews are high in fat and should be stored in the refrigerator to keep them from turning rancid.

INGREDIENT	Amount Market Form	Yield Equivalent	For Purpose of	Amount	Substitution	Instructions
Caster Sugar (Superfine Sugar) See Sugar						
Catfish See also Fish/Shellfish			All Recipes	1 lb. 1 lb.	1 lb. freshwater perch 1 lb. sablefish	

Cooking and Preparation Hints
* Catfish has to be skinned before cooking. Cut around the fish just in back of the gills, then pull the skin off.
* Herbs and spices that complement catfish include tarragon, garlic, black pepper, white pepper, ground red pepper, oregano, dill weed, bay leaf and fennel seed.
* Catfish can be frozen for 4 to 6 months.

INGREDIENT	Amount Market Form	Yield Equivalent	For Purpose of	Amount	Substitution	Instructions
Catsup See Ketchup						
Cauliflower See also Vegetables	1 medium head 1 lb. fresh 10 oz. frozen	1 1/2 - 2 lb. 1 1/2 c. 2 c.				Include paprika, parsley, white pepper, chives, rosemary, caraway seed, celery salt, dill weed, mace, tarragon and nutmeg.

Cooking and Preparation Hints
* To keep cauliflower white while cooking, add a little milk or ascorbic acid to the cooking water.
* To counteract any cooking odors, drop 2 or 3 cloves into the cooking water.
* Herbs and spices that complement cauliflower
* Cauliflower flowerets should be blanched for 3 minutes before freezing. Frozen cauliflower will keep for up to 12 months.

INGREDIENT	Amount Market Form	Yield Equivalent	For Purpose of	Amount	Substitution	Instructions
Caviar	1 oz.	2 T	All Recipes	1 T sturgeon roe 1 T sturgeon roe 1 T sturgeon roe	1 T lumpfish caviar (1) 1 T whitefish caviar (1) 1 T salmon caviar (1)	(1) While sturgeon roe is considered the true caviar, these others are good and much less expensive substitutes. The eggs of the substitutes will be smaller and they will differ in color from the grayish sturgeon roe. Lumpfish caviar is black; whitefish caviar is golden; and salmon caviar is red.

Cooking and Preparation Hints
* The quality of caviar is judged by the size of the eggs and the amount of salt. The larger the eggs and the less salt, the better the caviar.
* Fresh caviar should be refrigerated — preferably at 28° to 32°. It will not freeze at that temperature because of its salt content. Properly stored it will keep a week. Small-grain caviar can be frozen at 0° without adverse effects, but large-grain caviar eggs may burst if frozen.
* Pasteurized caviar has been partially cooked to give it a longer shelf life. It does not have to be refrigerated before opening and will keep unopened for 6 months. Once opened, it should be kept cold and eaten immediately.
* Do not serve caviar in silver dishes or with silver utensils because caviar tarnishes silver very quickly.
* Caviar, except for the golden, will discolor other ingredients you mix it with.

INGREDIENT	YIELD			SUBSTITUTION		
	Amount Market Form	Yield Equivalent	For Purpose of	Amount	Substitution	Instructions
Cayenne Pepper See Red Pepper, Chili Pepper						
Celeriac See Celery Root						
Celery See also Vegetables	1 medium stalk 1 lb. raw	1/2 c. chop'd or sliced 4 servings cooked	Cooked Recipes		1 lb. lovage stalks 1 lb. stalks	

Cooking and Preparation Hints
* Celery that is badly wilted can never be made crisp again. However, if it's only slightly wilted, you can restore it. Cut a few notches in the root end of the stalks and stand them upright in a glass of water for about 1 hour.
* To make celery "fans," cut the stalks into 1 1/2" pieces. From one or both ends of the piece of celery, make thin cuts toward the middle without cutting all the way through the stalk. Place the cut celery pieces in water, and the ends will fan out.
* An easy and practical way to stuff celery is to fill a plastic storage bag with the stuffing mixture. Cut off a corner of the bag and squeeze out the filling.
* Cooked celery is complemented by tarragon and thyme.
* Celery can be frozen without blanching. Chop or dice it, then quick-freeze on a tray. Store it in small freezer bags or containers.

INGREDIENT	Amount Market Form	Yield Equivalent	For Purpose of	Amount	Substitution	Instructions
Celery Knob See Celery Root						
Celery Root (Celeriac, Celery Knob) See also Vegetables	1 lb. fresh 1 lb. fresh 1 lb. fresh	1 small 4 c. sliced 3 1/2 c. julienne strips				

Cooking and Preparation Hints
* Celery root will keep up to 1 week in the refrigerator in a plastic bag.
* Celery root must be peeled before cooking. It darkens once it is cut; so put the cut pieces immediately into lightly acidulated water (3 to 4 t. lemon juice or vinegar per 5 c. water) to preserve its white color.
* The peel of the celery root is hard on garbage disposals, so dispose of it in another way.
* Celery root is complemented by dill weed, tarragon, parsley and chives.

INGREDIENT	Amount Market Form	Yield Equivalent	For Purpose of	Amount	Substitution	Instructions
Celery Salt See also Herbs/Spices	1 oz.	2 T	All Recipes	1 t.	3/4 t. salt + 1/4 t. crushed celery seed	
Celery Seed See also Herbs/Spices	1 oz.	4 T	Pickling	1 T	1 T dill seed	

Cooking and Preparation Hints
* Celery seed complements such foods as breads, egg dishes, dressings, salads, soups, fish, shellfish, turkey, chicken, beef, tomatoes, tomato juice, beets, cabbage and cauliflower.

INGREDIENT	Amount Market Form	Yield Equivalent	For Purpose of	Amount	Substitution	Instructions
Cèpe See Mushroom						

A B C D E F G H I J K L M N O P Q R S T U V W X Y Z

INGREDIENT	YIELD		SUBSTITUTION			
	Amount Market Form	Yield Equivalent	For Purpose of	Amount	Substitution	Instructions
Cereals See also individual listings	**Cooking and Preparation Hints** * If ready-to-eat breakfast cereals become soggy, you can recrisp them by baking them spread out on a cookie sheet for 2 to 3 minutes at 350°. * Unopened ready-to-eat cereals will keep in the cupboard for 6 to 12 months; opened, they will keep for 2 to 3 months.					
Chanterelle See Mushroom						
Chard See Swiss Chard						
Chayote (Mirliton)	1 lb. fresh	1 large	**Cooking and Preparation Hints** * Chayote can be stored up to 1 month in a plastic bag in the refrigerator.		* Chayote has a mild flavor and needs substantial seasoning. Herbs and spices that complement chayote include basil, oregano, nutmeg and thyme.	
Cheddar Cheese See also Cheese	4 oz.	1 c. shredded	Dips or Cooked Recipes	1 c. shredded sharp	1 c. shredded mild cheese + 1/4 t. Worcestershire sauce + 1/8 t. dry mustard	
Cheese See also individual listings	3 1/2 oz. hard cheese 5 oz. hard cheese 3 oz. can grat'd hard chse 4 oz. firm cheese 4 oz. blue cheese 8 oz. cream cheese 8 oz. cottage cheese	1 c. shredded 1 c. finely grated 3/4 c. 1 c. shredded 1 c. crumbled 1 c. 1 c.	All Recipes/Non-Dairy Cooked Recipes/Non-Dairy	1 c. 1 c.	1 c. soy cheese (1) 1 c. tofu (2)	(1) Soy cheese does not melt well; so the consistency of cooked dishes will be different. Soy cheese is also bland; you may want to increase seasonings to compensate. (2) Tofu is especially effective in dishes such as lasagna, manicotti and enchiladas. Because tofu is bland, adjust the seasonings to compensate.

Cooking and Preparation Hints

* To store cheeses, refrigerate them wrapped tightly in plastic wrap or in a damp cloth. If you're using plastic wrap, rewrap the cheese each time you use it in fresh plastic. The damp cloth will restore moisture to the cheese and should be dampened frequently. To prevent moisture loss and extend the life of some cheeses you can: (1) run the flat of a knife over the cut surface to seal the pores of the cheese; or (2) rub the surface of the cheese lightly with butter before wrapping and refrigerating. Hard cheeses keep longer than soft ones.

* For the best flavor, most cheeses should be served at room temperature. The length of time it takes to bring a cheese to room temperature depends on the type of cheese and the temperature of the room. In general, remove a hard cheese from the refrigerator 45 minutes to 3 hours before serving; remove a medium-firm cheese 30 minutes to 2 hours before serving; and remove a soft cheese 15 minutes to 1 hour before serving. Soft,

unripened cheeses such as cottage cheese and cream cheese should be served chilled.

* Excessive heat and prolonged cooking will cause cheese to become tough and stringy. To avoid this: (1) Use low temperatures (325° to 350°); (2) Bring the cheese to room temperature before cooking; (3) Grate or shred the cheese so it will melt more quickly; (4) Use a double-boiler rather than direct heat; (5) Blend the cheese with the other ingredients before cooking to reduce its density; and (6) Add cheese at the last minute, if possible.

* Aged cheeses have more flavor than young, mild ones. As a result, you can use less of the aged cheeses for seasoning purposes.

* When using shredded or grated cheese as a topping for casseroles, mix the cheese with bread crumbs to prevent the cheese from becoming tough and stringy. Mix 1 part bread crumbs and 3 parts cheese.

* To prevent cheeses such as blue or Roquefort from crumbling when you cut them, use a heavy thread, wire or dental floss.

* If you're grating cheese by hand, spray the grater with nonstick cooking

INGREDIENT	YIELD		For Purpose of	SUBSTITUTION		
	Amount Market Form	Yield Equivalent		Amount	Substitution	Instructions
Cheese continued	**Cooking and Preparation Hints (continued)** spray first. It makes the grater easier to clean. * Refrigerated and frozen cheese is easier to grate than cheese at room temperature. * If mold appears on a soft cheese such as cream cheese or Brie, throw the cheese away. For mold on harder cheeses, cut off 1/2" of the cheese under and around the mold before eating. * Freezing will damage the body and texture of most cheeses,					causing them to become mealy and crumbly. For best results, freeze cheese in its original, unopened package. For large pieces of cheese, cut them into 1 lb. segments and wrap tightly before freezing. Freeze as quickly as possible. Thaw slowly and unopened in the refrigerator. Some varieties of cheese (brick, cheddar, Muenster, mozzarella, Swiss, provolone, Edam, Gouda, Camembert) can be frozen for up to 6 months.
Cherry See also Fruit	1 lb. fresh unpitted 1 lb. fresh unpitted 1 lb. fresh unpitted 16 oz. can 21 oz. can cherry filling 10 oz. frozen 2 oz. dried	80 cherries 2 1/3 c. pitted 1 1/2 c. cherry juice 1 1/2 c. 2 c. 1 c. 1/2 c.	**Cooking and Preparation Hints** * Adding almond extract to cherries, either fresh or canned, gives them a more intense cherry flavor. * Unopened, dried cherries will keep in the cupboard for 18 months. * Cherries can be quick-frozen on trays and then transferred to a freezer storage bag and kept for 6 to 12 months.		Cherries can also be frozen in a dry sugar pack using 3/4 c. sugar per 1 qt. fruit. Or cherries can be frozen in a 40% to 50% syrup pack. For the syrup, dissolve 3 to 4 3/4 c. sugar and 1/2 t. ascorbic acid in 4 c. water and refrigerate. Add 1/2 to 2/3 c. syrup per pt. of fruit. They can be frozen for 12 to 16 months.	
Chervil See also Herbs/Spices	1 T chopped fresh	1 t. dried	**Cooking and Preparation Hints** * The mild flavor of chervil is diminished when it is boiled; add it near the end of cooking. * Chervil complements such foods as soups, savory sauces, beef,	Seasoning	1 T chopped fresh	1 T chopped fresh parsley (1)	(1) The taste of chervil is more delicate with just a hint of anise.
					pork, lamb, veal, sausages, chicken, duck, turkey, fish dishes, egg dishes, rice, pasta, potatoes, asparagus, beets, celery, carrots, cucumbers, eggplant, greens, peas, spinach, tomatoes, squash and tomato juice.	
Chestnut See also Nuts	1 1/2 lb. in shell 1 lb. in shell 8 1/4 oz. can puree	1 lb. shelled 35 - 40 whole 2 1/2 c. peeled 1 c.	**Cooking and Preparation Hints** * To remove the shell and inner skin of chestnuts, cut a strip of the shell from the outside curve of each chestnut. Put the chestnuts in a pan of cold water to cover and bring to a boil. Boil for 1 minute. The			chestnuts must be warm to remove the shells, so work on 1 at a time. Strip off the outer shell and peel off the brown inner skin. If any chestnut is recalcitrant, drop it back in boiling water and try again.	
Chicken See also Poultry	3 lb. broiler/fryer 3 lb. broiler/fryer 1 medium breast half 9 medium breast halves 1 whole breast 2 thighs 2 drumsticks 1 drumstick/thigh	2 1/2 c. cook'd meat 5 servings 1/2-3/4 c. cook'd meat 5 c. cooked meat 2 servings 1 serving 1 serving 1 serving	All Recipes		1 lb. boneless breasts 1 lb. chicken pieces	1 lb. turkey breast slices 1 lb. rabbit pieces (1)	(1) Rabbit is more finely textured meat than chicken. It should be cooked longer and at a lower temperature.

INGREDIENT	YIELD		SUBSTITUTION			
	Amount Market Form	Yield Equivalent	For Purpose of	Amount	Substitution	Instructions
Chicken continued						

Cooking and Preparation Hints
* To avoid any bacterial contamination from raw chicken, always thoroughly wash your hands, cutting board, knives and other utensils immediately after cutting the raw chicken. And don't let any raw chicken juices come in contact with cooked chicken. Chicken is completely cooked when the meat is opaque and the juices are yellow.

* Herbs and spices that complement chicken include basil, dill weed, ginger, nutmeg, oregano, marjoram, thyme, celery seed, chives, bay leaf, garlic, dry mustard, parsley, paprika, rosemary, sage, tarragon, poultry seasoning, saffron and sesame seed.
* Whole chickens can be frozen for up to 12 months; pieces can be frozen for up to 9 months; and cooked chicken can be frozen for up to 1 month.

INGREDIENT	Yield Equivalent
4 wings	1 serving
1 lb. boneless cuts	4 servings

Chicken Stock
See Stock

Chickpea
See Garbanzo Bean

Chili Pepper (Chile, Hot Pepper) See also Vegetables	Amount Market Form	For Purpose of	Amount	Substitution	Instructions
	Anaheim (fresh form)	All Recipes	Anaheim (fresh)	Bell pepper (1)	(1) A mild Anaheim is slightly hotter.
	Poblano (fresh form)		Anaheim (fresh)	Pimiento (1)	(2) The cayenne is hotter.
	Chilaca (fresh form)		Anaheim (fresh)	Sweet banana pepper (1)	(3) The habañero is hotter.
	Mirasol (fresh form)		Cayenne (fresh)	Serrano (2)	
	Colorado (dried form)		Cayenne (fresh)	Jalapeño (2)	
	Ancho (dried form)		Cayenne (fresh)	Habañero (3)	
	Pasilla (dried form)		Habañero (fresh)	Cayenne (3)	
	Guajillo (dried form)		Serrano (fresh)	Cayenne (2)	

Cooking and Preparation Hints
* There are more than 200 varieties of chili peppers. The determining factor in whether or not they are interchangeable is the degree of heat they provide.
* If a fresh chili is too hot for its intended use, you can reduce its potency by removing the seeds and veins. You can also soak the chili in cold salt water for an hour.
* Always wear plastic or rubber gloves when working with chili peppers; or be sure to wash your hands thoroughly with soap and water immediately after handling them. Their oils can remain on your skin and can cause serious skin and eye irritations.
* To peel fresh chilies, broil them 4" to 6" from the heat turning them often until their skins are blistered on all sides. Put them into a paper bag to steam for 15 minutes.

* The skins will come off easily.
* Chopping dried chilies is easier with scissors than with a knife.
* Before you can use whole dried chillies, you will have to soak them in hot water for about an hour. Then slit them and remove the seeds.
* Fresh chillies will keep for up to 2 weeks in the refrigerator. Wrap them in paper towels rather than a plastic bag; plastic inhibits air circulation and will cause them to rot faster. Chilies do not freeze well; they lose flavor and texture.
* Dried chillies can be wrapped in plastic and refrigerated indefinitely.
* If you eat a chili pepper that is too hot for you, don't drink water; it will just spread the capsaicin — the chemical responsible for the burning. Eat something starchy (like bread or rice) or drink milk, beer or wine; they will all counteract the burning.

INGREDIENT	YIELD		For Purpose of	SUBSTITUTION		Instructions
	Amount Market Form	Yield Equivalent		Amount	Substitution	
Chili Pepper continued			All Recipes	Serrano (fresh)	Jalapeño (4)	(4) The jalapeño is hotter.
				Serrano (fresh)	Mirasol	
				Jalapeño (fresh)	Cayenne (2)	
				Jalapeño (fresh)	Mirasol (4)	
				Jalapeño (fresh)	Serrano (4)	
				Mirasol (fresh)	Jalapeño (4)	
				Mirasol (fresh)	Serrano	
				Hungarian Wax (fresh)	Serrano	
				Poblano (fresh)	Anaheim	
				Poblano (fresh)	Bell pepper	
				Pimiento (fresh)	Red bell pepper	
				Guajillo (dried)	Hontaka	
				Pasilla (dried)	Mulato	
			Seasoning	1 T chopped fresh	1 T chopped pickled	
				1 small red chili	1/4 t. ground red pepper	
				1 small red chili	1/2 t. crushed red pepper	
				1 small red chili	1/2 t. hot chili paste	
				1 small red chili	1/2 t. hot pepper sauce	
Chili Powder See also Herbs/Spices			Seasoning	2 1/2 t.	1 t. cumin + 1/2 t. ground red pepper + 1/2 t. garlic powder + 1/2 t. oregano	**Cooking and Preparation Hints** * Chili powder will last up to 2 years if refrigerated.
				1 T	1 mild dried red chili pod	
				1 t.	1 t. liquid chili	
Chili Sauce	12 oz.	1 1/4 c.	All Recipes	1 c.	1 c. ketchup	
				1 c.	1 c. tomato sauce + 1/2 c. sugar + 2 T vinegar	
Chinese Cabbage See Bok Choy						
Chinese Gooseberry See Kiwi						
Chinese Parsley See Coriander						
Chinese Snow Pea See Snow Pea						

C-10

INGREDIENT	YIELD		For Purpose of	SUBSTITUTION		
	Amount Market Form	Yield Equivalent		Amount	Substitution	Instructions
Chive See also Herbs/Spices	1 T fresh chopped	1 t. freeze-dried	Flavoring	1 T chopped	1 T chopped scallions	

Cooking and Preparation Hints
* Chives complement such foods as carrots, beans, tomatoes, corn, squash, turnips, peas, cauliflower and mushrooms.
* So that they retain their flavor, chives should be added toward the end of cooking.

* Chives can be frozen raw but should be used within 3 months. Freezing causes them to lose their crispness and become tough and highly flavored. Chop or snip fresh chives and pack them in small freezer bags.

INGREDIENT	Amount Market Form	Yield Equivalent	For Purpose of	Amount	Substitution	Instructions
Chocolate See also Cocoa	1 square	1 oz.	All Cooked or Melted Recipes	1 oz. unsweetened	3 T cocoa powder + 1 T shortening	(1) Decrease the shortening in the recipe by 1 T and the sugar by 1/4 c.
	1 oz.	4 T chopped or grated		6 oz. unsweetened	6 oz. semisweet chips (1)	(2) Use water or a liquid called for in the recipe.
	4 oz.	1 c. grated		1 oz. unsweetened	3 T carob powder + 2 T liquid (2)	(3) Liquid chocolate was developed especially for baking and needs no melting.
	9 oz.	1 c. melted		1 oz. unsweetened	1 oz. liquid chocolate (3)	This product is different than chocolate syrup.
	6 oz. chips	1 c.		1 oz. bittersweet	1 oz. semisweet chocolate (4)	(4) Do not substitute milk chocolate.
	1 envelope liquid chocolate	1 oz.		1 oz. semisweet	1/2 oz. unsweetened chocolate + 1 T sugar	It is difficult to melt.

chocolate will retain its original shape until it's stirred.
* When adding melted chocolate to cake and cookie mixtures, first let it cool to about 80°.
* To decorate desserts with drizzled melted chocolate, put the chocolate inside a plastic zipper-type storage bag and melt it in the microwave. Then snip a small piece off of 1 corner of the bag and drizzle the chocolate through the opening.
* One way to make chocolate curls is with a vegetable peeler. Heat a chocolate bar in the microwave on half power for 10 to 20 seconds. Then pull the vegetable peeler across the bar. The more quickly you pull the peeler, the tighter the curls. Another method is to melt the chocolate, then spread it in a thin layer over the surface of a cookie sheet or bottom of a jelly-roll pan. Refrigerate it for a few minutes until the chocolate is firm but not hard. Use a metal spatula to scrape strips of chocolate to form curls.
* In very hot weather, you can store chocolate in the refrigerator, but you run the risk of it absorbing odors from other foods.

				Amount	Substitution
				1 oz. semisweet	3 T cocoa powder + 1 T shortening + 1 T sugar
				1 oz. liq.chocolate	3 T cocoa powder + 1 T oil or melted shortening
				1 oz. Mexican choc.	1 oz. semisweet chocolate + 1/2 t. ground cinnamon + 1/8 t. almond extract

Cooking and Preparation Hints
* The whitish-gray film that sometimes appears on chocolate is due to being exposed to varying temperatures. It does not affect the quality or the taste of the chocolate.
* Chocolate will stiffen and turn grainy ("seize") if it is overheated during melting or if it comes in contact with a drop or 2 of water (as would happen if the pan were not dry). To prevent seizing, use low, even heat or a double boiler or melt the chocolate in the microwave. If you must add liquid to the melting chocolate, make sure you use at least 1 T of liquid for each 1 oz. of chocolate.
* If chocolate stiffens while being melted, you can rescue it by adding 1 t. vegetable oil or melted shortening for each 1 oz. of chocolate and stirring vigorously until smooth. Don't add butter to stiffened chocolate; it contains water and will only exacerbate the problem.
* Melting chocolate in the microwave is faster and helps the chocolate stay smooth. Unwrap the squares, put them in an uncovered, microwave-safe dish and heat on high for 1 to 2 minutes. The

| INGREDIENT | YIELD | | For Purpose of | Amount | SUBSTITUTION | Instructions |
	Amount Market Form	Yield Equivalent			Substitution	
Chutney	12 1/2 oz. jar	1 c.				
Cilantro See Coriander						
Cinnamon See also Herbs/Spices	1 whole stick	1/8 - 1/2 t. ground				pork, ham, lamb, chicken, fish, fruits, applesauce, sweet potatoes, winter squash, pumpkin, spinach, beets, carrots, onions, tomatoes, cakes, pies, cookies, custards, coffees and spiced wines.

Cooking and Preparation Hints
* A cinnamon stick can be reused. Taste it to determine if it has retained some flavor. Be sure to dry it completely before storing or it will become moldy.
* Cinnamon complements such foods as

| INGREDIENT | YIELD | | For Purpose of | Amount | SUBSTITUTION | Instructions |
	Amount Market Form	Yield Equivalent			Substitution	
Citric Acid			Flavoring	1 T powder	1/2 c. lemon juice	
Citron	6 1/2 oz. jar chopped	1 c.				

Cooking and Preparation Hints
* Citron should be stored in the freezer.

| INGREDIENT | YIELD | | For Purpose of | Amount | SUBSTITUTION | Instructions |
	Amount Market Form	Yield Equivalent			Substitution	
Clam See also Fish/Shellfish	6 - 12 clams	1 serving				
	8 qt. in shell	1 qt. shucked				
	1 qt. shucked	6 servings				
	1 qt. shucked	2 - 3 c. chopped				
	6 1/2 oz. can minced	1/2 c. drained				
	6 1/2 oz. can minced	1/2 c. juice				

Cooking and Preparation Hints
* There are 2 types of clams: hard shell and soft shell. While all clams are interchangeable in clam recipes, the soft shell "steamer" is preferred for steamed clams. Hard shell clams include littleneck, cherrystone, chowder, pismo and butter clam. Soft shell clams include steamer, razor and geoduck.
* Clams should be alive when you buy them. This is indicated by a tightly closed shell. If the shell is open (and clams may even open in the refrigerator), give it a tap. If it closes, it's alive. If it doesn't close, discard it. For a soft shell clam, touch the neck. If it moves, it's alive and safe to eat.
* To remove any sand or mud from clams before opening or cooking them, cover them with salt water (1/3 c. salt per 1 gallon water) for several hours. For additional help in eliminating the sand, add 1/4 to 1/2 c. cornmeal to the soaking water.
* To make clams easier to open, put them in the freezer for 15 to 20 minutes. After you remove them from the cold and their bodies warm up, the muscles relax and the shells open slightly.
* Herbs and spices that complement clams include black pepper, parsley, garlic, chervil, oregano, marjoram and thyme.
* Live clams can be refrigerated up to 2 days; shucked clams, up to 4 days.
* To freeze clams, shuck them and save the liquid. Rinse the clams with salt water (1 T salt to 1 qt. water), place them in a rigid freezer container and cover them with the reserved liquid. If necessary, add fresh salt water to cover.

INGREDIENT	YIELD		SUBSTITUTION			Instructions
	Amount Market Form	Yield Equivalent	For Purpose of	Amount	Substitution	
Clove See also Herbs/Spices	5 - 6 whole	1/8 - 1/2 t. ground			les, relishes, cakes, cookies, pumpkin pie and mulled wine.	**Cooking and Preparation Hints** * Cloves complement such foods as ham, stews, pork roasts, roasted poultry, curried dishes, marinades, barbecue sauce, beef and bean soups, beans, squash, sweet potatoes, fruit dishes, pick-
						* The flavor of cloves strengthens during the freezing process; keep that in mind when adding cloves to dishes that will be frozen.
Cocktail Sauce	12 oz.	1 1/4 c.	All Recipes	1 c.	1 c. ketchup or chili sauce + 3 T horseradish + 1 T lemon juice + 2 t. Worcestershire sauce	**Cooking and Preparation Hints** * Cocktail sauce keeps well in the freezer.
Cocoa Mix			All Recipes	6 1/2 c.	5 c. instant nonfat dry milk + 3/4 c. sugar + 3/4 c. cocoa powder	
Cocoa Powder See also Chocolate	1 lb. 4 oz.	4 c. 1 c.	All Recipes Baking	1 c. "Dutched" cocoa 1 T 1/4 c.	1 c. regular cocoa (1) 1 T carob powder (2) 1/2 c. semisweet chocolate chips (3)	(1) Dutching is a process that neutralizes the natural acidity of cocoa powder, making it less bitter, easier to mix with liquids and darker in color. (2) While the color and texture of carob powder are similar to cocoa powder, the products made with carob powder will lack a real chocolate flavor; they will have a distinctive carob taste. Carob powder is high in natural sugars; if you are substituting a large amount of carob powder, you may want to reduce the amount of sugar in the recipe. (3) Decrease the shortening called for in the recipe by 1 T and the sugar by 1/4 c.

Cooking and Preparation Hints
* Instant cocoa mixes should not be used as a substitute for cocoa powder.
* Cocoa powder does not mix easily with liquids. To prevent lumps, mix the cocoa with the sugar called for in the recipe or mix the cocoa with some of the liquid from the recipe in a blender in advance of cooking.
* Cocoa will retain its quality and freshness almost indefinitely stored in the cupboard. Avoid moisture and high temperatures which will cause the cocoa to turn gray and clump (although neither condition will adversely affect the flavor or quality).

INGREDIENT	YIELD		SUBSTITUTION			Instructions
Coconut	1 medium 1 medium 4 oz. flaked 4 oz. shredded	3 - 4 c. grated 1/2 - 1 c. liquid 1 1/2 c. 1 1/3 c.	All Recipes	1 c. unsweetened	1 c. sweetened (1)	(1) Rinse the sweetened coconut well in cold water and drain before using it in the recipe.

Cooking and Preparation Hints
* You can drain the liquid from a whole coconut by piercing the "eyes," or indentations, with an ice pick or screwdriver.
* If a coconut will not crack open easily, heat it in a 350° oven for about 15 minutes. At the end of this time the coconut will have cracked or it will crack easily with one blow of a hammer. Another method, if you have more time, is to put the coconut in the freezer for 1 to 2 hours.
* If coconut has dried out, you can restore moisture by (1) soaking it in milk for a few minutes and straining or (2) steaming it in a strainer over boiling water.
* A whole coconut can be stored at room temperature for up to 6 months. Grated fresh coconut can be refrigerated covered tightly for up to 4 days and frozen for up to 6 months. Canned coconut can be stored in the cupboard for up to 18 months. Coconut sold in plastic bags can be stored for up to 6 months. If the can or bag has been opened, refrigerate the contents. Dried coconut will keep unopened in the freezer for about 18 months; or once opened, it will keep in a tightly sealed container at room temperature for up to 1 month.

INGREDIENT	YIELD			SUBSTITUTION		
	Amount Market Form	Yield Equivalent	For Purpose of	Amount	Substitution	Instructions
Coconut Milk	16 oz. can	2 c.	All Recipes	1 c. 2 c. 1 c. 1 c.	1 c. fresh chopped coconut + 1 c. hot water (1) 7 oz. unsweetened coconut + 2 c. milk or cream (2) 3 T canned cream of coconut + 7/8 c. hot water or milk 1 c. milk or cream + 1 t. coconut flavoring	(1) Put coconut into a food processor and grate. Add water and process until the mixture is of a puree consistency. Strain the liquid through a double thickness of cheesecloth, squeezing out as much liquid as possible. Coconut milk made with water is especially good for fish, meat and vegetable recipes. (2) Heat and stir coconut and milk in a saucepan until it reaches a slow boil. Let it cool to room temperature. Strain the liquid though a double thickness of cheesecloth, squeezing out as much liquid as possible. Coconut milk made with milk or cream is good for dessert recipes.

Cooking and Preparation Hints
* Coconut milk contains coconut oil which may affect people on low-cholesterol diets.

INGREDIENT	YIELD			SUBSTITUTION		
Cod See also Fish/Shellfish, Salt Cod			All Recipes	1 lb. 1 lb.	1 lb. haddock 1 lb. rockfish	

Cooking and Preparation Hints
* "Scrod" is a term used for young cod weighing under 2 1/2 lb. or for small fish in the cod family including haddock, pollock and cusk.
* Herbs and spices that complement cod include parsley, bay leaf, tarragon, dill weed, black pepper, white pepper, chives and basil.
* Cod can be frozen for 4 to 6 months.

INGREDIENT	YIELD			SUBSTITUTION		
Coffee	1 lb. beans 1 lb. ground 2 T ground 1 lb. ground 4 oz. instant 4 oz. instant 4 oz. freeze-dried 4 oz. freeze-dried	5 c. ground 80 T 3/4 - 1 c. brewed 40 c. brewed 1 1/2 c. powder 50 c. prepared 1 3/4 c. crystals 60 c. prepared	All Recipes All Recipes/Reducing Caffeine	1 c. brewed 1 c. brewed 1 c. brewed 1 c. brewed 1 c. brewed 1 c. brewed	1 c. prepared instant 1 c. brewed decaffeinated 1 c. prepared instant decaffeinated 1 c. prepared grain beverage (1) 1 c. prepared from roasted soybeans 1 c. brewed from dandelion roots (2)	(1) These beverages are typically made from roasted barley and chicory. (2) Wash and chop unpeeled dandelion roots. Roast in an oven at 180° for 2 hours or until the pieces are medium brown and dry. Grind in a coffee grinder and brew like coffee. Use a little less dandelion root than you would coffee beans.

Cooking and Preparation Hints
* Ground coffee turns stale more quickly than whole coffee beans. If possible, grind only the amount you will use right away.
* The more coffee surface that is exposed to the water, the more flavor the coffee will have. Fine grind the coffee to impart the most flavor, and use fresh cold water.
* To make iced coffee, brew coffee at double strength and pour it over ice.
* Whole roasted beans can be stored in an airtight container at room temperature for up to 2 weeks or frozen for up to 3 months. Ground coffee should be refrigerated in an airtight container and will keep for up to 2 weeks. Instant coffee will keep unopened in the cupboard for 1 to 2 years; opened it will keep for up to 2 months.
* You can use leftover coffee by freezing it in ice cube trays and using the cubes in iced coffee.

Colewort
See Kale

A B C D E F G H I J K L M N O P Q R S T U V W X Y Z

INGREDIENT	YIELD		SUBSTITUTION			
	Amount Market Form	Yield Equivalent	For Purpose of	Amount	Substitution	Instructions
Collard Greens See also Greens, Cooking	1 lb. fresh 15 oz. can 10 oz. frozen	2 c. cooked 2 c. 1 1/2 c. cooked				* Blanch collard greens 3 to 4 minutes before freezing. They can be frozen for up to 12 months.
						Cooking and Preparation Hints * The tough stems and ribs of collard greens should be removed and discarded.
Conch See also Fish/Shellfish			All Recipes	1 lb. 1 lb. 1 lb.	1 lb. whelk 1 lb. abalone 1 lb. squid	**Cooking and Preparation Hints** * Conch requires tenderizing before eating. One way is to break down the connective tissue by pounding it with a mallet. Or you can parboil it, then pound it until the flesh is tender.
Confectioners' Sugar (Powdered Sugar) See Sugar						
Consommé See Stock						
Cookies	18 choc. wafers (2") 24 vanilla wafers (2") 17 gingersnaps 9 macaroons (2 1/2") 12 Oreo cookies	1 c. crumbs 1 c. crumbs 1 c. crumbs 1 c. crumbs 1 c. crumbs	All Recipes/ Non-wheat	1 cookie	1 gluten-free cookie	dough before putting it in the oven. If your sheet is less than half full, put an inverted baking pan on the empty half. * To improve results when baking cookies at high altitudes, alter the recipe by slightly decreasing the amounts of baking powder, baking soda, fat and sugar; increasing slightly the flour and liquid ingredients; and slightly increasing the oven temperature. * Cookies can be frozen either before or after baking.
						Cooking and Preparation Hints * To keep cookie dough from sticking to a rolling pin, freeze the pin in the freezer before rolling. This will eliminate or reduce the need for flouring the rolling pin. * To prevent sticking, dip cookie cutters in flour before cutting the dough into shapes. * To keep from burning cookies use flat, shiny pans. Dark cookie sheets with sides are more likely to cause burning. Also, fill the sheet with cookie
Cooking Banana See Plantain						
Cooking Greens See Greens, Cooking						
Coriander (Chinese Parsley, Cilantro) See also Herbs/Spices						**Cooking and Preparation Hints** * Coriander is available as a fresh herb (whose leaves are also referred to as Chinese parsley and cilantro) and as seeds. The two forms have completely different tastes and cannot substitute for one another. * Fresh coriander leaves should be stored with their stems in a glass of water and a plastic bag over the leaves in the refrigerator. They will keep fresh for up to 1 week.
						* Coriander leaves complement such foods as guacamole, salsa, pork, sausages, poultry, duck, egg dishes, corn, tomatoes and cauliflower. * Coriander seeds complement such foods as cakes, pastries, sweet breads, soup stocks, curried dishes, beef, lamb, pork, sausages, poultry stuffings, onions, spinach, tomatoes and chutneys. * Coriander leaves can be chopped and frozen in small quantities in freezer containers for 6 to 9 months.

INGREDIENT	YIELD		SUBSTITUTION			
	Amount Market Form	Yield Equivalent	For Purpose of	Amount	Substitution	Instructions
Corn See also Vegetables	2 medium ears 16 oz. can 10 oz. frozen 16 oz. can cream-style	1 c. kernels 1 3/4 c. drained 1 3/4 c. 2 c.				ear in the tube, hold the ear with one hand and slice the kernels off with a knife in your other hand. The kernels will land in the pan. * Herbs and spices that complement corn include chill powder, oregano, chives and black pepper. * Corn should be blanched on the cob before freezing. If you plan to freeze it on the cob, quick-freeze it first on trays and then pack in freezer bags. If you plan to freeze just the kernels, slice them off the cob after blanching. Then pack and freeze. Frozen corn will keep for 8 to 12 months.
	Cooking and Preparation Hints * Corn continues to mature once it's picked. The corn's sugar quickly turns to starch making the corn more chewy and less sweet. It's important to buy corn that is just picked and to cook corn the same day you purchase it. When boiling corn, don't salt the water because the salt will toughen the kernels. And cook it as briefly as possible until the corn milk is coagulated — about 4 to 5 minutes after the water returns to a boil. * An efficient way to cut the kernels off an ear of corn is to use a cake tube pan. Place the husked					
Corn Flour See Flour						
Corn Grits See Grits						
Corn Syrup	16 oz.	2 c.	All Recipes	1 c. light 1 c. light 1 c. dark	1 1/4 c. granulated sugar + 1/3 c. liquid (1) 1 c. light treacle 3/4 c. light corn syrup + 1/4 c. light molasses	(1) Combine the sugar with 1/3 c. liquid called for in the recipe. Boil the mixture and cook until it becomes syrupy.
	Cooking and Preparation Hints * Before measuring corn syrup, spray the measuring cup with nonstick cooking spray. The corn syrup will pour right out.			and cleanup will be easier. * Corn syrup will keep up to 3 years in the cupboard if it is unopened or tightly reclosed.		
Cornflakes See also Cereals	4 oz. flakes	1 c. crumbs				
Cornish Hen (Cornish Game Hen, Rock Cornish Hen) See also Poultry	1 medium bird 1 bird	2 lb. 1 serving				
	Cooking and Preparation Hints * Herbs and spices that complement Cornish hens include basil, dill weed, ginger, nutmeg, oregano, marjoram, thyme, celery			seed, chives, bay leaf, garlic, dry mustard, parsley, paprika, rosemary, sage, tarragon, poultry seasoning, saffron and sesame seed.		
Cornmeal See also Grains	1 lb. 1 c.	3 c. 4 c. cooked				
	Cooking and Preparation Hints * Yellow cornmeal comes from yellow corn; white cornmeal comes from white corn. They will produce the same taste and texture. * Regular steel-ground cornmeal can be stored					almost indefinitely in a cool, dry place. Stoneground cornmeal contains some of the outer bran layer and should be kept in an airtight container in the refrigerator (up to 4 months) or in the freezer to prevent it from turning rancid.

INGREDIENT	YIELD		For Purpose of	Amount	SUBSTITUTION	
	Amount Market Form	Yield Equivalent			Amount	Substitution	Instructions

Cornstarch
See also Flour

Market Form	Yield Equivalent	For Purpose of	Amount	Substitution	Instructions
1 lb.	3 c.	Thickening	1 T / 1 T / 1 T / 1 T	2 T flour (1) / 1 T arrowroot (2) / 2 T quick-cooking tapioca (3) / 2 eggs (4)	(1) Flour will produce an opaque sauce in contrast to the clear sauce produced with cornstarch. (2) Like cornstarch, arrowroot produces a clear sauce and is recommended for thickening very acid fruits. (3) Like cornstarch, tapioca is recommended for thickening very acid fruits. (4) If you have used eggs for thickening and want to reheat the sauce, don't boil it or the sauce will curdle.

Cooking and Preparation Hints
* Cornstarch should be mixed with a little cold liquid (about 1 t. cornstarch to 1 T cold liquid) before being added to a hot liquid to prevent lumps.
* 1 T cornstarch will thicken 1 1/2 to 2 c. liquid.
* Once cornstarch has been added to a hot liquid, bring the mixture to a boil over medium heat so that the starch granules can swell to their full capacity. Stir continuously but gently to avoid lumping. If you're adding other ingredients to the sauce after thickening, remove the mixture from the heat and stir in the other ingredients quickly and carefully.
* Overcooking, too high a temperature or overstirring will cause cornstarch-thickened sauces to thin out.
* Before adding acid ingredients to a cornstarch-thickened sauce, remove the sauce from the heat. Otherwise, the thickening ability of the cornstarch will be reduced.

Cottage Cheese
See also Cheese

Market Form	Yield Equivalent	For Purpose of	Amount	Substitution	Instructions
8 oz.	1 c.	All Recipes	8 oz. dry / 8 oz. dry / 8 oz. dry / 8 oz. dry / 8 oz. dry / 8 oz. dry	8 oz. creamed cottage cheese, drained / 8 oz. ricotta cheese / 8 oz. baker's cheese / 8 oz. farmer cheese / 8 oz. hoop cheese / 8 oz. pot cheese	(1) Substituting tofu is especially good in dishes such as lasagna and manicotti where it assumes the taste of the sauce it's combined with.
		Pasta Dishes	1 c.	1 c. mashed tofu (1)	
		All Recipes/Reducg Fat	8 oz.	8 oz. low-fat/nonfat cottage cheese	

Cooking and Preparation Hints
* Dry cottage cheese can be frozen in wax cartons or freezer containers for 2 to 3 months. Creamed cottage cheese doesn't freeze well; it becomes crumbly and mealy and tends to separate when defrosted.

Cow Cabbage
See Kale

Cowpea
See Black-Eyed Pea

Crab
See also Fish/Shellfish

Market Form	Yield Equivalent	For Purpose of	Amount	Substitution	Instructions
1 lb. whole	6 - 7 oz. meat	All Recipes	1 lb.	1 lb. surimi (imitation crab) (1)	(1) Surimi is made from pollock and other fish and flavored to resemble crab. It is lower in calories and cholesterol than real crab but may be higher in sodium.
1 - 2 lb. whole	2 servings	Salads	1 c.	1 c. poached skate	
1 lb. claws	1 serving				
1 lb. cooked meat	2 1/2 - 3 c.				
1 lb. cooked meat	3 - 4 servings				
16 oz. can	3 c. flaked				

INGREDIENT	YIELD		For Purpose of	SUBSTITUTION		
	Amount Market Form	Yield Equivalent		Amount	Substitution	Instructions
Crab continued						under cold, running water because the claws and legs may separate from the body. * Herbs and spices that complement crab include crab boil, dry mustard, dill weed, black pepper, red pepper, tarragon and parsley. * Cooked crabmeat freezes well and will keep for up to 3 months.

Cooking and Preparation Hints
* All kinds of hard shell crabs (Dungenous, blue crab, king crab, stone crab, snow crab) can be substituted for one another.
* Soft shell crabs are blue crabs that have shed their hard shells during molting. They should be cooked within 2 days of purchase but can be frozen for up to 12 months. When thawing soft shell crabs, do so in the refrigerator. Do not try to thaw them

INGREDIENT	Amount Market Form	Yield Equivalent	For Purpose of	Amount	Substitution	Instructions
Cracked Wheat See Wheat, Cracked						
Crackers	15 graham crackers or squares 28 saltine squares 26 Ritz crackers 10 oz. soda cracker crumbs	1 c. crumbs 1 c. crumbs 1 c. crumbs 4 c.	Breading	1 c.	1 c. dry bread crumbs	

Cooking and Preparation Hints
* Recrisp soggy crackers by baking them at 350° for 2 to 3 minutes.
* Crackers freeze well. Put the unopened box or bag in a freezer storage bag.

INGREDIENT	Amount Market Form	Yield Equivalent	For Purpose of	Amount	Substitution	Instructions
Cranberry See also Fruit	1 lb. fresh 1 lb. fresh 8 oz. can whole 16 oz. can sauce	4 c. 3 c. cook'd sauce 1 c. 1 2/3 c.			* Cranberries can be refrigerated in a plastic bag for up to 1 month or frozen, unsweetened, for 9 to 16 months.	

Cooking and Preparation Hints
* Sort and discard any soft berries before cooking because they can cause an off flavor.

INGREDIENT	Amount Market Form	Yield Equivalent	For Purpose of	Amount	Substitution	Instructions
Crayfish (Crawfish) See also Fish/Shellfish	1 lb. in shell 1 lb. in shell 12 crayfish	10 crayfish 3/4 c. meat 1 serving	All Recipes	1 lb.	1 lb. small shrimp	

Cooking and Preparation Hints
* Herbs and spices that complement crayfish include crab boil, bay leaf, thyme, garlic, oregano, fennel seed, black pepper and parsley.

INGREDIENT	Amount Market Form	Yield Equivalent	For Purpose of	Amount	Substitution	Instructions
Cream See also Sour Cream	1 c. whipping cream	2 c. whipped	Whipped Cream	1 c. whipping cream 1 c. whipping cream 1 c. whipping cream 1 c. sweetened whipped	2/3 c. evaporated milk + 4 t. lemon juice or vinegar (1) 1/2 c. nonfat dry milk + 1/3 c. water + 1 T lemon juice (2) 1 c. light cream + 1 egg white (3) 4 oz. frozen whipped topping, thawed	(1) Chill milk to just below 32° so that ice crystals form. Beat until thick. The milk will increase 2 to 3 times in volume. Fold the lemon juice or vinegar into the whipped milk to increse its stability. When refrigerated, the whipped milk will remain stiff for 45 minutes to 1 hour. (2) Combine the milk and the water and chill. Whip until soft peaks form and add the lemon juice. Whip again until thick. This will produce about 1 3/4 c. whipped milk. (3) Whip the cream and the egg white separately and fold together.

* "cream" is not applied to products with less than 18% fat. Half and half has 10.5% to 18% fat.
* Ultrapasteurized cream has been exposed to higher temperatures to kill the microorganisms that cause cream to sour. While the process extends the shelf life of the cream, it also reduces its whipping ability.

Cooking and Preparation Hints
* The varieties of cream are categorized by the amount of butterfat they contain. Heavy cream (sometimes called heavy whipping cream) has a minimum of 36% fat. Whipping cream has 30% to 36% fat. Light cream (also called coffee cream or table cream) has 18% to 30% fat. The term

C-17

INGREDIENT	YIELD			SUBSTITUTION		
	Amount Market Form	Yield Equivalent	For Purpose of	Amount	Substitution	Instructions

Cream continued

Cooking and Preparation Hints (continued)

* For successful whipped cream, start with very cold cream and utensils. Try freezing the bowl and beaters for 30 minutes. Begin beating slowly and gradually increase speed until soft peaks form; then slow again. Improper beating can cause your cream to curdle. Add sweeteners and flavorings after the cream has started to thicken. If added too soon, the cream may not thicken properly; if added too late, the extra beating may cause the cream to curdle.
* If you suspect your cream is not as fresh as it should be for whipping, add 1/8 t. baking soda for each 1 c. cream before beating. This should keep the cream from curdling.
* Overbeating usually means you have to start over with a new batch of cream. However, as a last ditch effort, try whipping in 2 T cold milk. Sometimes it works to retrieve the whipped cream.

For Purpose of	Amount	Substitution	Instructions
Whipped Cream	1 c. sweetened whipped	1 1/4 oz. dessert topping mix, prepared	* There are several ways to stabilize whipped cream for frosting or decorating cakes. (1) For each 1 c. cream, dissolve 1 t. unflavored gelatin in 2 T cold water. Heat so that the gelatin dissolves, then cool completely. As your cream thickens with beating, slowly add the gelatin mixture and beat until stiff. (2) Combine 1/2 whipped cream and 1/2 non-dairy dessert topping. (3) Sweeten whipped cream with confectioners' sugar. It contains cornstarch which acts as a stabilizer.
Soups/Sauces	1 c. whip'g cream	3/4 c. milk + 1/3 c. butter	
	1 c. light cream	7/8 c. milk + 3 T butter	* Whipped cream freezes well. You can freeze it in individual portions in small paper cups for use as a dessert topping. Or you can freeze dollops or piped rosettes for use as garnishes for cakes and other desserts. First quick-freeze them on a wax paper-lined cookie sheet. Then put them in a freezer storage bag.
	1 c. light cream	1/2 c. whipping cream + 1/2 c. milk	
	1 c. half and half	7/8 c. milk + 1 1/2 t. butter	
	1 c. half and half	1/2 c. light cream + 1/2 c. milk	
Soups & Sauces/ Reducing Fat	1 c. cream	1 c. evaporated milk	
	1 c. light cream	1 c. low-fat or nonfat milk + 2 t. cornstarch + 1 T water (4)	(4) Combine the water and cornstarch in a saucepan until smooth. Gradually add the milk. Bring to a boil, stirring, over medium heat until the mixture thickens slightly. (5) Heat and reduce to 1 c.
Non-Dairy	1 c. light cream	1 c. non-dairy cream substitute	
	1 c. light cream	2 c. non-dairy milk substitute (5)	

INGREDIENT	Amount Market Form	Yield Equivalent	For Purpose of	Amount	Substitution	Instructions
Cream Cheese See also Cheese	3 oz.	6 T	All Recipes/ Reducing Fat	1 c.	1 c. creamed cottage cheese, drained	(1) The dry cottage cheese should be pressed through a sieve.
	8 oz.	1 c.		1 c.	1 c. dry cottage cheese (1)	(2) Neufchatel is like cream cheese except it has slightly less butterfat. It is smoother and spreads more easily.
				1 c.	1 c. Neufchatel cheese (2)	
				1 c.	1 c. low-fat/nonfat cream cheese	(3) 3 c. nonfat plain yogurt will yield 1 c. yogurt cheese. Line a colander with a double thickness of cheesecloth. Set the colander over a large bowl. Spoon in the yogurt, cover with plastic wrap and refrigerate for at least 8 hours. Transfer the cheese to another container, and discard the liquid. The cheese will keep for 1 week.
				1 c.	1 c. yogurt cheese (3)	

Cooking and Preparation Hints

* Cream cheese can be refrigerated for up to 2 weeks. Freezing is not recommended; it makes the cheese dry and crumbly.

ABCDEFGHIJKLMNOPQRSTUVWXYZ

INGREDIENT	YIELD			SUBSTITUTION			
	Amount Market Form	Yield Equivalent	For Purpose of	Amount	Substitution	Instructions

Cream of Tartar

| | | | Stabilizing Egg Whites | 1 t. | 1 t. lemon juice |
| | | | | 1 t. | 1 t. vinegar |

Cooking and Preparation Hints
* As a stabilizer, cream of tartar keeps beaten egg whites from deflating. Add 1/8 t. per egg white, 1 t. per 1 c. of egg whites, and for meringues add 1/8 t. for each 2 egg whites.

Crème Fraîche

			All Recipes	1 c.	1 c. whipping cream + 1 T buttermilk (1)	(1) Combine the ingredients and heat until just lukewarm. Pour mixture into a lightly covered jar and let sit at room temperature until thickened — several hours or overnight. Refrigerate for up to 2 weeks.
				1 c.	1 c. whipping cream + 1 T yogurt (1)	(2) Whisk the ingredients until the mixture is lightly thickened. Let it sit at room temperature for several hours to thicken and sour. Refrigerate for up to 2 weeks.
				1 c.	1/2 c. whipping cream + 1/2 c. sour cream (2)	(3) The butterfat content is the same, but the taste is different.
				1 c.	1 c. whipping cream (3)	

Cucumber
See also Vegetables

| 12 oz. fresh | 2 1/2 c. sliced |

Cooking and Preparation Hints
* To avoid bitterness, remove the seeds of an older cucumber. As a cucumber ages, its seeds grow larger and bitter. Another method is to cut a small piece from the stem end, then rub the cut side of the stem end in a circular motion against the cut side of the remaining cucumber piece. A white foam will form which you can remove by simply slicing off.

* To make a cucumber crisp, slice it, salt it and let the pieces stand for an hour. Then rinse off the salt. The salt draws out the extra moisture.
* Herbs and spices that complement cucumbers include basil, mint, dill weed, tarragon, black pepper and chives.
* Cucumbers can't be frozen raw and whole. They will turn mushy.

Cumin
See also Herbs/Spices

| 1 t. whole seeds | 1/2 t. ground |

Cooking and Preparation Hints
* As a rule-of-thumb, 1/2 t. ground cumin is adequate for a dish serving 6.

* The taste of cumin is much more intense in cold foods. It mellows as the food is cooked.

Curaçao
See also Spirits

| | | | All Recipes | 1 c. | 1 c. triple sec |
| | | | | 1 c. | 1 c. Cointreau |

C-19

INGREDIENT	YIELD			SUBSTITUTION		
	Amount Market Form	Yield Equivalent	For Purpose of	Amount	Substitution	Instructions
Currant See also Fruit	1 lb. dried	3 c.	All Recipes	1 c. dried 1 c. dried	1 c. raisins 1 c. chopped dates	

Cooking and Preparation Hints

* Fresh currants and dried currants are really 2 different fruits. Fresh currants are small berries related to the gooseberry; red, white and black varieties are available. Dried currants are actually sun-dried Black Corinth grapes.
* To plump dried currants, cover them with hot tap water and let them soak for 5 to 15 minutes. Alternatively, you can wash and drain them, then heat them, covered, in a 350° oven until they puff up.
* There are several methods for chopping dried currants without having them stick to the knife, scissors or food processor blades. (1) Coat the knife or scissors with a little oil. (2) Toss the currants themselves with oil (1 t. oil per 1 c. currants). (3) Lightly flour the currants with some of the flour called for in the recipe. (4) Freeze the currants, then chop them in a food processor or blender.
* Fresh currants can be frozen unsweetened, in a dry sugar pack (3/4 c. sugar per 1 qt. currants) or in a 50% syrup pack. For the syrup, dissolve 4 3/4 c. sugar in 4 c. water and refrigerate. Add 1/2 to 2/3 c. syrup per 1 pt. of fruit.

INGREDIENT	YIELD			SUBSTITUTION		
Curry Paste	5 oz.	1/2 c.				
Curry Powder See also Herbs/Spices			All Recipes	2 T	1 t. ground ginger + 1 t. coriander + 1 t. cardamom + 1 t. ground red pepper + 1 t. turmeric + 1 t. cumin (1)	(1) Recipes for curry powder can contain up to 20 ingredients. You may also include ingredients such as mustard seeds, fennel seeds, nutmeg, poppy seeds, cloves, mace, allspice, cinnamon and garlic.
Cusk See also Fish/Shellfish			All Recipes	1 lb. 1 lb. 1 lb. 1 lb. 1 lb.	1 lb. haddock 1 lb. cod 1 lb. pollock 1 lb. whiting 1 lb. hake	

INGREDIENT	YIELD		SUBSTITUTION			
	Amount Market Form	Yield Equivalent	For Purpose of	Amount	Substitution	Instructions
Dandelion Greens See also Greens, Cooking	1 lb. fresh	2 3/4 c. cooked				after the flowers have appeared. Harvest the plants by cutting 1" to 2" below the surface. When selecting a harvesting site, make sure the area has not been treated with chemicals, and avoid plants along heavily-traveled roadsides which may have been contaminated by automobile exhaust.

Cooking and Preparation Hints
* Unlike other greens, the taste of dandelion greens does not improve with long cooking. About 15 minutes is adequate.
* If you want to pick your own dandelion greens, look in early spring before the yellow flowers have bloomed. The leaves become increasingly bitter

INGREDIENT	Amount Market Form	Yield Equivalent	For Purpose of	Amount	Substitution	Instructions
Date See also Fruit	1 lb. unpitted 1 lb. pitted	2 c. pitted 2 1/2 c. chopped	All Recipes	1 c. chopped 1 c. chopped 1 c. chopped 1 c. chopped	1 c. chopped raisins 1 c. chopped figs 1 c. chopped prunes 1 c. date crystals + 1/3 c. liquid (1)	(1) Allow the mixture to stand until the crystals have softened.

Cooking and Preparation Hints
* If dates are stuck together, you can separate them easily by putting them in a warm oven for a few minutes.
* An unopened package of dried dates can be stored at room temperature for 4 to 6 months. An opened package should be kept tightly covered in the refrigerator and will keep for up to 2 months. Stored in the freezer, they will keep almost indefinitely.
* To freeze fresh dates, wash, drain and pit them if desired. They can be frozen unsweetened or in a 50% syrup pack. For the syrup, dissolve 4 3/4 c. sugar in 4 c. water and refrigerate. Add syrup to the fruit at the rate of 1/2 to 2/3 c. for each pt. of fruit.

INGREDIENT	Amount Market Form	Yield Equivalent	For Purpose of	Amount	Substitution	Instructions
Date Sugar See Sugar						
Dewberry See also Fruit			All Recipes	1 c. 1 c. 1 c. 1 c.	1 c. blackberries 1 c. boysenberries 1 c. loganberries 1 c. youngberries	sugar pack (3/4 c. sugar per 1 qt. berries) or in a 40% to 50% syrup pack. For the syrup, dissolve 3 to 4 3/4 c. sugar in 4 c. water and refrigerate. For each pt. of fruit, add 1/2 to 2/3 c. syrup. Dewberries in syrup can be frozen for up to 16 months.

Cooking and Preparation Hints
* Dewberries can be frozen unsweetened. Quick-freeze them on a tray for two hours, then transfer them to a plastic freezer bag. They will last for 6 months. Dewberries can also be frozen in a dry

INGREDIENT	Amount Market Form	Yield Equivalent	For Purpose of	Amount	Substitution	Instructions
Dill (Dill Seed, Dill Weed) See also Herbs/Spices	1/2 oz. fresh 1 T chopped fresh	1/2 c. leaves 1 t. dried	Seasoning	1/4 t. dried	1/4 t. liquid dill	

Cooking and Preparation Hints
* Fresh dill loses its fragrance when heated; so add the leaves toward the end of cooking.
* Dill complements such foods as salmon, shrimp, pork, lamb, chicken, beets, cabbage, potatoes, cucumbers, eggs, carrots, squash, beans, tomatoes, Brussels sprouts, turnips and, of course, dips.
* A rule-of-thumb for pickling is to add 1 1/2 t. dill seed per 1 qt. of pickling liquid.
* Heating dill seeds in a small amount of water will release their flavor.
* You can store fresh dill in the refrigerator wrapped in paper towels for 1 to 2 weeks.
* Fresh dill sprigs can be frozen whole for up to 1 year.

A B C D E F G H I J K L M N O P Q R S T U V W X Y Z

INGREDIENT	YIELD		For Purpose of	SUBSTITUTION		Instructions
	Amount Market Form	Yield Equivalent		Amount	Substitution	
Dolphinfish See Mahi Mahi						
Dorado See Mahi Mahi						
Dressing See Salad Dressing or Stuffing Mix						
Dried Beans See Beans, Dried						
Dried Cod See Salt Cod						
Duck (Duckling)	1 1/2 lb.	1 serving				

Cooking and Preparation Hints
* A duckling averages 5 lbs. One duckling will serve 2 people generously with lots of leftovers.
* A duck has much more fat than a chicken or turkey. Be sure to prick the skin well so that the fat will drain out as it cooks. This also insures that the skin will be crispy.
* Herbs and spices that complement duck include thyme, black pepper, rosemary, bay leaf, ginger and dry mustard.
* Ducks frozen whole or cut up will last for 6 to 7 months.

INGREDIENT	YIELD		SUBSTITUTION			
	Amount Market Form	Yield Equivalent	For Purpose of	Amount	Substitution	Instructions
Eaux-de-vie See Spirits						
Edam Cheese See also Cheese	8 oz.		All Recipes	8 oz.	8 oz. gouda cheese (1)	(1) They are similar in flavor although edam is made from partly skim milk and gouda from whole milk.

Cooking and Preparation Hints
* Edam is better as an eating cheese than one for grating and cooking.
* Edam may be frozen for up to 6 months.

INGREDIENT	YIELD		SUBSTITUTION			
	Amount Market Form	Yield Equivalent	For Purpose of	Amount	Substitution	Instructions
Edible Flowers See Flowers						
Egg See also Meringue, Soufflé	1 extra large	4 T	Thickening	1 whole	1 T flour	
	1 extra large	1 T + 1 t. yolk		1 whole	1 1/2 t. cornstarch	
	1 extra large	2 T + 1 t. white		1 whole	1 1/2 t. arrowroot	
	1 large	3 T + 1/4 t.		1 whole	2 egg yolks + 1 T cold liquid	
	1 large	1 T + 1/4 t. yolk				
	1 large	2 T white	All Cooked Recipes	1 whole	3 1/2 T thawed frozen egg	
	1 medium	2 T + 1 1/2 t.		1 whole	1/4 c. liquid egg substitute	
	1 medium	1 T yolk		1 whole	2 1/2 T dried whole egg + 2 1/2 T water	

Cooking and Preparation Hints
* Eggs should be refrigerated. They will deteriorate more in one day at room temperature than a week in the refrigerator. Store eggs in a closed carton to keep them from absorbing odors through their shells. Keep them away from strong smelling foods such as fish, cabbage, onions and apples. Arrange them with the large ends up to help the yolks remain centered.
* To test the freshness of an egg, place it in a large bowl of cold water. If it's very fresh, it will sink to the bottom. If it drops midway down, it's about 3 days old. And if it floats, it's more than 3 days old.
* Stored properly in the refrigerator, eggs will keep for 3 to 5 weeks. Separated whites and yolks will keep for 2 to 4 days. Hard-cooked eggs will last a week. Thawed liquid egg substitute will remain fresh for 10 days unopened or 3 days when the container has been opened.
* If eggs stick to the carton, wet the carton. You can then remove the eggs without having them crack.
* Some recipes call for eggs at room temperature, which you can achieve by immersing them in warm tap water for a couple of minutes. The only times eggs need to be at room temperature are when: (1) You plan to beat the whites. (They achieve better volume that way.) Or (2) when the eggs will be combined with fat and sugar. (Cold eggs can harden the fat, causing the batter to curdle and affecting the texture of the finished product.)
* Most recipes for baked goods are based on the use of large size eggs.
* If you are halving a recipe and need half an egg, use a white only to substitute for the half egg.
* For thickening, use 1 egg for each 1 c. of liquid.
* If you're thickening with egg yolks, use 2 to 3 yolks for each 1 c. of liquid. Never add the yolks directly to the hot liquid or you'll have what looks like scrambled eggs. Stir the yolks first to break them up, then add a small amount of the hot liquid to the yolks. When the yolks are warm, add the mixture gradually to the hot liquid and stir over low heat until the liquid is thickened. Do not boil the liquid or it will curdle.
* To prevent an egg from cracking when it is boiled, pierce the large end with an egg piercer or pin before cooking.

INGREDIENT	YIELD		SUBSTITUTION			
	Amount Market Form	Yield Equivalent	For Purpose of	Amount	Substitution	Instructions
Egg continued	1 medium	1 T + 2 1/2 t. white	All Cooked Recipes	1 yolk	3 1/2 t. thawed frozen yolk	
	1 small	2 T + 1 t.		1 yolk	2 T dried egg yolk + 2 t. water	
	1 small	3/4 T yolk				
	1 small	1 T + 2 t. white		1 white	2 T thawed frozen white	
	12 extra large	3 c.		1 white	1 T dried egg white + 2 T water	
	12 extra large	1 c. yolk				
	12 extra large	1 3/4 c. white				
	12 large	2 1/3 c.	Baking	1 whole	4 oz. tofu (1)	(1) Mix into other ingredients well.

Cooking and Preparation Hints (continued)

* When an egg has cracked during boiling, add about 1 t. salt or a few drops of vinegar or lemon juice to prevent the whites from seeping out into the water.
* For easier peeling of hard-cooked eggs, select eggs that are at least a week old. As an egg ages an air cell forms between the shell and the egg, ultimately making peeling easier. Piercing the large end of the egg shell with an egg piercer or pin before cooking will facilitate peeling as well. The puncture allows a small amount of water to enter the egg, separating the shell and the egg. When eggs are done, plunge them immediately into cold water.
* Occasionally in hard-cooked eggs, a greenish tinge will appear on the surface of the yolk. This usually happens when the egg has been cooked over too high a heat, has been cooked too long or has been stored several days before peeling. Correcting any of these will help. Also, after cooking, plunge the eggs immediately into cold water; this will stop the eggs from cooking and help prevent discoloration.
* Hard-cooked eggs can be stored, shelled or unshelled, in the refrigerator for a week.

* If you've stored hard-cooked eggs in their shells and can't remember which eggs are cooked and which ones are raw, try this test. Spin an egg around on its side, then stop it. A cooked egg will spin and stop easily. A raw egg, because of its liquid interior, will not spin easily and may start moving again after it is stopped.
* For easy and attractive deviled eggs, put the cooked yolks and other stuffing ingredients into a plastic food storage bag and knead until blended. Cut off a corner of the bag and squeeze the mixture decoratively into the egg whites.
* To prevent tough scrambled eggs, add salt after, not before, cooking. Salt promotes coagulation of eggs and toughens them.
* Adding milk or water to scrambled eggs and omelets will produce a moister, softer result. The recommended amount for scrambled eggs is 2 to 5 t. per egg, and the amount for omelets is 2 to 3 t. per egg.
* Creamy scrambled eggs can be achieved by adding a little softened cream cheese.
* Before frying eggs, preheat the pan over medium heat. Eggs will cook unevenly in a pan that is not preheated. If the heat is too high, the eggs will overcook on the bottom before they're set on top.

	12 large	7/8 c. yolk	Baking/Reducing Fat	1 whole	1/3 c. liquid egg substitute (2)	(2) In cake recipes that call for only 1 to 2 whole eggs, use 1/3 c. for each egg. In recipes with 3-4 eggs, use 1/4 c. liquid egg substitute for each egg and reduce the amount of liquid in the recipe by 2 T to compensate for the additional liquid from the egg substitute. For a recipe with more than 4 eggs, the liquid egg substitute will not produce a satisfactory result.
	12 large	1 1/2 c. white		1 whole	1 banana (3)	
	12 medium	2 c.		1 whole	1/4 c. unsweetened applesauce (3)	
	12 medium	3/4 c. yolk		1 yolk	1/4 c. liquid egg substitute (4)	
	12 medium	1 1/3 c. white				
	12 small	1 3/4 c.	All Recipes/	1 whole	2 egg whites (5)	(3) This works best for recipes with up to 3 eggs and is not recommended for recipes that depend on eggs for leavening such as angel food and sponge cakes. The products using this substitution may have to be baked longer. Whether or not this substitution will affect the taste depends on the other flavorings that are used.
	12 small	2/3 c. yolk	Reducing Cholesterol	1 whole	2 egg whites + 1 t. unsaturated oil (6)	
	12 small	1 1/4 c. white		1 whole	1/4 c. low-cholesterol liquid eggs (7)	

INGREDIENT	YIELD			SUBSTITUTION		
	Amount Market Form	Yield Equivalent	For Purpose of	Amount	Substitution	Instructions

Egg
continued

Instructions (continued column):

(4) Recipes requiring more than 2 egg yolks do not have satisfactory results when made with liquid egg substitutes.

(5) This substitution can be used for half of the eggs called for in scrambled eggs, quiches and custards.

(6) When using this substitution for baked goods, subtract 1 1/3 T of the liquid in the recipe for each whole egg that is being replaced.

(7) This product is pasteurized and can be used raw in recipes for eggnog, mayonnaise or hollandaise sauce. It can be beaten to a thick pale yellow color. When used for cooking, this product will cook a little faster, and baked goods will brown more quickly.

Substitution / Amount column (Cooking and Preparation Hints continued):

residue of fat in the bowl will prevent the whites from developing volume.

* Fat inhibits the foaming of egg whites; so if a yolk breaks into the whites during separation, you may have to start over. If it's just a drop of yolk, however, you may be able to remove it without a trace. You can try removing it with a spoon or with the corner of a moistened paper towel. If the yolk has blended with some of the whites, you can use a piece of soft white bread to move the whites containing the yolk up one side of the bowl. Hold the tainted whites there and pour the remaining clear egg whites into another container.

* Salt reduces the foaming ability of egg whites when beaten; so add any salt called for in the recipe to the other ingredients.

* When folding beaten egg whites with another mixture, you want to retain as much volume as possible. To do this, add the whites to the other mixture instead of adding the mixture to the whites. First stir about 1/4 of the whites into the other mixture to loosen it. Then add the rest of the egg whites and fold another 7 or 8 times until blended. Do not overblend or you will deflate the egg whites.

* Sugar beaten into egg whites should be added after the whites start to become a foamy white. If added earlier, the sugar can cause a decrease in volume.

For Purpose of column (Cooking and Preparation Hints continued):

* If you like your fried eggs to have the whites set but the yolk runny, try this method. Break the egg into a heated pan, cover, remove from heat and let stand 3 to 4 minutes.

* For poached eggs, adding a little salt, vinegar or lemon juice to the water will speed coagulation and help the whites retain their shape.

* Eggs can be separated easily through a funnel. The white slides through while the yolk stays on top.

* Egg whites will increase in volume 6 to 8 times when beaten and will achieve their greatest volume if allowed to stand at room temperature for 30 minutes before beating.

* Beaten egg whites can lose their volume easily and, for that reason, need a stabilizing agent. You can add cream of tartar, vinegar or lemon juice. As a rule-of-thumb, add 1/8 t. per egg white or 1 t. per 1 c. of egg whites. If you are beating the egg whites for a meringue, add 1/8 t. for each 2 egg whites. Beating the whites in a copper bowl will also stabilize the foam, but don't use both a copper bowl and cream of tartar because the whites will take on a greenish color.

* When selecting a bowl in which to beat egg whites, avoid aluminum because the whites will turn gray and, especially, avoid plastic and wood because they tend to absorb fat. Any

Yield Equivalent column:

1 c. whole   4 - 7 whole
1 c. yolks   12 - 18 yolks
1 c. whites   7 - 11 whites

Amount column (Cooking and Preparation Hints continued):

* If you overbeat your egg whites, you can reconstitute them by simply adding another egg white and beating briefly until smooth.

* If your recipe calls for beating egg yolks until they are thick and lemon-colored, you can count on 3 to 5 minutes of beating at high speed with an electric mixer.

* Raw eggs can be frozen, but not in the shell. For convenience, whole eggs, yolks or whites can be frozen in ice cube trays and transferred to freezer bags when solid.

Instructions column (Cooking and Preparation Hints continued):

Each cube holds approximately 1 whole egg, 2 egg yolks or 2 egg whites. Whole eggs can be stored for 6 to 9 months; yolks for 4 to 6 months; whites for 9 to 12 months.

* To prevent coagulation when freezing egg yolks, you must add either salt or sugar, depending on the final use, before freezing. The rule-of-thumb is 1/8 t. salt per 1/4 c. egg yolks (4 yolks) for main dishes and 1 1/2 t. sugar or corn syrup per 1/4 c. yolks for baking or desserts.

* Use thawed eggs within 24 hours.

| INGREDIENT | YIELD | | For Purpose of | SUBSTITUTION | | Instructions |
	Amount Market Form	Yield Equivalent		Amount	Substitution	
Egg Noodle See Pasta						
Eggnog						

Eggnog — Cooking and Preparation Hints
* Eggnog can be frozen. The commercially made product can be frozen in the carton. For homemade, pour it into a rigid freezer container and leave 1/2" headspace for expansion.
* For serving a punch bowl of eggnog, freeze some of the eggnog in ice cube trays and add to the punch bowl so that the eggnog stays cold but is not watered down.

Eggplant (Aubergine) See also Vegetables	1 lb. 1 lb. 1/3 lb.	1 medium 3 c. diced 1 serving				

Eggplant — Cooking and Preparation Hints
* Most varieties of eggplant can be used interchangeably. Their skins differ in appearance, but their cream-colored interiors are similar. The most common type found in U.S. markets is the deep-purple globular eggplant whose flesh is somewhat more bitter than other varieties.
* Eggplant is very perishable and should be cooked as soon as possible after purchase because it becomes bitter when stored longer than a few days. It is best not to refrigerate an eggplant, but if you must, wrap it loosely in paper towels and put it into a plastic bag.
* Eggplant may become too watery when cooked. You can reduce the moisture beforehand by salting the eggplant slices, letting them stand for an hour, then rinsing and draining. This process will also reduce any bitterness and reduce the amount of oil that is absorbed if the eggplant is fried.
* Eggplant discolors quickly once it's cut. You can retard the process by sprinkling the slices with lemon juice.
* Aluminum pans will discolor eggplant; so use glass, enamel or stainless steel cookware.
* If you plan to bake eggplant whole, first pierce the skin or the buildup of steam will cause the vegetable to burst.
* When adding already-sautéed eggplant pieces to a stew, do so a few minutes before serving. That way, the eggplant pieces will absorb the sauce yet retain their shape and texture.
* Eggplant is complemented by herbs and spices such as marjoram, oregano, basil, pepper, parsley and thyme.
* Eggplant can be frozen, but its texture deteriorates. However, when eggplant is frozen in casseroles or stews, there is little change in texture.

Emmenthal Cheese See also Cheese			All Recipes	8 oz. 8 oz.	8 oz. Swiss cheese 8 oz. Gruyère cheese	
Endive See Belgian Endive						
Eschalot See Shallot						
Extracts						

Extracts — Cooking and Preparation Hints
* In general, the difference between an extract and a flavor is that an extract contains alcohol and a flavor does not.
* The shelf life of an extract is about 4 years. Keep the bottle tightly closed to prevent the evaporation of the alcohol.
* To test the potency of an extract, pour 3 drops into a mixture of 1/2 c. water and 1 t. sugar. If the aroma is weak, it is time to replace the extract.
* All extracts are not equal in strength; so a one-to-one substitution is not always recommended. In general, the fruit flavors (with the exception of orange and lemon) are the mildest, and the mint flavors are the strongest in flavor.

INGREDIENT	YIELD		For Purpose of	SUBSTITUTION		Instructions
	Amount Market Form	Yield Equivalent		Amount	Substitution	
Farina	1 lb.	3 c.				
	1 c.	5 1/2 c. cooked				
Farmer Cheese			All Recipes	8 oz.	8 oz. dry cottage cheese	(1) You may want to add a little salt to taste.
				8 oz.	8 oz. hoop cheese (1)	(2) Pot cheese and baker's cheese are not as dry
				8 oz.	8 oz. creamed cottage cheese, drained	as farmer cheese.
				8 oz.	8 oz. pot cheese (2)	
				8 oz.	8 oz. baker's cheese (2)	
Fats			Baking	1 c.	1 c. prune paste (1)	(1) To make 1 c. prune paste, put 8 oz. pitted prunes into food processor. Add 1/2 c. water for each oz. of prunes) and process until paste consistency. Baked goods will have a chewier and denser texture than those made with fat. When added to a chocolate recipe, the chocolate taste is less pronounced in the finished product.
See also Butter, Margarine, Oil, Shortening				1 c.	1 c. dried fruit puree (2)	
				1 c.	1 c. applesauce	
				1 c.	1 c. fresh fruit puree (3)	(2) To make 1 c. dried fruit puree, combine 1 1/3 c. dried fruit (such as apricots, dates, figs), 1/2 c. water and 1 1/2 t. vanilla in food processor and puree. Dried fruit that is pliable rather than hard will have a better result. Be careful not to overmix the batter or dough because it will toughen the final product. Mixing by hand is preferable.
				1 c.	1 c. mashed sweet potato (4)	

Cooking and Preparation Hints

* In low-fat baking, adding beaten egg whites to the batter will help to create a lighter texture; and adding corn syrup can help make cakes moist and tender.
* To remove fat from soup or gravy, try any of the following methods:

(1) Drop ice cubes into the mixture and remove immediately. The grease will stick to the cubes.
(2) Wrap paper towels around the ice cubes and skim the surface.
(3) Refrigerate the mixture until the fat solidifies on the surface. It is then easily removed.

(3) It is important not to overmix or overbake these batters. Cakes made with fruit purees tend to get moister, rather than drier, as they stand.

(4) Use the dark-skinned type because it offers a sweeter flavor and richer consistency. You may want to reduce the amount of sugar called for in the recipe.

For Purpose of	Amount	Substitution	Instructions
Baking	1 c.	16 t. (2 envelopes) Butter Buds ® Mix + 1 c. liquid (5)	(5) Butter Buds ® Mix, liquified, can be used to replace 1/4 to 1/2 the fat in cakes; 1/2 the fat in pie crusts and muffins; and up to 100% of the fat in quick breads. For cookies, the dry mix alone can replace 1/4 to 1/2 the fat in the recipe.
	1 c.	1/4 c. Butter Buds ® Sprinkles (6)	(6) Butter Buds ® Sprinkles can replace 1/4 to 1/2 of the fat in cakes (decrease the amount of flour slightly); 1/2 to 2/3 of the fat in brownies (add a little water to the batter); 1/4 to 1/2 of the fat in cookies (reduce the flour by 25%); 1/2 of the fat in
Greasing Pans	1 T	1 second nonstick cooking spray	

A B C D E F G H I J K L M N O P Q R S T U V W X Y Z

INGREDIENT	YIELD Amount Market Form	Yield Equivalent	For Purpose of	SUBSTITUTION Amount	Substitution	Instructions
Fats continued						muffins (increase the liquid by the same amount of the fat that is removed); and up to 3/4 of the fat in quick breads.
Fava Bean (Broad Bean)	5 lb. fresh unshelled 20 oz. can	4 c. cooked 2 c.	All Recipes	1 c.	1 c. lima beans (1)	(1) Lima beans take slightly less time to cook.
Fennel (Finocchio, Florence Fennel) See also Herbs/Spices, Vegetables	9 oz. whole bulb with leaves 1 lb. bulb 1 T fresh leaves	1 1/2 c. trimmed, sliced 4 c. sliced 1 t. dried				both raw and cooked. The bulb, the seeds and the feathery leaves have a licorice-like flavor similar to anise.

Cooking and Preparation Hints
* All parts of the fennel plant are edible. The bulb is the swollen leaf-base of the plant and is served

INGREDIENT	Amount Market Form	Yield Equivalent	For Purpose of	Amount	Substitution	Instructions
Fig See also Fruit	1 lb. fresh 1 lb. fresh 1 lb. fresh 1 lb. can 1 lb. dried 1 lb. dried	9 medium 12 small 2 2/3 c. chopped 12 - 16 whole 44 whole 3 c. chopped				* To freeze fresh figs, wash in ice water, remove the stems and peel if desired. They can be frozen unsweetened or in a 35% syrup pack. For the syrup pack method, dissolve 2 1/2 c. sugar in 4 c. water and refrigerate. Add 1/2 to 2/3 c. of the syrup for each pt. of figs. Add 3/4 t. ascorbic acid for each qt. of fruit.

Cooking and Preparation Hints
* When chopping dried figs by hand with kitchen scissors or knife, dip the blades in warm water occasionally to prevent sticking.
* To keep dried figs from sticking when chopping them in a food processor, add a little of the sugar that's called for in the recipe.

INGREDIENT	Amount Market Form	Yield Equivalent	For Purpose of	Amount	Substitution	Instructions
Filbert See Hazelnut						
Fines Herbes			Seasoning	4 T	1/2 c. fresh parsley + 2 t. dried chervil + 2 t. dried chives + 1 1/2 t. dried tarragon (1)	(1) Chop together until mixture is a fine consistency.

Cooking and Preparation Hints
* Fines herbes complement such foods as fish, eggs, chilled soups, sauces and salads.

INGREDIENT	Amount Market Form	Yield Equivalent	For Purpose of	Amount	Substitution	Instructions
Finocchio See Fennel						
Fish/Shellfish See also individual listings	1 lb. whole fish 1/2 - 3/4 lb. dressed fish 1/3 - 1/2 lb. steak 1/4 - 1/3 lb. fillet	1 serving 1 serving 1 serving 1 serving	Mixing with other ingredients	8 oz. fresh	8 oz. canned fish or shellfish (1)	(1) To remove any "canned" flavor, soak the fish or shellfish in fresh packing liquid — fresh water if it was water-packed or fresh oil if it was oil-packed.

INGREDIENT	YIELD				SUBSTITUTION		
	Amount Market Form	Yield Equivalent	For Purpose of	Amount	Substitution	Amount	Instructions

Fish/Shellfish
continued

Cooking and Preparation Hints

* The "Canadian Method" is a good rule-of-thumb for cooking fish. It recommends 10 minutes of cooking for every inch of fish thickness regardless of the cooking process used. To measure, lay the fish on its side and use a ruler to determine the thickness at its thickest point. If you are preparing a rolled fillet, measure it after rolling. Fish less than 1/2" thick does not have to be turned when cooking. Add 5 minutes to the cooking time if the fish is cooked in foil or sauce.

* To achieve the best flavor, fish should be cooked just until the center is opaque. By the time it gets to the point where it "flakes easily with a fork," it's overcooked.

* For scaling fish easily and without a mess, soak it in cold water for a few minutes before you begin scaling or hold it under water while scaling.

* Marinating fish with lemon, wine, vinegar, ginger or garlic will reduce any fishy tastes or odors.

* An efficient way to marinate fish is in a self-closing plastic bag which you can turn easily and discard afterward.

* To make sure the breading stays on when frying fish, coat the fish with flour before dipping it into the egg and bread crumbs.

* If you can't serve your fish immediately after cooking and want to keep it warm, put the fish on a warm platter in a very low oven and keep the oven door open. In the case of fillets and steaks, also cover them with a warm, damp cloth.

* For poaching fish, good seasonings to add to the liquid are bay leaf, whole peppercorns, whole allspice, plus some slices of lemon.

* For grilling, use a meaty fish with a strong flavor such as swordfish, tuna, salmon, mackerel and bluefish. Their natural oils will insure they stay moist.

* If you plan to serve fish cold, remove the skin while it is still warm. It's much easier to remove that way.

* In general, fish can be refrigerated for 1 to 2 days and frozen for up to 6 months. Oily types of fish can't be frozen that long.

* Live shellfish can be refrigerated for 1 to 2 days. Cover the container with a damp cloth so that it is not airtight. Discard any shellfish that die. Shellfish can be frozen for 3 to 6 months.

* To freeze fish that are high in fat, rub them with lemon juice or a solution of ascorbic acid. Low-fat fish should be rinsed in a saltwater solution before freezing.

* Frozen fish should be thawed in the refrigerator. Count on 24 hours per lb. of fish. Fish that has been slowly thawed loses less juice and is more delicate when cooked than quickly thawed fish. If a quicker thawing method is necessary, place individual packges of fish in cold water. Allow 1 to 2 hours per lb. to thaw.

* Frozen fillets, steaks and dressed fish can be cooked without thawing. Just allow additional cooking time. It can take up to twice as long to cook.

* Once fish has thawed, cook it right away or throw it out because fish can spoil very quickly.

* When preparing a fish "en papillote," the best paper to use is parchment paper because it has been specially treated with oils to keep juices inside and prevent leaks. Aluminum foil is the second best choice. Wax paper will become soggy and paper bags may contain unhealthy chemicals.

* Some pointers on pickling fish: (1) Pure granulated salt or sack salt is best, but table salt is acceptable. Avoid salt containing calcium or magnesium compounds because they can produce "off color" and "off flavor." (2) Avoid hard water, especially water with a high iron, calcium or magnesium content. (3) Use distilled white vinegar with at least 4 1/2% acetic acid to prevent bacterial growth. (4) Use pickled fish within 4 to 6 weeks.

* Canned fish stored in a dry area at a temperature below 70° will maintain its nutritional and eating quality for 5 years or more.

INGREDIENT	Amount Market Form	Yield Equivalent	For Purpose of	Amount	Substitution	Amount	Instructions
Five Spice Powder			Seasoning		1 T peppercorns + 1 T fennel seeds + 8 star anise + 6 cloves + 1 1/2" cinnamon stick, crushed (1)	4 T	(1) Toast mixture in the oven for 20 minutes at 250°. Cool. Crush until finely ground.
Flavorings See Extracts							
Florence Fennel See Fennel							

INGREDIENT	YIELD		SUBSTITUTION			Instructions
	Amount Market Form	Yield Equivalent	For Purpose of	Amount	Substitution	
Flounder See also Sole, Fish/Shellfish			All Recipes	1 lb. 1 lb. 1 lb. 1 lb.	lb. sole 1 lb. sandab 1 lb. filleted halibut 1 lb. orange roughy	

Cooking and Preparation Hints
* Herbs and spices that complement flounder include parsley, peppercorns, bay leaf, tarragon, dill weed, chives and basil.

* Flounder is best cooked and served in the same dish because it tends to break apart when moved after cooking.
* Flounder can be frozen for 4 to 6 months.

INGREDIENT	Amount Market Form	Yield Equivalent	For Purpose of	Amount	Substitution	Instructions
Flour	1 lb. all purpose (white) 1 lb. all purpose 7/8 c. all purpose, unsifted 1 lb. bread 1 lb. buckwheat 1 lb. cake 1 lb. cake 1 lb. corn	3 1/2 c. unsifted 4 c. sifted 1 c. sifted 4 c. sifted 3 1/4 c. sifted 4 1/8 c. unsifted 4 5/8 c. sifted 4 c. unsifted	Thickening	2 T all purpose 2 T all purpose 2 T all purpose 2 T all purpose 2 T all purpose 2 T all purpose 2 T all purpose	1 T cornstarch (1) 1 T arrowroot (2) 2 t. kudzu (3) 2 large eggs (4) 2 T quick-cooking tapioca (5) 2 T instant flour (6) 2 T cake flour (7) 1 T potato flour (8)	(1) Cornstarch will produce a clearer sauce than flour. It should be added toward the end of preparation. (2) Arrowroot will produce a clearer sauce than flour. It has no holding power; so serve as soon as possible after thickening. Arrowroot should be added toward the end of preparation. It should be mixed into a cold liquid before being added to a hot mixture. A sauce thickened with arrowroot can't be reheated successfully. (3) Like arrowroot, kudzu will produce a light, translucent sauce. Dissolve kudzu in a small amount of cold liquid first. Then add to liquid to be thickened and bring to a high heat, stirring constantly. (4) Do not boil the thickened sauce or it will curdle. (5) Tapioca is a delicate thickener for milk and egg puddings and is especially good for fruit fillings because it produces a clear sauce that does not hide the flavor of the fruit. (6) Instant flour is specially designed as a thickener and cannot substitute for all purpose flour for other uses. (7) Cake flour causes less cloudiness than all purpose and has slightly greater thickening properties. (8) Potato flour produces a translucent liquid with a glossy sheen. It requires less simmering than does all purpose flour. Avoid excessive heating and stirring because the sauce will thin out. Potato flour has no holding power; so serve as soon as possible after thickening.

Cooking and Preparation Hints
* Flours milled from hard wheats have the highest gluten content. Gluten provides the elasticity that allows bread dough to expand. Flours with the highest gluten produce breads with the biggest volume and the lightest texture. High gluten flours are not recommended for cakes because they will toughen a cake's texture. Flours milled from soft wheats have a low gluten content. Cakes benefit from low-gluten, high-starch flours that produce a moist, tender and delicate texture.
* All purpose flour combines both hard and soft wheats and is satisfactory for most household cooking purposes. It has enough gluten to produce good yeast breads but not too much to preclude equally good quick breads and cakes.
* Sifting flour is recommended

when: (1) a light product is the primary objective; or (2) dry ingredients such as baking powder, baking soda, and cocoa need to be incorporated evenly throughout the batter.
* For génoise and angel food cakes, sift the flour first before folding it into the batter to keep the beaten eggs from deflating.
* The leaveners in self-rising flour become less effective with age. For the best results the flour should be fresh. It can maintain its freshness for up to 18 months.
* To improve the nutritional content of all purpose flour, add 2 t. of powdered wheat germ or ground oat flour or peanut flour to each c. of all purpose flour.
* Flour does not work well as a thickener in the presence of acidic fruits such as strawberries, cranberries and tart cherries. Cornstarch, tapioca and arrowroot are better choices.

* To thicken sauce with flour, make a paste using 1 part flour to 2 parts water. Add the paste to the sauce, heat until it thickens, then continue to heat for another 3 minutes to eliminate the raw taste of the flour.
* To prevent a "skin" from forming on your sauce or gravy after it has been sitting for a few minutes, use a high-starch, low-protein flour for thickening such as cake flour or pastry flour or bleached all purpose flour.
* Too much sugar will reduce the thickening property of flour and other starches. Add only as much as the recipe calls for.
* Add acids such as vinegar or lemon juice to a flour-thickened sauce after the thickening is completed. If added before, the mixture will not thicken as well.

Ingredient	Amount Market Form	Yield Equivalent	For Purpose of	Amount	Substitution	Instructions
Flour continued	1 lb. gluten	3 1/4 c. sifted	Thickening	2 T all purpose	1 T rice flour (9)	(9) Rice flour will produce a clear sauce. Try to use a waxy type rice flour which reduces lumpiness and promotes the stability of sauces so they can be reheated without separating.
	1 lb. instant	3 5/8 c. unsifted		2 T all purpose	1 T waxy corn flour (10)	(10) Waxy corn flour will produce a clear sauce.
	1 lb. pastry	4 1/2 c. sifted		2 T all purpose	2 T ground oat flour	(11) The vegetables used in preparing soups and sauces can be pureed and returned to the liquid for thickening.
	1 lb. Potato (potato starch)	4 c. sifted		2 T all purpose	2 T biscuit mix	(12) Self-rising flour contains baking powder and salt; so omit those 2 ingredients from the recipe. If a second leavening such as baking soda is
	1 lb. rice	3 c. unsifted		2 T all purpose	4 T instant mashed potatoes	called for, it will have to be added. Self-rising flour is made from soft wheat flours and produces
	1 lb. rice	3 1/2 c. sifted	Baking	2 T all purpose	Pureed vegetables as needed (11)	lighter cakes and quick breads. It is not good for sponge or angel food cakes or popovers because the additional baking powder causes them to rise,
	1 lb. rye (light)	5 c. sifted		1 c. all purpose	1 c. self-rising flour (12)	then collapse. It is also not recommended for yeast bread. Pastry crusts made with self-rising
	1 lb. rye (dark)	3 1/2 c. sifted		1 c. all purpose	1 c. + 2 T cake flour (13)	flour will turn out spongy rather than flakey.

(13) Cake flour provides a fine and crumbly texture in baked goods. It is especially good in baking powder-leavened and egg-leavened batters for chiffon, génoise, angel food and sponge cakes. All purpose flour with its high gluten content is better for heavier batters such as pound cakes and yeast coffee cakes.

Cooking and Preparation Hints (continued)

* Avoid lumps in flour-thickened sauces by stirring constantly. Thickening occurs more quickly at the sides and bottom of the pan and causes lumping if not stirred.
* Flour and other starch-thickened sauces should be heated quickly for best results. Too gradual heating will produce a heavy, gummy consistency.
* When thickening sauces, use a wide, shallow pan. A thin layer of liquid thickens more quickly and more uniformly.
* For each 1 c. of liquid to be thickened, add 1 T of flour for a thin sauce, 2 T of flour for a medium thickness, 3 T for a thick sauce and 4 T for a very thick sauce.
* An easy way to measure 7/8 c. flour is to measure 1 c. flour and then remove 2 T.
* Bleaching of all purpose flour has no effect on baking except that the bleached product may absorb slightly less liquid. The bleached flour has a little less vitamin E, a somewhat lower protein content and a slightly coarser texture.
* You can create a handy device for flouring greased cake pans by filling an empty spice jar with a shaker top with flour.
* 1 c. of flour will yield about 20 2-inch cookies.
* Whole-grain flours should be stored in the refrigerator if they will be used in a few days. For longer periods, store in the freezer. Bring the flour to room temperature before using.
* When adding flour to cookie dough, mix only until incorporated to prevent toughness.

	1 lb. self-rising	4 c. sifted	Baking	1 c. self-rising	1 c. all purpose flour + 1 1/2 t. baking powder + 1/2 t. salt	(14) The cornstarch promotes tenderness in cakes.
	1 lb. soy (full fat)	7 1/2 c. sifted		1 c. cake	7/8 c. all purpose flour + 2 T cornstarch (14)	(15) Working the pastry dough will activate the gluten in the flour and give the dough body. But don't overwork it or the dough will become tough and rubbery.
	1 lb. soy (low fat)	5 1/2 c. unsifted		1 c. all purpose	1 c. pastry flour (15)	(16) If using for cakes, use 1 T less per c. than the recipe calls for.
	1 lb. whole wheat (graham)	3 1/3 c. stirred		1 c. all purpose	1 c. presifted flour (16)	(17) This is best in muffins, cookies and pancakes.
				1 c. all purpose	1/4 c. barley flour + 3/4 c. all purpose flour (17)	(18) Oat flour may produce a sticky texture. It contains very little gluten and should be used in combination with wheat flour.
				1 c. all purpose	1/3 c. oat flour + 2/3 c. all purpose flour (18)	(19) Soy flour is high in both protein and fat. Because of the fat, it's easier to cream it with the shortening or blend it with the liquids rather than
				1 c. all purpose	2 T soy flour + 7/8 c. all purpose flour (19)	adding it to the dry ingredients. The amount of liquid and leavening in the recipe should be slightly increased.
				1 c. all purpose	1/2 c. buckwheat flour + 1/2 c. all purpose flour (20)	
				1 c. all purpose	1/4 c. matzo cake meal + 3/4 c. potato flour	

A B C D E F G H I J K L M N O P Q R S T U V W X Y Z

INGREDIENT	YIELD		SUBSTITUTION			
	Amount Market Form	Yield Equivalent	For Purpose of	Amount	Substitution	Instructions
Flour continued						Soy flour browns quickly; so reduce oven temperature by 25°. Soy flour doesn't contain gluten — which provides cohesiveness in dough — and must always be used in conjunction with all purpose flour. (20) This substitution is especially good for pancakes, waffles, quick breads, muffins, cookies and gingerbread. You can grind your own flour by whirling whole or coarse kasha in a food processor for about 3 minutes until pulverized. Dark buckwheat flour has a stronger flavor than the light.
			Baking	1 c. ground nut flour	1 c. other ground nut flour (21)	(21) Wheat flour is not a good substitute because it lacks the oils and texture of nuts. Ground almonds, walnuts, pecans and hazelnuts are all interchangeable. If you want to use a food processor to make your own nut flour, grind each 1 c. nuts with 2 T of sugar or flour from the recipe. Without the addition of sugar or flour, the nuts will release too much of their oil and turn into a paste instead of flour.
			Baking/Non-Wheat (22)	1 c. all purpose	1 c. ready-mixed wheat-free flour	(22) Each kind of flour functions differently in relation to the other ingredients in a recipe. As a result, these substitutions will not be entirely accurate for all recipes, and you will have to experiment. Cakes made with non-wheat flour tend to be dry. Frosting them and storing them in closed containers will help preserve their moisture.
				1 c. all purpose	5/8 c. potato flour (23)	(23) To avoid lumps, either mix the flour with the sugar or cream the flour with the shortening before adding the liquid ingredients. Potato flour is best used in combination with other flours.
				1 c. all purpose	1/2 c. potato flour + 1/2 c. cornstarch (23)	
				1 c. all purpose	1/2 c. rice flour + 1/2 c. cornstarch (24)	(24) Rice flour alone produces a heavy, tasteless product. It is the least allergic flour, but is best used in combination with other grains. Avoid waxy types of rice flour which are better for thickening than baking.
				1 c. all purpose	1 c. tapioca flour	
			Yeast Bread	1 c. all purpose	1 c. bread flour (25)	(25) Bread flour has a high gluten content which gives the dough elasticity and allows it to expand more than all purpose flour. The high rising dough produces a large volume bread and a light texture.
				1 c. bread flour	1 c. minus 1 t. all purpose flour + 1 t. gluten flour	

INGREDIENT

	YIELD			SUBSTITUTION			
	Amount Market Form	Yield Equivalent	For Purpose of	Amount	Substitution	Instructions	

Flour
continued

For Purpose of	Amount	Substitution	Instructions
Yeast Bread	1 c. all purpose	1/2 c. bran flour + 1/2 c. all purpose flour 1/2 c. whole wheat flour + 1/2 c. all purpose flour (26)	(26) The all purpose flour is added to produce a lighter and larger volume bread.
	1 c. all purpose	1/2 c. rye flour + 1/2 c. all purpose flour (27)	(27) Because of its low gluten content, rye flour is supplemented with all purpose. Rye flour alone will produce a sticky rather than an elastic dough.
	1 c. all purpose	2 T soy flour + 7/8 c. all purpose flour (28)	(28) Soy flour is used mainly to enrich a dough and cannot be used alone.
	1 c. all purpose	1/2 c. potato flour + 1/2 c. all purpose flour (29)	(29) Potato flour enhances fermentation, makes kneading easier and produces a moist bread that is slow to stale.
	1 c. all purpose	1/3 c. powdered wheat germ + 2/3 c. all purpose flour (30)	(30) Lightly toast the wheat germ before incorporating into the dough.
	1 c. all purpose	1/4 c. barley flour + 3/4 c. all purpose flour (31)	(31) Barley flour will make leavened breads only when combined with a wheat flour. The leavened bread will have a cakelike texture. Barley flour is ideal for Scandinavian flatbreads.
	1 c. all purpose	1/6 c. oat flour + 5/6 c. all purpose flour (32)	(32) The bread will be chewy. You can make your own oat flour by pulverizing rolled oats in a blender or food processor.
Yeast Bread/Non-Wheat	3 c. all purpose	2 c. rice flour + 2/3 c. potato flour + 1/3 c. tapioca flour + 3 1/2 t. xanthan gum (33)	(33) Xanthan gum replaces the gluten in wheat flour.
Flowers (Edible Flowers) All Recipes		1 orange blossom 1 lemon or lime blossom 1 light color rose 1 dark color rose (1)	(1) The darker shaded roses have a stronger flavor than the lighter ones.

Cooking and Preparation Hints
* Some flowers are poisonous. Do not eat the following: azalea, crocus, daffodil, foxglove, oleander, rhododendron, jack-in-the-pulpit, lily of the valley, poinsettia and wisteria. Also, avoid flowers that have been sprayed with pesticides, flowers from the florist and flowers growing along the roadside which may be tainted with exhaust fumes.
* Flowers that are edible include borage, carnation, chive, chrysanthemum, clover, cornflower (bachelor's button), dandelion, day lily, elder, gardenia, gladiolus, hibiscus, hollyhock, honeysuckle, jasmine, lavender, lemon blossom, lilac, lime blossom, marigold, nasturtium, orange blossom, pansy, primrose, rose, rosemary, squash blossom, tulip, violet, woodruff, yarrow and yucca.
* In general the more fragrant the flower is, the more flavor it will have.
* Before using flowers in recipes, wash and thoroughly dry them.
* When using a multipetaled flower such as carnation, chrysanthemum,

marigold or rose, pull the petals all at once from the stem. Then snip off the white bottom from the petals because it can have a bitter taste.
* There are several ways to make candied, or crystallized, flowers: (1) Lightly beat an egg white and use it to coat the front and back of each petal. Dip the coated flower in superfine granulated sugar and dry on wax paper. They will last in an airtight container for up to 2 days. (2) Beat an egg white with enough confectioners' sugar to produce a thin cream. Brush the flowers with the mixture, sprinkle on some superfine granulated sugar and dry. They will keep for 2 days. (3) Boil 1 c. sugar and 1/2 c. water until it forms a syrup and spins a thread. Cool to room temperature. Dip the flower or petals in the syrup, shake off the excess, and dip into superfine sugar. Dry on wax paper. They will keep for a week.

INGREDIENT	YIELD			SUBSTITUTION		
	Amount Market Form	Yield Equivalent	For Purpose of	Amount	Substitution	Instructions
Game/Game Birds See also individual listings	**Cooking and Preparation Hints** * Game spoils quickly, especially in muscles damaged by shot. Because of that and because of its limited seasons, it is a good condidate for freezing. Plan to use large or small game meat within 6 months of freezing. * Vinegar is a good tenderizer for game meat. It can be used in a marinade consisting of 1/2 c. vinegar and 1 c. liquid bouillon. * Herbs and spices that complement game meat include pepper,				marjoram, thyme, bay leaf, juniper berry and garlic. * Game birds can be frozen and should be prepared beforehand as they would be for cooking. They can be stored for up to 9 months. The exception is wild duck which, because of its fat content, should be used within 6 months. * Game birds are complemented by such herbs and spices as thyme, dry mustard, celery salt, parsley and paprika.	
Garbanzo Bean (Chick Pea, Cec) See also Beans, Dried	1 lb. dried 1 lb. dried 1 c. dried 8 oz. can	2 1/4 c. 5 1/2 c. cooked 2 1/2 c. cooked 1 c. drained				
Garden Beet See Beet						
Garlic	1 bulb or head 1 medium clove 1 clove elephant garlic	8 – 15 cloves 1/8 t. minced 2 regular cloves	Flavoring	1 medium clove 1 medium clove 1 medium clove 1 medium clove 1 medium clove	1/8 t. garlic powder 1/2 t. garlic salt (1) 1/8 t. garlic chips (2) 1/2 t. garlic juice 1 t. garlic paste	(1) Reduce added salt in the recipe by 1/2 t. (2) Rehydrate in a small amount of water if little liquid is called for in the recipe.

Cooking and Preparation Hints
* The longer garlic cooks, the more delicate the flavor becomes. Garlic is most pungent raw and either minced or put through a press. For a milder flavor, leave the cloves whole or cut in large pieces when adding to cooking foods.
* Putting garlic through a press may produce a slightly more pungent taste than by chopping because it exposes more of the surface. Garlic loses some of its strength as it ages; so you may want to put older garlic through a press to achieve greater flavor.
* If you are putting a garlic clove through a press, you don't need to peel it.
* For easy peeling, rinse the cloves in hot water before peeling. The hot water tends to loosen the skin. Or drop the cloves in boiling water for a few seconds, then rinse in cold water.
* Retrieving garlic cloves from a sauce or stew after cooking can be made easy if, beforehand, you put the cloves on skewers and then into the sauce for cooking. When the sauce is done, simply remove the skewers.
* Garlic burns easily and takes on a bitter taste that can ruin your dish. If you do burn the garlic while cooking, simply remove the cloves with

a spoon and replace with fresh garlic.
* In order not to waste the garlic juices that remain on your cutting board after mincing, pour the salt that is called for in your recipe directly into the minced garlic. The salt will absorb the juices and also make it easier to scoop up the little garlic pieces from the board.
* When garlic has been stored for some time, sprouts may develop. It is still good, but will have a somewhat milder flavor. If the center of the clove turns green, remove the green part. It is edible but will taste bitter.
* You can remove garlic odor from your hands by rubbing them with salt or lemon juice, then rinsing with cold water.
* 2 to 3 cloves are adequate for 2 lb. of meat, 3 c. of tomato-based sauce, 3 c. of soup, 1 qt. of pickled foods or 2 pt. of chutney or relish.
* Garlic becomes stronger in flavor during freezing. Keep this in mind when preparing a dish that will be frozen.
* Elephant garlic is a jumbo form of garlic with a milder flavor.
* Green garlic is fresh garlic (not dried and cured bulbs) which looks similar to and can be used in place of leeks and scallions — including the green leaves.

INGREDIENT	YIELD Amount Market Form	Yield Equivalent	For Purpose of	SUBSTITUTION Amount	Substitution	Instructions
Garlic Butter			All Recipes	1/4 c.	1/4 c. butter	
			Flavoring/Reducing Fat	1 t.	+ 1 clove garlic, minced Garlic butter flavored sprinkles to taste	

Cooking and Preparation Hints
* Garlic butter can be frozen into logs and ready to use on a moment's notice. Mash garlic into butter, add herbs if desired, form into logs, wrap in plastic and freeze. Slice as needed.

INGREDIENT	YIELD Amount Market Form	Yield Equivalent	For Purpose of	SUBSTITUTION Amount	Substitution	Instructions
Garlic Powder			Flavoring	1/8 t.	1 clove garlic minced	(1) Reduce added salt in the recipe by 1/2 t.
				1/8 t.	1/2 t. garlic salt (1)	
				1/8 t.	1/8 t. garlic chips	
				1/8 t.	1/2 t. garlic juice	
				1/8 t.	1 t. garlic paste	

Cooking and Preparation Hints
* If the amount of garlic powder is not specified in the recipe, you can safely add 1/8 t. for a dish that serves 4 to 6 people.

INGREDIENT	YIELD Amount Market Form	Yield Equivalent	For Purpose of	SUBSTITUTION Amount	Substitution	Instructions
Garlic Salt			Flavoring	1/2 t.	1 clove garlic minced (1)	(1) In substituting other forms of garlic for garlic salt, you may want to add salt to taste to the original recipe.
				1/2 t.	1/8 t. garlic powder (1)	
				1/2 t.	1/8 t. garlic chips (1)	
				1/2 t.	1/2 t. garlic juice (1)	
				1/2 t.	1 t. garlic paste (1)	

* You can make your own garlic salt by burying 3 peeled and flattened garlic cloves in 1/2 c. salt. Add pepper to taste and store in a jar for a few days. Remove garlic and use the salt as desired for flavoring.

Cooking and Preparation Hints
* 1/2 t. garlic salt is usually sufficient for a dish that serves 4 to 6. Add salt to the recipe only after the garlic salt has been added and after tasting.

INGREDIENT	YIELD Amount Market Form	Yield Equivalent	For Purpose of	SUBSTITUTION Amount	Substitution	Instructions
Gelatin	1 envelope	1/4 oz. granules	Gelling	1 T	2 t. agar (1)	(1) This will gel 2 c. liquid. Soften the agar first in 1/2 c. of the cold liquid. Then add the remaining 1 1/2 c. hot liquid to dissolve.
	1 envelope	1 T granules		1 T	2 - 3 T Irish moss (2)	(2) Irish moss should be rinsed and soaked for 10 minutes before using. Avoid using it as a substitute when an acid (lemon juice, vinegar) is called for in the recipe because the mixture will thin in the presence of an acid.
	1 envelope	6 (3X8) sheets	Salads and Desserts	3 oz. pkg. flavored	1 envelope unflavored gelatin + 2 c. fruit juice	
	1 (3X8) sheet	1/2 t. granules				
	1 oz. granules	4 T				
	1 oz. granules	1/4 c.				

INGREDIENT	YIELD			SUBSTITUTION		
	Amount Market Form	Yield Equivalent	For Purpose of	Amount	Substitution	Instructions
Gelatin continued						* If you are creating your own recipe for a sweetened gelatin dish, add no more than 3 T of sugar per 1 c. of liquid. More than that will retard setting. * If you plan to add wine to an aspic recipe, add it after the gelatin is dissolved. * To keep gelatin dishes firm during the hot summer months, add 1 t. of vinegar to the recipe. However, don't add more than 2 T per 1 c. of liquid or proper setting will be affected (not to mention the taste). * To speed up setting time, you can: (1) use a metal mold; (2) chill the mold in a container of ice water before refrigerating; (3) substitute 2 c. ice for each 1 c. of cold water called for in the recipe. Stir for about 3 minutes to melt the ice, then remove any unmelted ice and refrigerate. * If it looks like the mold is not going to set, remove the gelatin and heat it in a pan. Then add a little more gelatin that has been softened and dissolved in hot water. Remold and refrigerate. * For easy unmolding, spray the mold with nonstick cooking spray before filling it. To unmold, insert a knife around the edges of the mold to release the vacuum. Invert it onto a serving dish. Then wrap the mold in a hot, damp dish towel. If the mold does not lift off, reheat the towel and repeat the process. * To center the mold on a serving plate, first chill the plate. Moisten it slightly. Then invert the mold onto the plate. It won't stick, and you can easily position it where you want it.

Cooking and Preparation Hints
* 1 envelope of gelatin will gel 2 c. of liquid.
* When doubling a recipe that requires 2 c. of liquid, use only 3 3/4 c. of liquid in the doubled recipe.
* Unflavored gelatin has to be softened in cold water for at least 1 minute before it can be dissolved. Use 1/4 c. water for 1 T gelatin. Add hot water and make sure the gelatin is completely dissolved before continuing with the recipe; otherwise, the dish will not set properly.
* Some fresh and frozen fruits (pineapples, figs, mangoes, papayas, kiwi) contain an enzyme that prevents gelatin from setting. However, you can use these fruits in canned form successfully.
* Drain canned fruits and vegetables well before adding them to the gelatin mixture. Too much liquid will prevent the dish from gelling. If you want the added flavor of the juice from the can, substitute the juice for the liquid in the recipe.
* If you want to test gelatin to be sure of its strength, put 1 T of the mixture in the freezer. It should set in about 5 minutes.
* Ingredients added to gelatin increase the time needed for setting. Depending on the size and shape of the mold used and the quantity of food added, a gelatin dish will require from 3 hours to overnight to set properly.
* Let the gelatin thicken some before adding solid food to the mixture. Otherwise, the food will settle to the bottom and, when unmolded, will be crowded at the top.

INGREDIENT	YIELD			SUBSTITUTION		
Ghee See Butter						
Ginger (Ginger Root) See also Herbs/Spices	1/4 lb, 1 medium root 1" X 1" piece fresh 1 t. fresh chopped	1 medium root 3/4 c. grated or chopped 2 T grated or chopped 1/4 t. ground	Flavoring	1 t. fresh chopped 1 t. fresh chopped	1/2 t. dried whole (1) 2 t. crystallized chopped (2)	(1) Soak in cold water for several hours, then chop or grate. (2) Wash off sugar before using.

Cooking and Preparation Hints
* Fresh ginger will keep in the refrigerator for 3 to 4 weeks. Wrap it loosely in paper towels, put into a plastic bag and refrigerate.
* To keep peeled ginger fresh and moist indefinitely, place it in a jar, cover with sherry and refrigerate. You can also use the ginger-flavored sherry for cooking; it's especially good for marinades.
* You can store fresh ginger in the freezer (although it tends to get soft and mushy when thawed). For handy use at a moment's notice: Peel, then either grate, slice or mince the ginger. Pile in 1 T portions on a baking sheet lined with wax paper. Freeze until hard. Wrap each portion individually and refreeze until ready to use. It will keep for 3 to 4 months.
* Avoid using carbon-steel knives when peeling ginger because both the knife and the ginger will become discolored.
* 1/4 to 1/2 t. ground ginger is usually adequate for a dish serving 4.

INGREDIENT	YIELD			SUBSTITUTION			
	Amount Market Form	Yield Equivalent	For Purpose of	Amount	Substitution	Instructions	

Ginger
continued

Cooking and Preparation Hints (continued)
* Don't let ginger burn. It will give the dish a bitter taste.
* Ginger will complement such foods as chicken, beef, carrots, winter squash, breads, cakes and cookies.

Instructions: * To make ginger juice, peel and grate a piece of ginger root. Then put the grated ginger through a garlic press to extract the juice. You can also put the grated ginger in cheesecloth and squeeze the juice out with your fingers.

Girolle
See Mushroom

Globe Artichoke
See Artichoke

Gluten Flour
See Flour

Golden Syrup
See Treacle

Goose
See also Poultry

Amount Market Form	Yield Equivalent
1 1/4 - 1 1/2 lb.	1 serving
1 small	8 - 10 lb.
1 medium	10 - 12 lb.
1 large	12 - 14 lb.

Cooking and Preparation Hints
* Goose has much more fat than chicken or turkey and should be well pricked so the fat can drain out as it cooks. It's also helpful every 30 minutes during roasting to drain the fat and pour 1/2 c. boiling water on the goose. The water helps to release the fat and keeps the breast moist.

Substitution: * To freeze goose, prepare it as you would for cooking, making sure to cut out any lumps of fat. Put it into a freezer bag. If any of the bones are in danger of piercing the bag, pad the bones with aluminum foil or plastic wrap. Goose can be stored up to 4 months.

Gooseberry
See also Fruit

Amount Market Form	Yield Equivalent
1 lb. fresh	3 c.
16 oz. can	2 c.

Cooking and Preparation Hints
* Use fully ripe gooseberries for pies and slightly underripe berries for jelly or preserves.
* Gooseberries can be frozen unsweetened, in a dry sugar pack using 2/3 c.

Substitution: sugar per 1 qt. of berries, or in a 50% syrup pack. For the syrup pack, dissolve 4 3/4 c. sugar in 4 c. water and refrigerate. Add 1/2 to 2/3 c. syrup per 1 pt. of fruit. Gooseberries can be stored for up to 1 year.

Gorgonzola Cheese
See also Cheese

Amount Market Form	Yield Equivalent	For Purpose of	Substitution
4 oz.	1 c. crumbled	All Recipes	8 oz. blue cheese
		8 oz.	8 oz. Roquefort cheese

Cooking and Preparation Hints
* To keep Gorgonzola from crumbling while cutting, use a wire, dental floss or heavy thread.

INGREDIENT	YIELD		SUBSTITUTION			
	Amount Market Form	Yield Equivalent	For Purpose of	Amount	Substitution	Instructions
Gouda Cheese See also Cheese			All Recipes	8 oz.	8 oz. edam cheese (1)	(1) They are similar in flavor although edam is made from partly skim milk and gouda from whole milk.

Cooking and Preparation Hints
* Gouda is better as an eating cheese than one for grating and cooking.
* Gouda can be frozen for up to 6 months.

INGREDIENT	Amount Market Form	Yield Equivalent	For Purpose of	Amount	Substitution	Instructions
Graham Cracker See Crackers						
Graham Flour (Whole Wheat Flour) See Flour						
Grains See also individual listings	1 c. uncooked	3 c. cooked				rancid. Use flakes and flours within 3 to 6 months. * Overstirring while cooking will cause grains to become sticky. * When adding salt to grains, do so toward the end of the cooking process to prevent toughness. * Cooked grains can be stored in the refrigerator for 2 days and can also be frozen.

Cooking and Preparation Hints
* Store whole grains in a cool, dry area. They will keep indefinitely, but the longer they are stored, the longer they take to cook.
* Flakes and flours cannot be stored as long as whole grains because milling has exposed the oil in the germ which causes the products to turn

INGREDIENT	Amount Market Form	Yield Equivalent	For Purpose of	Amount	Substitution	Instructions
Granulated Sugar See Sugar						
Grape See also Fruit	1 lb. fresh 1 lb. fresh 8 oz. can	2 1/2 - 3 c. 5 - 6 servings 1 c. drained				bunch in a freezer bag. * Grapes can also be frozen in a 40% syrup pack. Dissolve 3 c. sugar in 4 c. water and refrigerate. Add 1/2 to 2/3 c. syrup per 1 pt. of fruit and freeze.

Cooking and Preparation Hints
* Grapes can be frozen but become soft when thawed. Leave seedless grapes whole, and remove seeds from others. They can be quick-frozen on trays and put into freezer bags — or for short-term storage, they can be frozen as a

INGREDIENT	Amount Market Form	Yield Equivalent	For Purpose of	Amount	Substitution	Instructions
Grape Leaf	8 oz. jar	40 grape leaves				
Grapefruit See also Fruit	1 lb. fresh 1 medium 1 medium 1 medium 16 oz. can 13 1/2 oz. frozen	1 medium 1 1/2 - 2 c. sections 3/4 c. juice 3 T grated rind 2 c. sections 1 1/2 c. sections	All Recipes	1 medium, sectioned 1 medium, sectioned	1 1/2 - 2 oranges, sectioned 1 1/2 - 2 tangerines, sectioned	months. They can be frozen unsweetened, just covered with juice. Or they can be frozen in a 40% syrup pack. Dissolve 3 c. sugar and 1/2 t. ascorbic acid in 4 c. water and refrigerate. Add 1/2 to 2/3 c. syrup per 1 pt. of fruit.

Cooking and Preparation Hints
* In selecting a grapefruit, look for one that is heavy for its size with a smooth, firm skin. Thinner rinds generally mean juicier fruit. Pointed ends and puffy skin usually indicate dryness.
* Grapefruit sections can be frozen and stored for 8 to 12

A B C D E F G H I J K L M N O P Q R S T U V W X Y Z

INGREDIENT	YIELD		SUBSTITUTION			Instructions
	Amount Market Form	Yield Equivalent	For Purpose of	Amount	Substitution	
Grapefruit Juice			All Recipes	1 c.	1 c. other citrus juice (1)	(1) Others include orange juice, lime juice, and lemon juice. Differences in taste will result depending on the quantity called for in the recipe.

Cooking and Preparation Hints
* Grapefruit juice can be frozen for up to 1 year.

INGREDIENT	Amount Market Form	Yield Equivalent
Gravy	12 oz. can	1 1/3 c.
	18 oz. can	2 c.

Cooking and Preparation Hints
* Gravy can be thickened in a variety of ways. Among the ingredients you can use are: (1) Beurre manié (equal parts butter and flour kneaded into a paste). It should be added toward the end of the heating process. Use 2 T per 1 c. of liquid for a medium to thick consistency. (2) Flour. Use flours such as cake flour, pastry flour and bleached all purpose flour that are high in starch and low in protein to prevent the "skin" that forms when the gravy sits for a short time. (3) Instant mashed potatoes. These will thicken without causing lumps. (4) Commercial gravy thickener which consists of dehydrated meat extract plus thickening agents such as cornstarch or flour. (5) See also listings for arrowroot, cornstarch, flour.
* If your gravy becomes lumpy, put it into a blender or food processor and process until it's smooth. Then reheat.
* For a roast meat gravy, the amount of added salt will depend on the kind of meat and the flavor of the drippings. However, a rule-of-thumb is 1 t. salt for every 2 c. water.
* If your gravy is too salty, try adding a small amount of brown sugar or vinegar.
* Gravy can be frozen for up to 3 or 4 months. If you know in advance that you will be freezing the gravy, use as little fat as possible in its preparation. Gravies made with a high proportion of fat or with milk tend to separate when thawed and reheated. Another way to prevent separation is to mix the gravy with an electric mixer or in a blender or food processor before freezing. Gravies made with broth or tomato juice freeze well.

INGREDIENT	Amount Market Form	Yield Equivalent	For Purpose of	Amount	Substitution
Great Northern Bean See also Beans, Dried	1 c. dried	3 c. cooked	All Recipes	1 c. cooked	1 c. cooked small white beans
				1 c. cooked	1 c. cooked navy beans
				1 c. cooked	1 c. cooked cannellini beans
				1 c. cooked	1 c. cooked white kidney beans
				1 c. cooked	1 c. cooked marrow beans
				1 c. cooked	1 c. cooked pea beans

INGREDIENT	Amount Market Form	Yield Equivalent
Green Bean (String Bean, Snap Bean, Wax Bean) See also Vegetables	1 lb. fresh	3 c. trimmed
	1 lb. fresh	2 1/2 c. cooked
	1 lb. fresh	4 servings
	16 oz. can	2 c.
	9 oz. frozen	1 1/2 c.

Cooking and Preparation Hints
* The time it takes to cook green beans depends on their size and freshness. Select beans that are about the same size to ensure even cooking.
* While steaming beans helps to retain their vitamins, boiling produces greener beans.
* If you don't plan to serve your beans immediately, plunge them into cold water to stop the cooking and to set the color.
* If you're using beans in a salad, add the vinegar or lemon juice at the last minute to prevent them from turning gray.
* Green or wax beans can be frozen whole or cut. Blanch them for 3 minutes, then chill and pack. They can be stored for 8 to 12 months.
* Herbs and spices that complement green beans include chives, basil, marjoram, mint, mustard seed, oregano, savory, pepper, thyme, tarragon and dill weed.

Green Onion
See Scallion

INGREDIENT	YIELD		SUBSTITUTION			
	Amount Market Form	Yield Equivalent	For Purpose of	Amount	Substitution	Instructions
Greens, Cooking (Potherbs) See also individual listings	1 lb. fresh 1/2 lb. fresh 10 oz. frozen	3 c. cooked 1 serving 1 1/2 - 2 c.	**Cooking and Preparation Hints** * Although greens will differ in intensity of flavor, they can usually be used interchangeably or in combination. * Greens will stay fresh for up to 3 days. As they age they become tough. * Cleaning greens in lukewarm water rather than		cold will remove dirt or sand more easily. * Greens can be frozen for up to 12 months. Wash and remove tough stems. Blanch for 1 1/2 to 2 minutes (exceptions are Swiss chard and collard greens, which should be blanched for 3 minutes), chill and pack.	
Grits (Corn Grits, Hominy Grits) See also Grains	1 lb. 1 c.	3 c. 3 1/3 c. cooked	**Cooking and Preparation Hints** * Stone-ground grits retain the germ and the hull of the grain which are processed out of regular grits. As a result, stone-ground grits have more nutritive value and a		more pronounced flavor. They also require longer cooking than the other forms of grits (regular, quick and instant). * Grits can be stored at room temperature for 4 to 6 months.	
Grouper See also Fish/Shellfish			All Recipes	1 lb. 1 lb. 1 lb. 1 lb. 1 lb. 1 lb.	1 lb. sea bass 1 lb. tilefish 1 lb. drum 1 lb. halibut 1 lb. rockfish 1 lb. cod	**Cooking and Preparation Hints** * Herbs and spices that complement grouper include parsley, pepper, bay leaf, tarragon, dill weed, chives and basil.
Gruyère Cheese See also Cheese			All Recipes	8 oz. 8 oz. 8 oz.	8 oz. Swiss cheese 8 oz. Emmenthal cheese 8 oz. raclette cheese	

INGREDIENT	YIELD		SUBSTITUTION			
	Amount Market Form	Yield Equivalent	For Purpose of	Amount	Substitution	Instructions
Haddock See also Fish/Shellfish			All Recipes	1 lb. 1 lb.	1 lb. cod 1 lb. rockfish	
	Cooking and Preparation Hints * Herbs and spices that complement haddock include parsley, pepper, bay leaf, tarragon, dill weed, chives and basil. * Haddock can be frozen for 4 to 6 months.					
Hake See also Fish/Shellfish			All Recipes	1 lb. 1 lb. 1 lb. 1 lb.	1 lb. cod 1 lb. haddock 1 lb. pollock 1 lb. whiting	**Cooking and Preparation Hints** * Hake can be frozen for up to 9 months.
Halibut See also Fish/Shellfish			All Recipes	1 lb. 1 lb.	1 lb. cod 1 lb. fluke	
	Cooking and Preparation Hints * Herbs and spices that complement halibut include parsley, pepper, bay leaf, tarragon, dill weed, chives and basil. * Halibut can be frozen for 4 to 6 months.					
Ham See also Pork	1 lb. fresh — boneless 1 lb. fresh — bone-in 1 lb. can — boneless 2 1/2 oz. can deviled	4 - 5 servings 3 servings 12 oz. meat 4 1/2 T	**Cooking and Preparation Hints** * Ham labeled "fully cooked" requires no additional cooking, but all hams should be heated to 130° to 140° before eating for the best flavor. * Hams labeled "cook before eating" should be cooked to an internal temperature of 160° to 170°. * If you are boiling a ham, you can remove some of the salty taste by adding a little vinegar to the boiling water. * Country hams are salt cured and need to be soaked overnight in cold water before cooking to		remove some of the saltiness. * A canned ham that is unopened will keep in the refrigerator for 14 to 16 months. A whole cooked ham can be refrigerated for 1 week. Ham slices can be stored in the refrigerator for 3 to 4 days. * Ham does not freeze well. The salt content causes the fat in the meat to turn rancid. If you plan to freeze ham, store it no longer than 3 weeks. Smoked ham will keep in the freezer for 1 to 3 months.	
Hamburger See Beef						
Hare See Rabbit						
Hazelnut (Filbert) See also Nuts	2 1/4 lb. in shell 1 lb. in shell 1 lb. shelled	1 lb. shelled 1 3/4 - 2 c. chopped 3 1/3 - 4 c. chopped	All Recipes	1 c.	1 c. macadamia nuts (1)	(1) The macadamia is another delicately flavored nut and may be easier to use because it has no skin to remove.

INGREDIENT	YIELD			SUBSTITUTION		
	Amount Market Form	Yield Equivalent	For Purpose of	Amount	Substitution	Instructions
Heart See also Meat	1 lb. raw	5 servings				
Herb Tea (Tisane) See Tea						
Herbes de Provence			Seasoning	3 T	2 T dried thyme + 2 t. dried basil + 2 t. dried summer savory + 2 t. dried rosemary + 1 t. dried marjoram + 1/2 bay leaf (1)	(1) Grind all the ingredients together. You may also include chervil, sage, fennel, oregano or lavender.
Herbs/Spices See also individual listings	1 T fresh herb chop'd 1 T fresh herb chop'd	1 t. dried crumbled 1/2 t. ground				

Cooking and Preparation Hints

* Most herbs come from temperate climates and, in general, only the leaves are used as seasonings. (Exceptions are the seeds of such plants as dill, coriander, caraway and poppy.) Spices are mainly from tropical areas and are usually derived from bark, root or fruit.
* Leaves of herbs should be chopped finely. The more cut surface that is exposed, the more flavor will be absorbed. To chop a small amount, pack the leaves into a small glass. Insert kitchen scissors into the glass with the tips touching the bottom, and cut until chopped to the right consistency.
* When cooking with fresh herbs, they should be added at the end of cooking to maintain their flavor. Adding them earlier will produce a mellowed flavor.
* Dried herbs should be added at the beginning of cooking so that the flavors will permeate the dish.
* You can develop the flavor of dried herbs by soaking them for at least 10 minutes before adding to the recipe. You can use water, wine, stock or any liquid called for in the recipe.

* You can dry your own fresh herbs in the microwave. Wash and dry herbs. Then heat for 1-minute intervals on low power. Continue until the herbs are dry and fairly brittle. Then store them in airtight containers.
* A rule-of-thumb is to use 1/4 t. dried herbs for a dish serving 4.
* Some recipes call for roasting whole spices before grinding to enhance the flavor and to make grinding easier. To roast whole spices, add them to a hot skillet and heat them until they start to turn color and emit a fragrance. Remove them and let cool.
* When doubling a recipe, don't double the seasonings. Increase the amount 1 1/2 times, then add more if needed after tasting.
* Heat and moisture will cause dried herbs and spices to lose their flavor and will cause caking in the container. For those reasons, store herbs and spices away from the sink and the range.
* When adding seasonings to a boiling pot of food, add them with your fingers instead of directly from the container. The steam from the pot will be trapped in the container and cause caking.

Cooking and Preparation Hints (continued)

* When stored properly, herbs and spices will keep for 1 to 2 years. You can test for freshness by smell. Herbs and spices that have a strong aroma will add flavor; when the aroma is gone, so is the flavor.
* You can add flavor to grilled foods by sprinkling a handful of mixed herbs moistened with water over the hot coals.
* In general, herbs can be frozen for 6 to 9 months. You will need

about 2 times the amount of frozen herbs to equal the flavor of fresh. Whole spices such as cardamom and juniper berries can be frozen and can be used without thawing.
* Dishes that have been highly spiced and frozen should be cooked within 2 to 3 months or the spices may overpower the flavor of the other ingredients. However, the spicy flavor of chilies decreases with freezing.

INGREDIENT	YIELD			SUBSTITUTION			
	Amount Market Form	Yield Equivalent	For Purpose of	Amount	Substitution	Instructions	

INGREDIENT	Amount Market Form	Yield Equivalent	For Purpose of	Amount	Substitution	Instructions
Herring See also Fish/Shellfish	1 - 2 fresh	1 serving	All Recipes	8 oz. 8 oz.	8 oz. sardines 8 oz. pilchards	**Cooking and Preparation Hints** * Herring can be frozen for 3 to 6 months.
Hominy See also Grains	1 lb. whole 1 c. whole 15 oz. can	2 1/2 c. 6 2/3 c. cooked 1 3/4 c.				
Hominy Grits See Grits						
Honey	16 oz.	1 1/3 c.	Baking	1 c. 1 c.	1 1/4 c. sugar + 1/4 c. liquid 1 c. corn syrup	

Cooking and Preparation Hints
* There are more than 200 types of honey, and each one will impart a flavor as well as sweetness. A rule-of-thumb for selecting honey is that the darker it is, the stronger its taste will be. Much of the honey available in the market is a blend of varieties that ensures consistency in taste and color.
* Honey may crystallize when it's refrigerated or when it ages. It can be reliquified by heating it in a pan of water over low heat (not over 140°) or by placing the open container in the microwave at high power for 30 seconds or more depending on the quantity of honey. Be careful not to subject honey to too high a heat because the flavor and color will deteriorate.
* Store unopened containers of honey at room temperature and opened containers in the refrigerator to protect against mold.
* To keep honey from sticking to a measuring cup, first spray the cup with nonstick cooking spray. Or if your recipe calls for oil, measure that first.

INGREDIENT	Amount Market Form	Yield Equivalent	For Purpose of	Amount	Substitution	Instructions
Honeydew Melon See also Melon, Fruit	4 lb. 1 medium	1 medium 5 c. cubed				
Hoop Cheese See also Cheese			All Recipes	8 oz. 8 oz. 8 oz. 8 oz. 8 oz.	8 oz. baker's cheese 8 oz. farmer cheese 8 oz. pot cheese 8 oz. creamed cottage cheese, drained 8 oz. dry cottage cheese	

Cooking and Preparation Hints
* A ripe honeydew will have a velvety texture, a creamy yellow color and will be soft at the blossom end. Generally, a white melon with a greenish cast is not ripe and will not sweeten.
* You can freeze honeydew cubes in a sugar pack of 2 c. sugar for each 3 qt. of cut melon. Or you can freeze it in a syrup pack. Dissolve 3 c. sugar in 4 c. water and refrigerate. Add syrup to melon to cover, leave 1" headspace in freezer container and freeze.

INGREDIENT	YIELD		SUBSTITUTION			
	Amount Market Form	Yield Equivalent	For Purpose of	Amount	Substitution	Instructions
Horseradish	1 1/2 lb. fresh root 8 oz. prepared (bottled)	2 3/4 c. peeled, grat'd 1 c.	All Recipes	1 T fresh grated 2 T prepared	2 T prepared 1 T dried horseradish + 1 T vinegar + 1 T water (1)	(1) Add sugar and salt to taste. If possible, pre-pare dried horseradish not more than 30 minutes ahead of time because its pungency dissipates.
Cooking and Preparation Hints * Fresh horseradish can be frozen for 9 to 12 months. Peel and chop or grate before freezing.						
Hot Pepper See Chili Pepper						
Hot Pepper Sauce			All Recipes	1 t. 1 t.	1 1/2 t. black pepper 3/4 t. ground red pepper	
Huckleberry See also Fruit				can also be frozen in a 40% syrup pack. For the syrup pack, dissolve 3 c. sugar in 4 c. water and refrigerate. Add 1/2 to 2/3 c. syrup to each pt. of fruit.		
Cooking and Preparation Hints * Huckleberries can be frozen unsweetened. Quick-freeze them on a tray, then transfer them to a freezer storage container. They						

INGREDIENT	YIELD		For Purpose of	Amount	SUBSTITUTION	
	Amount Market Form	Yield Equivalent			Substitution	Instructions
Ice						Likewise, freeze fruit juices for use in punches. * To eliminate bubbles when making ice molds, boil the water first. Then pour it into the mold and let it cool to room temperature before freezing. You can also use distilled water.

Cooking and Preparation Hints
* You can freeze leftover coffee and tea in ice cube trays to use later in iced coffee and iced tea; that way the beverages will not become diluted as they do when regular ice cubes melt.

INGREDIENT						
Ice Cream						* After using some of the ice cream from the carton, press plastic wrap or aluminum foil over the exposed surface before closing and returning to the freezer. This will prevent ice crystals from forming.

Cooking and Preparation Hints
* Commercially prepared ice cream keeps in the freezer in the original carton for 2 to 4 months. Homemade ice cream, however, stores well for only 1 to 2 months.

INGREDIENT						
Icing (Frosting)	16 oz. can	1 3/4 c.				type icing will keep for 2 to 3 months. Seven-minute and boiled or fluffy white icing can be frozen for 1 month. Do not freeze cakes with cream or custard icing; the icing will seep into the cake during defrosting. * To thaw frozen frosted cakes, keep them wrapped until completely defrosted. * Cake icings made with a high proportion of egg whites will weep when thawed. * A cake that has been frozen without frosting should be completely thawed before icing.

Cooking and Preparation Hints
* The addition of meringue powder gives strength to icings that will be used for decorating.
* For quick cake decorating or writing purposes, fill a sturdy plastic storage bag with icing, snip off one corner and squeeze out the icing.
* If your icing hardens on the cake before you've had a chance to smooth it, heat the spatula under hot tap water, shake off the excess water and continue.
* Some iced cakes can be frozen. Cakes with butter or candy-

INGREDIENT			For Purpose of	Amount	Substitution	
Instant Flour See Flour						
Irish Moss (Carrageenan)			Gelling	2 T 2 T	1 T (1 envelope) gelatin granules 2 t. agar	* Irish moss will thin in the presence of an acid such as vinegar or lemon juice.

Cooking and Preparation Hints
* Use 2 to 3 T Irish moss to gel 2 c. liquid and 2 to 3 t. Irish moss to thicken 2 c. liquid to a thick paste consistency.

INGREDIENT			For Purpose of	Amount	Substitution	
Italian Seasoning			Seasoning	1 t.	1/4 t. dried basil + 1/4 t. dried marjoram + 1/4 t. dried oregano + 1/4 t. dried thyme	

INGREDIENT	YIELD		SUBSTITUTION			
	Amount Market Form	Yield Equivalent	For Purpose of	Amount	Substitution	Instructions
Jalapeño See Chili Pepper						
Jam/Jelly	**Cooking and Preparation Hints** * Using frozen berries instead of fresh for jams and jellies produces a fresher taste and better color. The freezing and thawing				process releases the juice and the natural fruit color. * Jams and jellies can be stored unopened in the cupboard for 12 months.	
Jamaica Pepper See Allspice						
Jerusalem Artichoke (Sunchoke) See also Vegetables	1 - 1 1/2 lb.	4 servings	**Cooking and Preparation Hints** * Like potatoes, Jerusalem artichokes will discolor quickly when cut or peeled. Put them immediately into a bowl of plain water or acidulated water to prevent darkening.		* Jerusalem artichokes do not freeze well raw, but they can be frozen for 6 to 9 months when they have been cooked and mashed or pureed. Do not add seasonings until after they are thawed and reheated for serving.	
Jewfish See Sea Bass						
Jicama (Mexican Potato, Yam Bean)	1 lb. fresh	4 c. shredded				
John Dory See also Fish/Shellfish			All Recipes	1 lb.	1 lb. porgy	
Juniper Berry See also Herbs/spices	4 berries	1/2 t. crushed	**Cooking and Preparation Hints** * Juniper berries complement game, lamb, pork and cabbage and will lighten oily or heavy dishes. * 3 to 4 crushed berries will season a dish for 4 people.			

INGREDIENT	YIELD			SUBSTITUTION			
	Amount Market Form	Yield Equivalent	For Purpose of	Amount	Substitution		Instructions
Kale (Cow Cabbage, Colewort, Borecole) See also Greens, Cooking	1 lb. fresh	3 c. cooked					* A variety of kale known as flowering kale or salad savoy is edible but is best used for decorative purposes. * To freeze kale, first blanch for 1 1/2 to 2 minutes. Then chill and pack.

Cooking and Preparation Hints
* Kale should be eaten as soon as possible after being harvested. Not only does kale become bitter with storage, but it also loses 1% to 5% of its vitamin C content each hour. Remove and discard the tough stems and ribs.
* Use only kale leaves.

Kasha See also Buckwheat, Grains	1 c.	2 1/2 - 3 c. cooked					breads, muffins and cookies. * Leftover cooked kasha can be frozen for later use in soups, stews and sauces. Freeze the kasha in ice cube trays, then store the cubes in plastic freezer bags.

Cooking and Preparation Hints
* You can grind your own buckwheat flour from kasha. Put it into a blender or food processor and process for about 3 minutes. You can replace half of the wheat flour called for in recipes for pancakes, waffles,

Ketchup (Catsup)	14 oz. bottle 24 oz. bottle 32 oz. bottle	1 1/3 c. 2 1/3 c. 3 c.	All Recipes	1 c. 1 c.	1 c. tomato sauce + 1/4 c. sugar + 2 T vinegar + 1/4 t. ground cloves 1 c. chili sauce		

Cooking and Preparation Hints
* Once a bottle of ketchup has been opened, refrigerator storage is recommended. Although it will keep well at room temperature, ketchup oxidizes quickly and will turn an unappetizing black. In the refrigerator, it will retain its color for a year or more.

Kidney See also Meat	1 lb. beef kidney 1 lb. lamb kidney 1 lb. pork kidney	4 servings 5 servings 5 servings					

Cooking and Preparation Hints
* Kidneys can be frozen for up to 2 months. Halve and remove all the fat and tubes.

Kidney Bean See also Beans, Dried	1 lb. dried 1 lb. dried 1 c. dried 16 oz. can	2 1/2 c. 6 1/4 c. cooked 2 1/2 c. cooked 2 c.	All Recipes	1 c. cooked 1 c. cooked 1 c. cooked	1 c. cooked pink beans (1) 1 c. cooked pinto beans (1) 1 c. cooked red beans (1)		(1) They are smaller than kidney beans.

Cooking and Preparation Hints

Kiwi (Kiwifruit) See also Fruit	5 medium fresh	2 1/3 c. sliced					* Kiwi has a natural enzyme that tenderizes meat. Try running a sliced half over the meat about 15 minutes before cooking.

Cooking and Preparation Hints

INGREDIENT	YIELD		For Purpose of	Amount	SUBSTITUTION	
	Amount Market Form	Yield Equivalent			Substitution	Instructions
Kohlrabi (Cabbage Turnip) See also Vegetables	4 small - medium bulbs; 2 lb. bunch with leaves; 4 medium bulbs	4 servings; 4 medium bulbs; 3 1/2 c. cubed, cooked				cubed for 6 to 12 months. Blanch 3 minutes for whole kohlrabi and 1 to 2 minutes for sliced or cubed before freezing.
Kosher Salt See Salt						
Kudzu (Kuzu)	1/2 oz.	3 1/4 t. crushed	Thickening	2 t.	1 T arrowroot (1)	(1) Both arrowroot and kudzu produce light, translucent sauces.
Kumquat See also Fruit	1/4 lb. fresh	9 - 15 medium				

Cooking and Preparation Hints (Kohlrabi)
* Kohlrabi is complemented by dill weed and chives.
* Kohlrabi can be frozen whole, sliced or cubed.

Cooking and Preparation Hints (Kudzu)
* To use kudzu, crush it into a powder and dissolve it in a small amount of cold liquid to form a thin paste. Add the paste to the liquid to be thickened and bring to a high heat stirring constantly.
* Kudzu will produce a crisp crust when used to coat food before frying.
* 2 t. kudzu will thicken 1 c. liquid.

Cooking and Preparation Hints (Kumquat)
* To make kumquat flowers, make cuts just through the skin from the top almost to the bottom of the kumquat. Peel back the "petals" and place in cold water for an hour. Drain before using as a garnish.

INGREDIENT	YIELD		SUBSTITUTION			
	Amount Market Form	Yield Equivalent	For Purpose of	Amount	Substitution	Instructions
Lamb See also Meat	1 lb. chops	2 - 2 1/2 servings				for 1 to 2 days; cooked leftovers can be refrigerated for 3 to 4 days.
	1 lb. leg roast — bone-in	2 1/2 servings				* Roasts can be frozen for 6 to 12 months; chops for 6 to 9 months; ground for 3 to 4 months; and cooked leftovers for 2 to 3 months.
	1 lb. leg roast — boneless	4 servings				
	1 lb. shank	2 servings				
	4 spareribs or riblets	1 serving				
	1 lb. ground	4 servings				

Cooking and Preparation Hints
* Herbs and spices that complement lamb include rosemary, thyme, marjoram, oregano, bay leaf, curry, celery seed, mint and juniper berries.
* Roasts and chops can be stored in the refrigerator for 3 to 5 days; ground can be stored

INGREDIENT	Amount Market Form	Yield Equivalent	For Purpose of	Amount	Substitution	Instructions
Lard See also Fats	8 oz.	1 c.	Baking	1 c.	1 c. vegetable shortening	

Cooking and Preparation Hints
* Because it is very rich, lard produces very tender and flaky pastries and biscuits.

INGREDIENT	Amount Market Form	Yield Equivalent	For Purpose of	Amount	Substitution	Instructions
Lasagna See Pasta						
Lechosa See Papaya						
Leek See also Vegetables	1/4 lb.	2 large	Flavoring	1 c. sliced	1 c. sliced scallions	
	1/4 lb.	3 medium		1 c. sliced	1 c. sliced ramp	
	1/4 lb.	1 1/2 - 2 c. sliced (white portion)		1 c. sliced	1 c. sliced shallots	
	1 large whole	1 serving		1 c. sliced	1 c. sliced green (fresh) garlic	

Cooking and Preparation Hints
* Leeks are complemented by chervil, parsley and tarragon.
* Leeks can be frozen for use in cooked dishes. Cut into thick slices, blanch for 2 minutes or sauté, and freeze. Blanched leeks can be stored for 9 months, sautéed for 6 months.

INGREDIENT	Amount Market Form	Yield Equivalent	For Purpose of	Amount	Substitution	Instructions
Lemon See also Fruit	1 lb. fresh	4 - 6 medium	Flavoring	1 slice	1 slice lime	it in warm water for a few minutes or put it in the microwave for up to 1 minute.
	1 lb. fresh	1 c. juice				* Lemon slices can be frozen to add to beverages. Grated peel can also be frozen.
	1 medium	3 T juice				
	1 medium	2 - 3 t. grated peel				

Cooking and Preparation Hints
* You'll get more juice from a lemon at room temperature than from a cold one. To warm a lemon that has been refrigerated, immerse

INGREDIENT	YIELD			SUBSTITUTION			
	Amount Market Form	Yield Equivalent	For Purpose of	Amount	Substitution	Instructions	

INGREDIENT	Amount Market Form	Yield Equivalent	For Purpose of	Amount	Substitution	Instructions
Lemon Extract See Lemon Peel See also Extracts						
Lemon Juice			All Recipes	1 c. fresh 1 c. fresh	1 c. frozen, thawed 1 c. bottled	
			Antidarkening Acidulation	1 t. 1 t. 1 t. 1 t.	1/4 t. ascorbic acid 1 t. other citrus juice 1 t. vinegar 1 t. white wine	
			Flavoring	2 T	1 t. grated peel	
Cooking and Preparation Hints * Fresh lemon juice will keep in the refrigerator for 3 days or in the freezer for 1 month. For convenience, freeze lemon juice in ice					* cube trays and transfer cubes to plastic freezer bags. * Bottled lemon juice can be stored unopened in the cupboard for 15 months and opened in the refrigerator for 6 months.	
Lemon Oil			Flavoring	1 drop	13 drops lemon extract	
Lemon Peel (Lemon Rind, Lemon Zest)			Flavoring	1 t. fresh, grated 1 t. fresh, grated 1 t. fresh, grated 1 t. fresh, grated	1 t. dried 1 t. other citrus peel, grated 1/2 t. lemon extract 2 T juice (1)	(1) The rind of the lemon has a high concentration of oil and, therefore, a more intense flavor than the juice.
Cooking and Preparation Hints * Use only the colored portion of the skin; the white underneath is bitter. An easy way to remove the colored portion is with a potato peeler.					* You can freeze grated or thin strips of peel for use in baking and beverages. * For easy cleanup, spray a hand grater with nonstick cooking spray before grating lemon peel.	
Lemongrass			Flavoring	2 fresh stalks	1 T grated lemon peel	
Cooking and Preparation Hints * Using only the bottom 6" of fresh lemongrass is recommended because of its fibrous texture.					* Unpeeled lemongrass is inedible and should be removed from cooked dishes before serving. To make lemongrass edible, remove the outer reed to expose the green stalk.	
Lentil See also Beans, Dried	1 lb. dried 1 lb. dried 1 c. dried	2 1/4 c. 5 c. cooked 2 1/4 c. cooked				
Cooking and Preparation Hints * The different types of lentils have slightly different flavors. The brown lentils have a meaty taste; the green ones have a more vegetable-like flavor; and the red ones are slightly sweet.					* While dried lentils do not require soaking before cooking, a preliminary soak can help them remain whole during cooking. Also, cooking them below the boiling point can help them stay intact.	

INGREDIENT	YIELD		For Purpose of	SUBSTITUTION		
	Amount Market Form	Yield Equivalent		Amount	Substitution	Instructions
Lettuce	1 lb. fresh	6 c. pieces				* Lettuce leaves for a salad must be dry, or the salad dressing will not adhere. Wet lettuce will also dilute the flavor of the dressing.
	1 lb. fresh	5 c. shredded				* You can make a salad ahead of time if the lettuce and dressing are not mixed. One way to achieve this is to pour the dressing in the bottom of a bowl. Place the sturdiest greens on top of the dressing and then more delicate greens and fruits or vegetables on top. Cover with plastic wrap and refrigerate until ready to serve.
	Cooking and Preparation Hints * Different varieties of lettuce are interchangeable according to your preference in flavor intensity and texture. * Do not store lettuce next to apples, plums, pears, avocados, tomatoes or melons. They produce ethylene gas which can spoil lettuce. * To core iceberg lettuce, hold the head above the counter with the core side down. Hit it hard on the counter top, and the core will come out easily.					
Liederkranz Cheese See also Cheese			All Recipes	8 oz.	8 oz. Limburger cheese (1)	(1) Both are made with whole milk. Limburger is somewhat heavier and stronger than Liederkranz.
Lima Bean (Butter Bean, Madagascar Bean)	3 lb. in pod 1 lb. dried 1 lb. dried 1 c. dried 15 oz. can 10 oz. frozen	3 3/4 c. shelled 2 1/3 c. 6 c. cooked 2 1/2 c. cooked 2 c. 1 3/4 c. cooked	**Cooking and Preparation Hints** * Herbs and spices that complement lima beans include marjoram, oregano, sage, savory, tarragon and thyme.			* Blanch limas before freezing — 3 minutes for baby limas and 4 minutes for large limas. They can be frozen for 6 to 12 months.
Limburger Cheese See also Cheese			All Recipes	8 oz.	8 oz. Liederkranz cheese (1)	(1) Both are made with whole milk, but Liederkranz is milder.
Lime See also Fruit	1 lb. fresh 1 lb. fresh 1 medium 1 medium	6 - 8 medium 1/2 c. juice 1 - 2 T juice 1 t. grated peel	Flavoring	1 slice 1 t. grated peel 1 t. grated peel	1 slice lemon 1 t. grated lemon peel 2 T juice	
Lime Juice			All Recipes Acidulation Flavoring	1 c. fresh 1 t. 2 T	1 c. bottled 1 t. other citrus juice 1 t. vinegar 1 t. grated peel	
	Cooking and Preparation Hints * Lime juice can be frozen. For handy use, freeze in ice cube trays and transfer cubes to a plastic freezer bag.					

INGREDIENT	YIELD		SUBSTITUTION			
	Amount Market Form	Yield Equivalent	For Purpose of	Amount	Substitution	Instructions
Lingcod (Long Cod) See also Fish/Shellfish	**Cooking and Preparation Hints** * Herbs and spices that complement lingcod include tarragon, pepper, oregano, dill weed, bay leaf, fennel seed				and red pepper. * Lingcod can be frozen for up to 9 months.	
Liqueur See Spirits						
Liver See also Meat	1 lb.	4 servings	**Cooking and Preparation Hints** * Liver can be frozen when it is very fresh and will keep for up to 2 months. Remove any outer membrane before freezing. Thaw in the refrigerator, rinse in cold water and pat dry with paper towels.			
Lobster See also Fish/Shellfish	1 lb. whole	1/3 - 1/2 c. cooked meat	All Recipes	1 lb. whole	1 lb. spiny lobster (1)	(1) The spiny lobster has no claws.
	1 - 1 1/2 lb. whole	1 serving				
	4 - 6 oz. cooked meat	1 serving	Salad	1 c. cooked meat	1 c. cooked monkfish	* To store live lobsters, put them in a perforated brown paper bag and refrigerate. * Herbs and spices that complement lobster are black pepper, dry mustard, chives and tarragon. * Overcooking will cause lobster to be tough. For boiled lobster, allow 5 to 6 minutes per lb. starting when the water returns to a boil. * Cooked lobster meat freezes well. To prevent ice crystals from forming and toughening the meat, pack it tightly in rigid containers.
			Cooking and Preparation Hints * The female lobster is considered preferable because it is more tender and because it contains the roe which is responsible for giving stews and sauces their pinkish color. To determine the gender, feel the underside of the lobster where the tail meets the chest. There will be 2 small appendages. In the female, they are fringed with fine hairs and will be soft to the touch. In the male, they are pointed and rough to the touch.			
Loganberry See also Fruit			All Recipes	1 c. 1 c. 1 c. 1 c.	blackberries boysenberries dewberries youngberries	refrigerate. Add 1/2 to 2/3 c. syrup to each pt. of fruit. Berries frozen in syrup will keep for up to 16 months. Unsweetened berries will keep for 6 months.
			Cooking and Preparation Hints * Loganberries can be frozen unsweetened, in a dry sugar pack using 3/4 c. sugar for each qt. of berries, or in a 40% to 50% syrup pack. For the syrup, dissolve 3 to 4 3/4 c. sugar in 4 c. water and			
Long Cod See Lingcod						

INGREDIENT	YIELD			SUBSTITUTION		
	Amount Market Form	Yield Equivalent	For Purpose of	Amount	Substitution	Instructions
Macadamia Nut See also Nuts	1 lb. shelled 5 oz. can whole	3 1/3 c. 1 c.	All Recipes	1 c.	1 c. almonds (1)	(1) Almonds need to have their skins removed to substitute for macadamias and bake them at 250°for 12 to 15 minutes, stirring often.
Cooking and Preparation Hints * Either raw or roasted macadamias can be used in most recipes. * To roast macadamias, spread the shelled nuts in a shallow pan					* Dry roasted and coconut oil roasted macadamia nuts are interchangeable in recipes.	
Mace See also Herbs/Spices			Seasoning	1 t. ground	1 t. ground nutmeg (1)	(1) While mace and nutmeg have the same origin (mace is the lacy fiber that covers the nutmeg), they are not identical in taste.
Cooking and Preparation Hints * Mace complements such foods as cakes, cookies, pies, fruit, custards, nut breads, fish, chicken, spinach and yellow vegetables.						
Mackerel See also Fish/Shellfish	16 oz. can	2 c.	All Recipes	1 lb. 1 lb. 1 lb.	1 lb. king mackerel 1 lb. Spanish mackerel 1 lb. jack mackerel	
Cooking and Preparation Hints * Mackerel is complemented by such herbs and spices as basil, thyme, marjoram, black pepper, tarragon, parsley,					dill weed, bay leaf, fennel seed, red pepper, oregano and rosemary. * Mackerel can be frozen for 4 to 6 months.	
Madagascar Bean See Lima Bean						
Mahi Mahi (Dolphinfish, Dorado)			Broiling/Grilling	1 lb. 1 lb.	1 lb. swordfish 1 lb. shark	
Maltose			All Recipes	1 c.	1 c. honey	
Mango See also Fruit	1 lb. fresh 1 lb. fresh	1 large 1 3/4 c. diced				
Cooking and Preparation Hints * You can hasten ripening of an underripe mango by putting it in a paper bag and letting it sit at room temperature. Do not refrigerate mangoes until they are fully ripe. * Some people, especially those who are allergic to poison ivy and poison oak, may be sensitive to the skin or sap of a mango. To be on the safe side, peel a mango under running water or wear plastic gloves. There is no problem once the skin is removed; eating the fruit will not cause a reaction.					* To make mango flowers, halve the mango off-center. Repeat on the other side so that you have 2 halves — without the long seed in the middle. Score the fruit cutting lengthwise and then crosswise at 1/2" intervals. Push the skin upward from underneath, turning the mango inside out and forming the flower. * Mangoes can be frozen in a dry sugar pack by adding 3/4 c. sugar for each qt. of fruit or in a 40% to 50% syrup pack. For the syrup, dissolve 3 to 4 3/4 c. sugar in 4 c. water and refrigerate. Add 1/2 to 2/3 c. syrup to each pt. of fruit.	

A B C D E F G H I J K L M N O P Q R S T U V W X Y Z

INGREDIENT	YIELD				SUBSTITUTION	
	Amount Market Form	Yield Equivalent	For Purpose of	Amount	Substitution	Instructions
Maple Sugar See Sugar						
Maple Syrup	12 oz.	1 1/2 c.	All Recipes	1 c. 1 c.	1 c. maple-flavored syrup (1) 1 c. pancake syrup (2)	(1) This is a combination of a less expensive syrup such as corn syrup and pure maple syrup. (2) This is corn syrup flavored with artificial maple extract.

Cooking and Preparation Hints
* An unopened bottle of maple syrup will keep in the cupboard for at least a year. Once opened, it should be refrigerated and will keep for 6 to 8 months.

INGREDIENT	Amount Market Form	Yield Equivalent	For Purpose of	Amount	Substitution	Instructions
Margarine See also Butter, Fats	1 lb. regular 1 lb. regular 1 stick regular 1/4 stick regular	4 sticks 2 c. 1/2 c. 2 T	All Recipes	1 c.	1 c. shortening + 1 t. salt + 1/2 t. butter flavor extract 1 c. soft margarine (1) 1 1/2 c. whipped margarine 1 c. diet margarine 1 c. soy-based margarine (2) 1 c. oil	(1) There will be a slight flavor difference because soft margarine has a high liquid oil content. (2) Recipes made with this will lack a buttery taste, but you can use butter flavoring to compensate.
			Stove Top Cooking	1 c. regular 1 c. regular 1 c. regular 1 c. regular 1 c. regular		

Cooking and Preparation Hints
* By law margarine must contain 80% fat unless it is intended as a diet product. In that case the package must be labeled "imitation" or "diet."

* Margarine can be frozen for 5 to 6 months in its original waxed carton and overwrapped with aluminum foil or freezer wrap.

For Purpose of	Amount	Substitution	Instructions
Baking	1 c. regular 1 c. regular	1 c. soft margarine (3) 1 c. shortening	(3) This substitution is not suitable for recipes that require the shortening to remain firm, such as for hard cookie dough, pastry shells and puff pastry.
Flavoring/Reducing Fat	2 t. 2 t. 2 T	1/2 t. Butter Buds ® Sprinkles 1 T liquified Butter Buds ® Mix (4) 1/8 t. butter flavor extract (5)	(4) Mix 1 t. Butter Buds ® Mix with 1 T liquid. (5) This amount is recommended for recipes that do not require cooking. If the dish will be cooked or baked, increase the amount of extract to 2 t. so that it will retain the flavor strength equivalent to 2 T margarine.
Spread/Reducing Fat	1 T	1 T nonfat margarine	
Baking/Reducing Fat	1 c.	8 t. (1 envelope) Butter Buds ® Mix + 1/2 c. liquid (6) + 1/2 c. margarine (6) 2 T Butter Buds ® Sprinkles + 1/2 c. margarine (7) 1 T shortening (8)	(6) For cookie recipes, eliminate the liquid and decrease the flour by 25%. (7) For best results when using the Sprinkles, slightly decrease the amount of flour in the recipe. Do not use the Sprinkles for pie crusts. (8) Shortening is better for dishes such as meringues or mixtures that contain sticky fruit.
Greasing Pans	1 c. 1 T 1 T	1 second nonstick cooking spray	
Greasing/Flouring Cake Pans	1 T	Cake pan coating spray as needed	

INGREDIENT	YIELD		SUBSTITUTION			Instructions
	Amount Market Form	Yield Equivalent	For Purpose of	Amount	Substitution	

Marinade

Cooking and Preparation Hints
* The main purpose of marinating is flavoring and, to a lesser extent, tenderizing. Most meat marinades contain an organic acid such as lemon juice, vinegar, wine or tomatoes which penetrate about 1/4" into the interior of the meat.
* For fish and lean meats such as chicken breasts, marinades help to moisten them and keep them from drying out when cooked. A small amount of oil in the marinade accomplishes this.
* Plan to use 1 c. marinade for every 1 lb. of food to be marinated. Foods do not have to be submerged in marinade. They can be placed in a lesser amount and turned frequently. A handy way to accomplish this is to put all the ingredients into a plastic storage bag,

seal tightly and turn as needed.
* Use glass or plastic containers for marinades that contain acidic ingredients. The acids might react with a metal container.
* Meat, fish and poultry should be marinated in the refrigerator. While warmer temperatures hasten the marinating process, they also encourage the growth of bacteria.
* Leftover meat marinade might contain bacteria. It is, therefore, the best idea to make extra marinade for basting and for sauces. The next best alternative is to boil the leftover marinade before using it.
* If the marinade recipe requires the ingredients to be cooked in advance, be sure to chill the marinade completely before using.

INGREDIENT	Amount Market Form	Yield Equivalent	For Purpose of	Amount	Substitution	Instructions
Marjoram (Sweet Marjoram) See also Herbs/Spices	1/2 oz. fresh 1 T fresh chopped	1/2 c. leaves 1 t. dried				

Cooking and Preparation Hints
* Marjoram complements such foods as beef, veal, poultry, fish, egg dishes, tomatoes, tomato-based soups and sauces, eggplant, squash, broccoli, asparagus, Brussels sprouts, celery, peas, potatoes and salad dressings.

* Fresh marjoram leaves can be frozen on their stems for up to 1 year. Wash and pat dry and store in plastic freezer bags or containers. Avoid crowding the herbs to prevent crushing them.

INGREDIENT	Amount Market Form	Yield Equivalent	For Purpose of	Amount	Substitution	Instructions
Marrow Bean See also Beans, Dried			All Recipes	1 c. cooked 1 c. cooked 1 c. cooked 1 c. cooked 1 c. cooked 1 c. cooked	cooked small white beans cooked navy beans cooked cannellini beans cooked great northern beans cooked white kidney beans cooked pea beans	
Marshmallow	1 large, cut up 11 large	10 miniature 1 c.				

Cooking and Preparation Hints
* To keep marshmallows from sticking to scissors when cutting, dip the scissors into cold water and cut the marshmallows while the blades are wet.
* If your marshmallows have hardened in the cupboard, you can add either a slice of apple or a slice of

fresh bread to the marshmallows and store them in an airtight container for 1 to 2 days.
* Marshmallows can be frozen for up to a year. When they thaw, they will still be moist. If you plan to cut the marshmallows, do so while they are still frozen.

INGREDIENT	YIELD			SUBSTITUTION		
	Amount Market Form	Yield Equivalent	For Purpose of	Amount	Substitution	Instructions
Marzipan See also Almond Paste	7 oz. tube	7/8 c.	All Recipes	2 1/2 c.	2 c. almond paste + 1 c. powdered sugar + 2 T corn syrup (1)	(1) Homemade marzipan is not as smooth as many commerical products but is adequate for most purposes. The exception is when the marzipan will be sculpted into decorations — where the extra graininess will be noticeable.

Cooking and Preparation Hints
* If you plan to frost a cake with marzipan, spread a thin layer of jam, preserves or icing over the cake first to help the marzipan adhere.
* Before molding or rolling marzipan, it should be kneaded to soften.

* To smooth rough edges or seams of marzipan, dip your fingers first in water or egg whites.
* An opened package of marzipan should be wrapped and refrigerated to prevent drying out and loss of flavor.

INGREDIENT	YIELD			SUBSTITUTION		
Mayonnaise	16 oz. Jar	2 c.	All Recipes	1 c. 1 1/2 c. bottled	1 c. salad dressing (1) 2 egg yolks + 1 t. Dijon mustard + 1 T lemon juice or vinegar + 1 c. oil + salt and pepper (2)	(1) Salad dressing is sweeter than mayonnaise. (2) Put all ingredients except the oil into a blender or food processor. Turn on machine and add oil in a thin stream until thickened.
				1 c. homemade	1 c. bottled mayonnaise + 1 t. lemon juice + 1 t. prepared mustard	

Cooking and Preparation Hints
* When making your own mayonnaise, be sure to have all ingredients at room temperature. Cold eggs will produce a soupy, rather than thick, result.
* If your homemade mayonnaise separates, you can salvage it by: (1) Putting a fresh egg yolk in a bowl and beating in the separated mixture plus 1/2 c. extra oil; or (2) Beating 1 t. prepared mustard with 1 T

of the separated mixture, slowly adding the remaining mayonnaise and beating until reconstituted.
* When stabilized, homemade mayonnaise will keep in the refrigerator for at least a week. To stabilize, add 2 t. boiling water or stock for each 1 c. of mayonnaise and beat until incorporated.
* Mayonnaise does not freeze well and will separate during the freezing and thawing process.

INGREDIENT	YIELD			SUBSTITUTION		
			All Recipes/Reducing Fat	1 c.	1 c. low-fat or nonfat mayonnaise	(3) To produce 1 c. mashed potatoes of the consistency of mayonnaise, cook a 12 oz. potato and mash with 8 T liquid such as chicken broth.
			All Recipes/Reducing Calories	1 c.	1 c. reduced calorie mayonnaise	
			All Recipes/Reducing Cholesterol	1 c.	1 c. low cholesterol mayonnaise	
			Dips/Reducing Fat and Calories	1 c.	1 c. mashed potatoes (3)	

INGREDIENT	YIELD			SUBSTITUTION		
	Amount Market Form	Yield Equivalent	For Purpose of	Amount	Substitution	Instructions
Meat See also individual listings	1 lb. lean, boneless cut 1 lb. boneless cut 1 lb. cut with some bone 1 lb. very boney cut	3 - 4 servings 2 c. ground 2 servings 1 serving	All Recipes Soups/Stews	8 oz. cooked 1 c. cooked, cubed 1 c. cooked, cubed 1 c. cooked, cubed	8 oz. cooked seitan (1) 1 c. tofu (2) 1 c. tempeh 1 c. cooked dried beans	(1) This "wheat meat" can be used as cutlets, cubes, slices or ground. The flavor will vary depending on the seasonings and broth used to cook the dough. Pre-cooked seitan is available but may contain salt as a preservative. (2) Freezing and then thawing tofu will give it a meaty texture.

Cooking and Preparation Hints

* Meat can be tenderized somewhat by marinating in some form of organic acid such as lemon juice, vinegar, wine or tomatoes. However, marinades penetrate only about 1/4" of the surface and, as a result, contribute more to flavor than to tenderness. Natural enzymes found in papaya, pineapple, figs, and kiwi can also act as tenderizers, but do not use them more than 10 to 15 minutes before cooking.

* Salt tends to draw out juices from meats while cooking. For this reason it is advisable not to salt meat before roasting or broiling. When cooking meat in a liquid, adding salt at any time is fine.

* The fat content of meat can change substantially according to the cooking method used. Broiling helps to reduce the fat content because the meat is cooked on a rack. As the fat melts from the heat, it drips off into the receptacle pan under the rack. Conversely, frying increases the fat content because (1) additional fat is added to the pan and (2) the fat from the meat does not drip off. In general, if you want to reduce the amount of fat, meats should not be floured or breaded before browning or roasting because the breading absorbs the fat from the meat.

* To prevent meat from turning gray when sautéing, make sure the meat is very dry before adding it to the pan, and don't overcrowd the pieces. Otherwise, the meat will steam instead of brown.

* If you don't want to cut into a piece of meat to determine if it is done, you can make the assessment by touch. Rare meat will be soft. Medium-cooked meat will have some resistance and spring back into place. Well done meat will be firm.

* If a recipe specifies a hot, medium or low charcoal temperature for grilling, you can determine the fire temperature by holding your hand, palm side down, over the coals at cooking height. If you can keep it there for 2 seconds, the temperature is hot; 3 seconds, medium-hot; 4 seconds, medium (the recommended temperature for cooking meat); 5 seconds, low; 6 to 7 seconds, very low.

* To prevent lower-fat meats and poultry from sticking to the barbecue grill, spray the grill with nonstick cooking spray before heating the grill or lighting the coals.

* If you're using metal skewers for kabobs, spray them with nonstick cooking spray before threading meats and vegetables for easy cleanup. If you're using wooden skewers, place the skewers in ice water to soak for several hours before cooking to prevent the skewers from burning.

* To prevent steaks and chops from curling when grilling, cut the fat around the edges of the meat at 2" to 3" intervals.

* For microwave cooking, boneless cuts of meat are preferred because bone has a reflective effect which causes uneven cooking.

* Large cuts of meat such as roasts should rest for a few minutes between cooking and carving. The rest period allows the juices to be absorbed back into the meat. The roast is both juicier and easier to carve. A rare roast should rest for 15 to 20 minutes in a warm place such as an open oven and should be loosely covered. A medium to well-done roast should rest for 7 to 10 minutes. During the standing time, the internal temperature of the roast will rise about 5°; consider this when calculating the cooking time.

INGREDIENT	YIELD			SUBSTITUTION		Instructions
	Amount Market Form	Yield Equivalent	For Purpose of	Amount	Substitution	

Meat (continued)

Cooking and Preparation Hints (continued)

* To easily thin-slice meat for stir frying, first freeze it for 45 minutes to 1 hour.
* The ideal temperature for meat storage is 28° to 32°. Most home refrigerators have temperatures of 36° to 40°. Storing meat in the coldest section of the refrigerator is suggested and can even double the shelf life of the meat.
* Leftover cooked meat should be left whole for refrigerator storage to prevent dryness and to inhibit bacterial growth.
* Variety meats such as brains, hearts, kidneys, liver, sweetbreads, tongue and tripe are more perishable than other meat and should be cooked as soon as possible after purchase.
* When preparing meat for freezing, do not salt it. Salt draws out moisture and oxidizes the meat fat which gives it a rancid taste. Trim away as much fat as possible. Also remove any protruding bones; they may tear the wrapping, leave the meat exposed and promote freezer burn.
* Raw meat can be frozen for 3 to 12 months, depending on the kind and cut of meat. When meat is reduced in size, the

Instructions:

increased surface area necessitates a shorter storage time. Ground meat can be frozen for 3 to 4 months. Steaks and roasts can be stored longer.
* Meat that is purchased on trays and wrapped in plastic can be frozen in the original store wrappings for up to 1 month. However, the plastic is not designed to protect against freezer burn, and the meat should be overwrapped for longer storage.
* The safest method for thawing meat is in the refrigerator. You can count on 4 to 7 hours per lb. for a large roast, 3 to 5 hours per lb. for a small roast and 12 to 14 hours total for a 1" thick steak.
* A frozen roast will require 30% to 50% more cooking time than a refrigerated roast.
* Broil frozen steaks, chops and patties farther from the heat than you would for defrosted meat. This will help to cook the inside to the desired level of doneness without burning the outside.
* Frozen steaks and chops that will be coated with eggs and crumbs need to be partially thawed so that the coating will adhere to the meat.

Melon
See also individual listings

Cooking and Preparation Hints
* To store ripe melons, place them in a plastic bag and refrigerate for up to 1 week.
* To freeze melon, cut into cubes, slices, balls or wedges. Melon can be frozen unsweetened covered with water or juice, in a dry

Substitution:

sugar pack with 2/3 c. sugar for each 1 qt. of fruit or in a 30% syrup pack. For the syrup, dissolve 2 c. sugar in 4 c. water, add 4 t. lemon juice and refrigerate. Add 1/2 c. to 2/3 c. syrup per 1 pt. of fruit. Melon can be frozen for 8 to 12 months. It will soften as it thaws; so serve while a few ice crystals still remain.

Meringue
See also Egg

Cooking and Preparation Hints
* For a soft meringue, add 2 T sugar per egg white. For a hard meringue, add 4 T sugar per egg white.
* Some cooks prefer confectioners' sugar over granulated sugar for meringues because it dissolves more quickly. To make sure granulated sugar dissolves, add the sugar gradually after the egg whites are beaten to the frothy stage — while they are still moist enough to dissolve the sugar. Undissolved granules produce a gritty texture and cause beads of syrup to appear on the baked meringue.
* If egg whites become stiff before all of the sugar has been added, beat in a small amount of water (not more than 1 T per white) and continue adding the sugar.

Substitution:

* Meringue will become tough and gummy if too much sugar is added, if it is underbeaten, if it is overbaked or if it is baked at too high a temperature.
* As long as they are baked very dry, meringue shells will keep for several days at room temperature loosely covered. They can be frozen for longer storage, then thawed at room temperature for about 10 minutes. If they become soft or soggy, dry them in the oven at 250° for about 15 minutes.
* To keep the meringue topping on a pie from shrinking when baked, be sure to use the correct amount of sugar (2 T per egg white) and spread the meringue so that it touches all sides of the pastry.

INGREDIENT	YIELD			SUBSTITUTION		
	Amount Market Form	Yield Equivalent	For Purpose of	Amount	Substitution	Instructions
Milk (Cow's Milk) See also Buttermilk	1 qt.	4 c.	All Recipes	1 c. whole	1/2 c. evaporated + 1/2 c. water	(1) Some recipes, particularly those for puddings, custards and sauces, rely on the dairy fat of whole milk for texture and flavor. In those cases add 2 1/2 t. butter.
				1 c. whole	1 c. nonfat (skim) (1)	
				1 c. whole	1 c. reconstituted nonfat dry milk + 2 1/2 t. butter	(2) The results will tend to be more crumbly than with whole milk.
				1 c. nonfat (skim)	1 c. reconstituted nonfat dry milk	
			Baking	1 c. whole	1 c. fruit juice (2)	
				1 c. whole	1 c. water (2)	

Cooking and Preparation Hints
* You can freeze milk for up to 3 weeks in its original 1 qt. wax-coated container. It separates during freezing and will not taste as good as fresh milk when consumed as a beverage, but it is acceptable for cooking. Thaw in the refrigerator.

* When a recipe calls for scalding milk, heat it to just below the boiling point — when bubbles begin to form around the edge of the pan. To facilitate cleanup, rinse the pan in cold water before pouring in the cold milk.

			All Recipes/Milk Allergies	1 c. whole	1 c. soy milk	
				1 c. whole	1 c. nut milk	
				1 c. whole	1 c. goat's milk (3)	(3) Goat's milk has a much higher fat content than cow's milk.

Cooking and Preparation Hints
* Unopened cans can be stored at room temperature. Milk that has been stored too long or that has been exposed to heat will darken and thicken. There is no health risk to using the milk, but it may affect the success of some recipes.

| **Milk, Condensed** (Sweetened Condensed Milk) | 14 oz. can | 1 1/4 c. | | | | |

| **Milk, Evaporated** | | | All Recipes | 1 c. | 1 c. cream | |

Cooking and Preparation Hints
* Unopened cans of evaporated milk will keep for up to 1 year. When opened, evaporated milk can be refrigerated in a tightly covered container for 7 to 10 days.

Milk, Nonfat Dry	1 lb.	3 2/3 c.				
	1 lb.	14 c. reconstituted				
	1/4 - 1/3 c.	1 c. reconstituted				

Cooking and Preparation Hints
* Unless a recipe specifically calls for reconstitution, dry milk can be added either to the dry or the liquid ingredients.

* Dry milk has a shelf life of 6 months. Once opened, store dry milk in an airtight container to prevent staling. As dry milk gets stale, it develops a sweet taste.

| **Millet** See also Grains | 1 c. | 3 1/2 c. cooked | | | | |

INGREDIENT	YIELD		For Purpose of	SUBSTITUTION		Instructions
	Amount Market Form	Yield Equivalent		Amount	Substitution	
Mint See also Herbs/Spices	**Cooking and Preparation Hints** * Mint complements such foods as lamb, veal, carrots, peas, spinach, bean dishes, new potatoes, yogurt, fruit, candies, jellies				and iced beverages. * Mint leaves can be chopped and frozen in small packs or rigid containers for 6 to 12 months.	
Mirin (Rice Wine)			Seasoning	1 T	1 T sake + 1 t. sugar (1)	(1) Cook until syrupy.
Mirliton See Chayote						
Miso	**Cooking and Preparation Hints** * Use miso at the end of cooking just before you remove the pan from the heat or without cooking at all. Like yogurt, miso is a liv-				ing food that contains bacteria and enzymes that will be destroyed by boiling. * Dark miso has a saltier taste and stronger flavor than the lighter varieties.	
Molasses	16 oz.	1 1/3 c.	All Recipes	1 c. unsulfured	1 c. sulfured molasses (1)	(1) Sulfured molasses is very thick and dark and will have a stronger molasses flavor. (2) The finished product will not be as sweet and will lack the molasses flavor. (3) You may want to increase the amount of spices called for in the recipe to compensate for the lack of molasses flavor.
			Baking	1 c. 1 c.	1 c. corn syrup (2) 3/4 c. sugar + 1/4 c. water (3)	
	Cooking and Preparation Hints * When the type of molasses is not specified in a recipe, use light, unsulfured molasses. * Blackstrap molasses should not be used in place of lighter molasses because of its astringency and dark cast.				* To keep molasses from sticking to a measuring cup, first spray the cup with nonstick cooking spray. Or if your recipe calls for oil, measure that first.	
Morel See Mushroom						
Mozzarella Cheese See also Cheese	8 oz.	2 c. grated	All Recipes	8 oz.	8 oz. Bel Paese cheese	**Cooking and Preparation Hints** * Mozzarella can be frozen up to 6 months.
Mullet See also Fish/Shellfish	**Cooking and Preparation Hints** * Mullet is complemented by such herbs and spices as tarragon, oregano, dill weed, bay leaf, fennel seed,				black pepper, white pepper, garlic and red pepper. * Mullet can be frozen for up to 3 months.	

INGREDIENT	YIELD				SUBSTITUTION		Instructions
	Amount Market Form	Yield Equivalent	For Purpose of	Amount	Substitution		

Mung Bean Sprouts
See Sprouts

Mushroom
See also Vegetables

Amount Market Form	Yield Equivalent	For Purpose of	Amount	Substitution
1 lb. fresh button	20 - 24 medium	Flavoring	4 oz. fresh	1 T powdered
1 lb. fresh button	5 c. sliced		2 oz. can	1 T powdered
1 lb. fresh button	2 c. sliced, cooked		3 T dried	1 T powdered
4 oz. can button, whole	3/4 c.			
4 oz. can button, sliced	3/4 c.			
1 lb. fresh button	3 oz. dried reconstituted			

Cooking and Preparation Hints

* With good storage, fresh mushrooms can last in the refrigerator for 5 days. Store them, unwashed, in a brown paper bag or on a plate covered with damp paper towels. Raw mushrooms require good ventilation as well as humidity; so remove any plastic from pre-wrapped packages.

* To clean mushrooms, just wipe them off with a damp cloth and cut off any tough stems. Mushrooms tend to absorb water; so don't immerse them for cleaning purposes. Peeling mushrooms is not necessary.

* Avoid using aluminum cookware when preparing light-colored mushrooms because it will turn the mushrooms dark.

* When microwaving mushrooms, no liquid and no cover are required.

* Mushrooms are complemented by parsley, tarragon, thyme and dry sherry.

* Mushrooms need to be blanched or sautéed before they are frozen or they will turn dark. To blanch whole mushrooms, add 1 T lemon juice for each 1 qt. of water and boil mushrooms for 3 to 4 minutes. Then cool in ice water. Drain, pack and freeze. The mushrooms will last in the freezer for 3 to 6 months and will have a somewhat softened texture when thawed.

* Cêpes (also called porcini, steinpilz and King Bolete) are available both fresh and dried. Avoid burning the fresh ones because it turns them bitter. The dried ones become more aromatic the longer and more slowly they are cooked.

* Morels are available fresh and dried. Dried morels have a much more pronounced flavor than the fresh. To prepare dried morels for cooking, soak them for only about 2 minutes or until they can be cut.

* Chanterelles (also known as pfifferlinge, girolle and egg mushroom) come fresh, dried and canned. Fresh are difficult to clean, but soil removal can be accomplished under running water. Pat dry immediately. Dried chanterelles require about an hour of soaking before cooking.

* The wood ear mushroom (also called cloud ear, tree ear and silver ear) is very bland and assumes the taste of the stronger-flavored ingredients in the recipe. This dried mushroom will increase in size 5 to 6 times when reconstituted.

* Shiitake mushrooms (also called black forest, golden oak, oriental black or Chinese black) are available fresh and dried. The stems of the fresh mushrooms can be used but should be cooked a few minutes ahead of the caps so that both are done at the same time. The stems of the dried mushrooms are too tough to eat but can be used to flavor cooking liquids. When reconstituting the dried mushrooms, add about 1 T oil to the soaking liquid.

Cooking and Preparation Hints (continued)

* Oyster mushrooms (also called tree oyster, shimeji, hiratake and abalone mushrooms) are usually available fresh but also dried. They have a delicate flavor that can be overpowered by too much fat or oil; try using cream or stock instead.

* Enoki mushrooms (also called enokitake, velvet stem, snow puff and golden needle) are available fresh and require very little preparation. In fact, do not cook them at all because they will become tough.

INGREDIENT	YIELD		For Purpose of	SUBSTITUTION		Instructions
	Amount Market Form	Yield Equivalent		Amount	Substitution	

Mussel
See also Fish/Shellfish

Amount Market Form	Yield Equivalent
1 qt. unshucked	25 mussels
1 qt. unshucked	1 1/2 lb.
1 qt. unshucked	1 c. meat
1 lb. unshucked	16 mussels
12 - 18 mussels	1 serving

Cooking and Preparation Hints
* Mussels should be alive when purchased — indicated by a closed shell. Their shells may open naturally, even in the refrigerator, but will close tightly when you tap them. If not, discard them. To clean mussels, scrape off the beards with a knife. Cultivated mussels are usually then ready to prepare. Wild mussels need further cleaning. Scrub the shells under cold water with a firm brush or remove any attached seaweed with a knife. A wild mussel may also contain sand — especially if it is noticeably heavy. Soak the mussels for 10 minutes in salt water (1/3 c. salt per 4 qt. water) and remove. If more than a little sand has been released into the water, soak the mussels again.
* If any mussel shells have failed to open during the steaming process, discard them.
* Shucked mussels will become plump and opaque when they are cooked and ready to eat.
* Mussels are complemented by herbs and spices such as bay leaf, parsley, thyme, black pepper, red pepper, garlic and oregano.
* Cooked mussels freeze well in their liquor and will keep for 2 to 3 months.

Mustard
(Mustard Seed)
See also Herbs/Spices

For Purpose of	Amount	Substitution	Instructions
All Recipes	1 T prepared	1 T dried mustard + 1 t. vinegar + 1 t. cold water + 1 t. sugar (1)	(1) Use this substitution when the volume of mustard as well as its flavor is important to the recipe. Let the mixture stand for 15 minutes to develop flavor. The sugar can be omitted, but the mustard will be much hotter.
Flavoring	1 T prepared 1 t. dried	1 t. dried 1 T prepared (2)	(2) This substitution is for addition to wet mixtures.

Cooking and Preparation Hints
* Prepared mustard is an excellent emulsifying agent for cold sauces. You can use it in vinaigrette dressings to hold the vinegar and oil together or as an addition to the egg yolks when making home-made mayonnaise.
* Because mustard thickens, always add it to a liquid before reducing for a hot sauce.
* Cooking will reduce the hotness of mustard.
* Mustard complements salty foods such as preserved meats and both sweet and sour sauces such as honey mustard sauce and lemon mustard sauce.

Mustard Greens
See also Greens, Cooking

Amount Market Form	Yield Equivalent
1 lb. fresh	1 1/2 c. cooked
1 lb. fresh	3 servings
15 oz. can	1 3/8 c.
10 oz. frozen	1 3/8 c.

Cooking and Preparation Hints
* Remove the leaves from the woody center rib and stem, and cook only the leaves.
* Mustard greens will discolor if you cook them in aluminum or iron pans.
* Before freezing, blanch mustard greens for 1 1/2 to 2 minutes. Then chill and pack. They will keep for up to 12 months.

YIELD · SUBSTITUTION

INGREDIENT	Amount Market Form	Yield Equivalent	For Purpose of	Amount	Substitution	Instructions
Navy Bean See also Beans, Dried	1 lb. dried 1 lb. dried 1 c. dried	2 1/3 c. 5 1/2 c. cooked 2 1/3 c. cooked	All Recipes	1 c. cooked 1 c. cooked 1 c. cooked 1 c. cooked 1 c. cooked 1 c. cooked	1 c. cooked small white beans 1 c. cooked great northern beans 1 c. cooked cannellini beans 1 c. cooked white kidney beans 1 c. cooked marrow beans 1 c. cooked pea beans	
Nectarine See also Fruit	1 lb. fresh 1 lb. fresh	3 medium 2 1/2 - 3 c. sliced	All Recipes	1 medium	1 medium peach	

Cooking and Preparation Hints
* Nectarines can be frozen: (1) Unsweetened. Pack slices or halves in freezer container and cover with acidulated water (1/2 t. ascorbic acid or 2 t. lemon juice per 1 qt. of water). Leave headspace for expansion. (2) Juice-packed. Cover slices with apple juice or white grape juice mixed with an equal amount of water and add 1/2 t. ascorbic acid or 2 t. lemon juice per 1 qt. of juice mixture. (3) In a dry sugar pack with 2 t. sugar and 1 t. lemon juice for each 1 c. of fruit. (4) In a 50% syrup pack. Dissolve 4 3/4 c. sugar in 4 c. water and add 1/2 t. ascorbic acid. Refrigerate, then add to nectarine slices.

INGREDIENT	Amount Market Form	Yield Equivalent	For Purpose of	Amount	Substitution	Instructions
Nutmeg See also Herbs/Spices	1 whole	2 - 3 t. grated	Seasoning	1 t. freshly grated 1 t. ground	1 t. ground (1) 1 t. ground mace (2)	(1) The ground is stronger, oilier and less sweet than freshly grated. (2) Mace is the lacy red membrane that surrounds the nutmeg. Although they have the same origin, they are not identical in taste.

Cooking and Preparation Hints
* Nutmeg complements such foods as cakes, cookies, custards, ground beef, white sauce, cream sauces, spinach, carrots, asparagus, sweet potatoes, stewed fruit and eggnog.

INGREDIENT	Amount Market Form	Yield Equivalent	For Purpose of	Amount	Substitution	Instructions
Nuts See also individual listings	1 lb. in shell 1/4 lb. shelled 1/3 c. raw nuts	1/2 lb. shelled 1 c. chopped 1 qt. nutmilk	Baking	1 c. chopped 1 c. chopped 1 c. chopped 1 c. chopped 1 c. chopped 1 c. chopped 1 c. chopped	1 c. bran 1 c. toasted and chopped soy nuts 1 c. sunflower seeds 1 c. coarse cookie crumbs 1 c. chopped candied fruit 1 c. uncooked kasha 1 c. cereal (1)	(1) You may want to add 1 - 2 drops of vanilla or nut extract to compensate for the lack of nut flavor.

Cooking and Preparation Hints
* Stored in a cool place, unshelled nuts will keep for 6 months; whole shelled nuts will keep for 3 months; and chopped nuts will keep for 4 to 6 weeks. For longer storage and to prevent the high fat content from turning the nuts rancid, store nuts in the freezer.
* When a recipe calls for chopped nuts, be sure to measure the nuts after chopping.
* If you plan to use chopped nuts for decoration, first shake them in a strainer to eliminate the dust and tiny pieces.
* A rule-of-thumb for adding nuts to cookie dough is 1/4 c. to 1/2 c. nuts for each 1 c. of flour in the recipe. Add nuts at the end of mixing.
* To prevent nuts from turning oily and into a paste when pulverizing them in a food processor or blender, add at least 1 T of granulated sugar.

* To blanch nuts, cover them with boiling water and let stand for a few minutes. Drain, cover with cold water and drain again. Pinch or rub off the skins. For hazelnuts, peanuts and pistachios, you may want to roast them instead.
* Roasting or toasting nuts will make them crisper and enhance their flavor. Bake them at 300° turning frequently. Remove from the oven before they look done because they will continue to cook after they've been removed from the heat.
* Nuts can also be toasted in the microwave. Cook the nuts in a shallow dish on high power. For 1/2 c. nuts, cook 1 1/2 minutes; for 1 c. nuts, cook 2 minutes. Stir, then cook again for 1 1/2 to 2 1/2 minutes.
* If only salted nuts are available, you can rinse them for use in dessert recipes.

A B C D E F G H I J K L M **N** O P Q R S T U V W X Y Z

INGREDIENT	YIELD		SUBSTITUTION			
	Amount Market Form	Yield Equivalent	For Purpose of	Amount	Substitution	Instructions
Oat Flour See Flour, Oats						
Oats (Oatmeal) See also Grains	1 lb. 1 c. 1 1/4 c.	5 3/4 c. 2 c. cooked 1 c. oat flour	Baking	1 c. rolled oats 1 c. oats	1 c. quick-cooking rolled oats (1) 3/4 c. all purpose flour	(1) Do not substitute instant oats. They have been precooked and will turn your baked goods soft and sticky. Also, do not substitute steel cut oats which are too large.

Cooking and Preparation Hints
* The only difference between regular oats and quick-cooking oats is the thickness of the flakes. The quick-cooking oats are rolled thinner to shorten cooking time.
* You can make your own oat flour by grinding regular or quick-cooking rolled oats in a blender or food processor for about 1 minute. Oat flour can be used with wheat flour in baked goods by substituting up to 1/3 of the amount of wheat flour.
* Oats are complemented by such spices as cinnamon, nutmeg, ginger and mace.

Ocean Pout See also Fish/Shellfish						

Cooking and Preparation Hints
* Ocean pout has a thin, colorless membrane between the skin and the flesh which should be removed when the fish is filleted. The membrane is edible but will cause the fillet to curl when cooked. An alternate method to prevent curling is to score the membrane at 1" intervals.

Octopus See also Fish/Shellfish	1/2 lb.	1 serving	Salads	8 oz. cooked	8 oz. cooked squid	

Cooking and Preparation Hints
* Choose an octopus under 2 lb. because it will be more tender than a larger one.

Oil See also Fats, Olive Oil			Baking	1 c. 1 c. 1 T	1 c. + 2 T butter (1) 1 c. + 2 T shortening (2) 1 T mustard (3)	(1) While oil is 100% fat, butter is only 80-85% fat. The rest is water. (2) While both oil and shortening are 100% fat, the air in shortening adds volume. (3) Mustard can replace part or all of the oil in vinaigrette dressings. The more mustard that is used, the more the dressing will require some sweetening.
			Salad Dressings/Reducing Fat			

Cooking and Preparation Hints
* The quality, or grade, of an oil depends on how it is extracted. The highest quality is cold pressed oil and comes from the first squeezing. One step down is semi-refined oil which is produced when the squeezed pulp is subjected to greater pressure and higher temperature. The lowest quality oil comes from the same pulp which now has to be treated with an organic solvent to extract the remaining oil. For practical purposes, use the highest quality oils where the flavor is paramount — for example a fresh green salad. On the other hand, for many cooking and sautéing purposes, the less expensive oil will be fine.
* Oils can be stored at room temperature. Cold-pressed oil will keep this way for 1 to 2 months; semi-refined and solvent-extracted (usually labeled "pure") will keep longer. To extend storage time, you can refrigerate oils. They may become cloudy or congeal, but returning them to room temperature will solve those problems.
* In general, non-flavored oils such as vegetable oil, corn oil and safflower oil are interchangeable. Do not substitute highly flavored oils such as olive oil or walnut oil unless a recipe specifically calls for them.

INGREDIENT	YIELD		For Purpose of	Amount	SUBSTITUTION	
	Amount Market Form	Yield Equivalent		Amount	Substitution	Instructions

Oil
continued

Cooking and Preparation Hints (continued)
* Oils with high smoking points (the point at which oil starts to decompose) are the best choices for frying; oils with low smoking points are better suited as seasoning oils. Following are some average smoking points: safflower oil, 510°; soybean oil, 495°; corn oil, 475°; peanut oil, 440°; sesame oil, 420°; olive oil, 375°.
* To keep deep-fried foods from absorbing excess fat, add 2 T white or cider vinegar to each 1 qt. of oil before heating the oil.
* To clarify used oil, filter it through a coffee filter fitted into a funnel.

Okra
See also Vegetables

Amount Market Form	Yield Equivalent
1 lb. fresh	2 1/4 c. chopped
1 lb. fresh	4 servings
15 1/2 oz. can	1 3/4 c. chopped
10 oz. frozen	1 1/4 c. chopped

Substitution: for each 1 lb. of okra used.

Cooking and Preparation Hints
* When cooked, okra releases a viscous natural juice that will thicken any liquid that it's cooked in. To prepare okra for soups or stews that are to be thickened, trim stem ends, then slice. For recipes that call for the whole pods, trim stems and tips without piercing the pod.
* To prevent okra from turning stringy in gumbo, add about 1 T distilled white vinegar

* Okra is complemented by such herbs and spices as black pepper, red pepper, chives and parsley.
* To freeze okra, remove stem end without cutting into the pod. Blanch 3 to 4 minutes for medium pods and 5 minutes for large pods. Chill. Leave whole or slice crosswise. Pack and freeze.

Olive

Amount Market Form	Yield Equivalent
6 oz. whole, pitted	56 medium
6 oz. whole, pitted	1 2/3 c.
6 oz. whole, pitted	1 1/3 c. chopped
2 1/4 oz. can sliced	2/3 c.
4 1/2 oz. can, chopped	1 c.

Cooking and Preparation Hints
* Use a cherry pitter to pit olives when appearance of the olives is important.

Olive Oil
See also Oil

Cooking and Preparation Hints
* Olive oil is made by first crushing, then pressing olives to extract the oil. Successive pressings require heat and solvents to extract the oil. The best quality olive oil comes from the first pressing and may be labeled "virgin," "extra virgin," "cold pressed," "first pressed" or "unrefined." Lesser grades may be labeled "fine" or "pure."

* Olive oil that is golden yellow in color comes from mature olives and has a mellow, sweet taste. Olive oil that has a greenish cast comes from olives that were harvested before they reached maturity and has a fruity, tart taste.
* Olive oil is not the best choice for deep-frying because it can't tolerate high temperatures. Use safflower oil, soybean oil, corn oil, peanut oil or avocado oil instead.

Ingredient	Amount Market Form	Yield Equivalent	For Purpose of	Amount	Substitution	Instructions
Onion See also Vegetables	1 lb. fresh 1 lb. fresh 1 medium 12 oz. frozen 1 large	4 medium 3 - 4 servings, cooked 1/2 c. chopped 3 c. chopped 4 t. juice	Flavoring	1/4 c. chopped 1/4 c. chopped 1/4 c. chopped 1/4 c. chopped 4 T chopped 8 T chopped 4 T chopped 1 T chopped	1/4 c. chopped shallots 1/4 c. chopped scallions 1/4 c. chopped leeks (1) 1/4 c. chopped ramp (2) 1 T minced dried onion 1 T onion powder 1 t. onion paste 2 T onion juice	(1) Leeks have a milder flavor than onions. (2) Ramps have a somewhat stronger flavor than onions.

Cooking and Preparation Hints
* Store onions in a cool, dark, dry place where air can circulate around them. Dampness and crowding promote root growth and decay. Do not store them in the refrigerator because the vegetable starch gets converted to sugar.
* To prevent tears when cutting onions, try refrigerating them first or put them in the freezer for 10 to 15 minutes before slicing. Another preventive measure is to cut them under cold running water.
* To peel onions, drop them into a pan of boiling water for 1 minute. Quickly drain them and plunge into cold water. Trim the root and stem ends carefully, keeping the bases intact. The skins can then be slipped off easily.
* To prevent whole onions from bursting when cooked, cut an "X" in the root end 1/8" deep.
* For crisp onion rings for salads, put the rings in ice water for an hour. Then drain and pat dry.
* Onions are complemented by such herbs and spices as caraway seed, mustard seed, nutmeg, oregano, sage and thyme.
* Chopped and sliced onions can be frozen raw and are convenient to have on hand. If you want to freeze whole onions, boil them for 3 to 7 minutes until the centers are heated. Quick-freeze them on trays, then pack in freezer bags or containers.
* Fresh onions become stronger in flavor when frozen. Keep that in mind when preparing dishes for freezing. You can effectively substitute minced dried onion for the fresh in those cases.

Ingredient	Amount Market Form	Yield Equivalent	For Purpose of	Amount	Substitution	Instructions
Onion Juice	1 large onion	4 t. juice	Flavoring	2 T 2 T 2 T	1/3 t. onion powder 3/4 t. minced dried onion 1/4 t. onion paste	

Cooking and Preparation Hints
* You can juice an onion just as you would an orange or lemon. Cut it in half, leaving the skin on. Then simply squeeze with your hands or with a reamer. Another method is to grate the onion and drain the juice.

Ingredient	Amount Market Form	Yield Equivalent	For Purpose of	Amount	Substitution	Instructions
Onion Powder			Flavoring	1 T 1 T 1 t.	2 T minced dried onion 2 t. onion paste 5 T onion juice	

Ingredient	Amount Market Form	Yield Equivalent	For Purpose of	Amount	Substitution	Instructions
Orange See also Fruit	1 lb. fresh 3 medium 1 medium 1 medium 2 medium 11 oz. can Mandarin sections	3 medium 1 c. juice 1/3 c. juice 10 - 12 sections 1 c. pieces 4 t. grated peel 1 1/4 c.	All Recipes	1 c. sections	1 c. tangerine sections	* You can increase the juiciness of an orange by immersing it in hot water, then rubbing it between your hands. Or you can put it in the microwave for 1 minute. * Orange sections can be frozen unsweetened, just covered with juice or water, or in a 40% syrup pack. For the syrup, dissolve 3 c. sugar and 1/2 t. ascorbic acid in 4 c. water and refrigerate. Add 1/2 to 2/3 c. syrup per 1 pt. of fruit and freeze.

Cooking and Preparation Hints
* The thinner the rind of an orange, the juicier it will be. Avoid oranges that are light in weight, puffy and spongy.
* To make oranges easier to peel, pour boiling water over them and let them stand for 5 minutes. You can do this at any time and refrigerate until you're ready to use them. This will also make the oranges juicier.

INGREDIENT	YIELD		For Purpose of	SUBSTITUTION		Instructions
	Amount Market Form	Yield Equivalent		Amount	Substitution	
Orange Extract See Extracts, Orange Peel						
Orange Juice	12 oz. frozen concentrate	6 c. reconstituted	All Recipes; Acidulation	1 c. fresh; 1 c. fresh; 1 t.	1 c. bottled; 1 c. reconstituted frozen; 1 t. other citrus juice	**Cooking and Preparation Hint** * You can use orange juice to replace water in a pie crust recipe. It doesn't add much flavor, but the acidity helps make the crust tender.
Orange Peel (Orange Rind, Orange Zest)			Flavoring	1 t. fresh, grated; 1 t. fresh, grated; 1 t. fresh, grated; 1 t. fresh, grated	1 t. dried; 1 t. other citrus peel, grated; 1/2 t. orange extract; 2 T orange juice (1)	(1) The rind of the orange has a high concentration of oil and, therefore, a more intense flavor than the juice.

Cooking and Preparation Hints
* Use only the colored portion of the skin; the white underneath is bitter. An easy way to remove the colored portion is with a potato peeler.
* You can freeze grated or thin strips of peel for use in baking and beverages.
* For easy cleanup, spray a hand grater with nonstick cooking spray before grating orange peel.

INGREDIENT	Amount Market Form	Yield Equivalent	For Purpose of	Amount	Substitution	Instructions
Oregano See also Herbs/Spices	1/2 oz. fresh; 1 T fresh chopped	1/2 c. chopped; 1 t. dried	Seasoning	1 t. dried; 1 t. dried	1 t. liquid oregano; 1 t. dried marjoram (1)	(1) Marjoram is a little sweeter.

Cooking and Preparation Hints
* Oregano complements such foods as grilled meats, poultry and game; stronger flavored fish; tomato-based soups, sauces and pasta dishes; poultry stuffing; and broccoli, eggplant, squash, cabbage, zucchini, bell peppers, dried beans, green beans, tomatoes, potatoes, peas, onions and spinach.
* Fresh oregano can be frozen for up to 1 year. Wash, pat dry and remove leaves from stems. Pack leaves in plastic freezer bags or containers without crowding to prevent crushing the herbs.

INGREDIENT	Amount Market Form	Yield Equivalent	For Purpose of	Amount	Substitution	Instructions
Oxtail See also Meat	1 tail	1 1/2 - 2 lb.				
Oyster See also Fish/Shellfish	6 large, in shell; 12 medium, in shell; 36 - 48 tiny, in shell; 1/4 - 1/2 pt. shucked; 6 1/2 oz. can smoked	1 serving; 1 serving; 1 serving; 1 serving; 24 oysters				

Cooking and Preparation Hints
* Oysters should be alive when you buy them in the shell. This is indicated by a closed shell. If the shell is open, tap it, and it should close. If not, discard the oyster.
* There are several methods that facilitate shucking oysters — although some of the flavor may be sacrificed: (1) Freeze the oysters for about 10 minutes. Insert a sharp knife and cut through the muscle that holds the 2 halves together. (2) Place the oysters in a 400° oven 5-7 minutes, then immerse them in ice water. Drain and cut muscle. (3) Place 6 oysters at a time in the microwave with the hinges facing out on a paper towel-lined plate. Cover with plastic wrap, heat on high power for 1-1 1/2 minutes until the oysters begin to open. Insert knife and cut muscle.
* Oysters are fully cooked when their edges begin to ruffle. Be careful not to overcook them.
* Herbs and spices that complement oysters include paprika, parsley, thyme and fennel seed.
* Freshly shucked oysters can be frozen for up to 3 months. Save liquid from shucking. Mix a salt solution of 1 T salt and 1 qt. cold water and wash oysters. Place oysters in a rigid freezer container and cover with the reserved liquid plus any fresh salt solution if necessary. Leave head space and freeze.

Oyster Plant See Salsify

INGREDIENT	YIELD		SUBSTITUTION			
	Amount Market Form	Yield Equivalent	For Purpose of	Amount	Substitution	Instructions
Pancakes			All Recipes/Non-Wheat	1 c. pancake mix	1 c. wheat-free pancake mix	their becoming tough. Stack the pancakes with wax paper in between and wrap well.
						* Thaw frozen pancakes at room temperature for 1 hour, separating individual pancakes after the first 15 minutes. You can reheat in the oven, covered, at 250° or fry in a lightly greased pan.

Cooking and Preparation Hints
* Tofu can replace the eggs in pancake batter at the rate of 2 oz. tofu for each egg. There will be only a slight taste difference.
* Pancakes freeze well and will keep for up to 2 months. For the best quality, cook the pancakes in as little grease as possible to prevent

INGREDIENT	Amount Market Form	Yield Equivalent	For Purpose of	Amount	Substitution	Instructions
Pancetta			Flavoring	6 oz.	6 oz. blanched salt pork	
				6 oz.	6 oz. blanched bacon	
			Cold Cut Recipes	6 oz. sliced	6 oz. sliced prosciutto	
				6 oz. sliced	6 oz. sliced unsmoked ham	
Papaya (Pawpaw, Lechosa, Fruta Bomba) See also Fruit	1 lb. fresh	2 c. sliced				dark place at room temperature for a few days. To speed up the process, put the papaya in a paper bag with a banana.
						* Papaya contains an enzyme that tenderizes meat. Rub a slice over the surface of the meat about 15 minutes before cooking.

Cooking and Preparation Hints
* Select a papaya that is partly or mostly yellow. Spottiness does not affect the quality. Judge the ripeness of a papaya by its feel rather than its look. It should have the same give as a ripe avocado.
* To ripen a partially ripe papaya, leave it in a

Paprika See also Herbs/Spices

Cooking and Preparation Hints
* The best paprika has a rich red color. It ages quickly and as it does so, it turns a darker, brownish color. To retain its color and flavor longer, store it in the refrigerator. It will last up to 2 years.
* Paprika complements such foods as chicken, veal, ham, fish, egg dishes, potatoes, cauliflower, cream soups, spreads and salad dressing.

INGREDIENT	Amount Market Form	Yield Equivalent	For Purpose of	Amount	Substitution	Instructions
Parma Ham			All Recipes	1 oz.	1 oz. prosciutto	
Parmesan Cheese See also Cheese	3 1/2 oz.	1 c. shredded	All Recipes	1 c. grated	1 c. grated Romano cheese	
	5 oz.	1 c. finely grated		1 c. grated	1 c. grated Sardo cheese	
	3 oz. can grated	3/4 c.		1 c. grated	1 c. grated Siciliano cheese	
				1 c. grated	1 c. grated Toscano cheese	
			Flavoring/Reducing Fat	1 c. grated	1 c. nutritional yeast	
Parsley See also Herbs/Spices	2 oz. bunch fresh	1 1/2 c. chopped	Seasoning	1 T fresh chopped	1 T chopped chervil (1)	(1) Chervil has a delicate flavor with a slight taste of anise.
	1 T fresh chopped	1 t. dried		1 t. dried	1 t. dried chervil (1)	

INGREDIENT	YIELD		For Purpose of	Amount	SUBSTITUTION	Instructions
	Amount Market Form	Yield Equivalent			Substitution	

Parsley (continued)

Cooking and Preparation Hints (continued)
* Curly leaf parsley and flat leaf (Italian) parsley can be used interchangeably.
* Parsley complements such foods as beef, lamb, pork, veal, poultry, fish, stews, stuffings, egg dishes, pasta dishes, salads, potatoes, carrots and peas.
* An easy method for chopping parsley is to put sprigs in a small glass and cut with kitchen scissors with the blades touching the bottom of the glass.

Instructions:
* To keep parsley fresh, rinse, pat dry, wrap in a paper towel or tea towel, put into a plastic bag and refrigerate.
* Parsley freezes well. Just wash, chop and wrap in aluminum foil. Use in 1 to 2 months.
* You can dry parsley by heating in the microwave on high power for 4 minutes.
* Refresh wilted chopped parsley by wrapping in a tea towel, immersing in cold water and squeezing dry.

Parsnip
See also Vegetables

	Amount Market Form	Yield Equivalent
	1 lb. without tops	4 medium
	1 lb. without tops	2 c. chopped
	1 lb. without tops	4 servings

Cooking and Preparation Hints
* To retain their nutrients, peel parsnips after, not before, boiling.
* Herbs and spices that complement parsnips include thyme, parsley, basil and tarragon.
* To freeze parsnips, peel, cut into 1/2" cubes and blanch for 2 minutes. Chill and pack.

Passion Fruit
See also Fruit

	Amount Market Form	Yield Equivalent
	5 - 6 whole	1/2 c. pulp

Cooking and Preparation Hints
* When selecting passion fruit, you should be able to hear the juice slosh around when you shake it. A passion fruit that looks slightly wrinkled is preferable to one that is full and round because the latter may not be ripe.
* The small black seeds of the passion fruit can be eaten or strained out of the pulp according to your taste.
* Passion fruit can be refrigerated for up to 10 days and can be frozen in plastic bags for several months.

Pasta

	Amount Market Form	Yield Equivalent	For Purpose of	Amount	Substitution
	1 lb. dry macaroni (1")	4 c. uncooked	All Recipes	4 c. cooked pasta	2 lb. whole spaghetti squash (1)
	1 lb. dry macaroni (1")	9 c. cooked		1 sheet lasagna	1 sheet instant lasagna (2)
	1 c. dry macaroni (1")	2 1/4 c. cooked	All Recipes/Reducing Cholesterol	1 lb. egg noodles	1 lb. cholesterol-free egg noodles
	1 lb. dry noodles (1")	6 1/2 c. uncooked	All Recipes/Non-Wheat	1 lb. pasta	1 lb. gluten-free pasta
	1 lb. dry noodles (1")	8 c. cooked			
	1 c. dry noodles (1")	1 1/4 c. cooked			
	1 lb. dry spaghetti (12")	7 c. cooked			
	2 oz. dry spaghetti (12")	1 c. cooked			

Instructions:
(1) Cut squash in half, cook until tender and remove strands from the shell with a fork. Serve with pasta sauce or in casseroles or cold salads.
(2) Instant lasagna is precooked and dehydrated and needs no boiling prior to assembly. Instant lasagna will rehydrate as it is cooked with other ingredients; or you can rehydrate it by soaking it in cold water for 15 minutes.

Cooking and Preparation Hints
* If you are making your own pasta, be sure to use finely ground semolina. You can use it alone or with all purpose flour. The semolina produces a smooth texture and has the gluten strength to prevent the noodles from losing shape and breaking easily.
* For homemade pasta, complete drying is essential before storing. Spread the noodles on trays and rotate occasionally for even drying. Store in airtight containers in the cupboard or in the freezer for several months.
* Salt added to the boiling water will shorten the cooking time for pasta somewhat but the real effect of salt is to season the pasta internally. Salt is dissolved in the water, and the water is absorbed into the pasta. For people on low sodium diets, just eliminate the salt when cooking.

INGREDIENT	YIELD			SUBSTITUTION		
	Amount Market Form	Yield Equivalent	For Purpose of	Amount	Substitution	Instructions
Pasta continued	**Cooking and Preparation Hints (continued)** * To prevent pasta from sticking together, use at least 4 qts. of water per 1 lb. of pasta so that the pasta can move freely, and stir the pasta immediately after it is added to the boiling water. Some cooks add oil to the cooking water, but that should not be necessary if you use enough water. * When your lasagna noodles won't fit into a round pan, try using a turkey pan set across 2 burners on your stove. You can easily cook 2 1-lb. boxes of noodles, and the noodles will stay straight without curling up. * To avoid starchiness, do not overcook the pasta; use enough				water so the pasta can move around freely; add dry pasta to the cooking water only after it has come to a boil. * Dry pasta will keep in the cupboard for up to 2 years. Egg-based pasta is best when used within 1 year. * When adding pasta to soups, a rule-of-thumb is 1 c. uncooked or 2 c. cooked pasta for 2 qt. soup. * To keep pasta from sticking together when making a cold pasta salad, mix it with a little of the dressing or a little oil, or spray the pasta with nonstick cooking spray before adding the other ingredients.	
	12 oz. orzo 3 oz. fresh pasta 1 lb. dry pasta	2 c. cooked 1 c. cooked 4 main course servings				
Pastry Dough See Pie Crust						
Pastry Flour See Flour						
Paté	2 - 4 oz.	1 first-course serving				
Pawpaw See Papaya						
Pea See also Vegetables	1 lb. fresh in pod 1 lb. fresh in pod 10 oz. frozen 16 oz. can 1 lb. dried, split 1 lb. dried, split	1 c. shelled 2 servings 2 c. 2 c. 2 1/4 c. uncooked 5 c. cooked				**Cooking and Preparation Hints** * If you have difficulty shelling peas, scald the pods in boiling water for 1 minute. * Boiling a few of the empty pods along with the peas will intensify the flavor. You can flavor soups with the pods as well. * Herbs and spices that complement peas include mint flakes, basil, chives and black pepper. * Peas must be blanched for 1 to 2 minutes before freezing. They will keep for up to 12 months.

P-3

A B C D E F G H I J K L M N O P Q R S T U V W X Y Z

INGREDIENT	YIELD			SUBSTITUTION			Instructions
	Amount Market Form	Yield Equivalent	For Purpose of	Amount	Substitution		
Pea Bean See also Beans, Dried	1 c. dried 1 c. dried	3 c. cooked 6 servings	All Recipes	1 c. cooked 1 c. cooked 1 c. cooked 1 c. cooked 1 c. cooked 1 c. cooked 1 c. cooked	1 c. cooked great northern beans 1 c. cooked white kidney beans 1 c. cooked navy beans 1 c. cooked cannellini beans 1 c. cooked small white beans 1 c. cooked marrow beans		
Peach See also Fruit	1 lb. fresh 1 lb. fresh 1 lb. fresh 1 lb. fresh 10 oz. frozen 16 oz. can 16 oz. can 1 lb. dried 1 lb. dried	3 - 4 medium 3 c. peeled, sliced 2 1/2 c. peeld, diced 2 c. peeled, pureed 1 c. slices 6 - 10 slices 2 c. slices 2 3/4 c. 5 1/2 c. cooked	All Recipes	1 fresh	1 fresh nectarine		

Cooking and Preparation Hints
* A peach that is picked prematurely will never ripen properly; it will just turn soft and mushy. To select a ripe peach or one that is "firm-ripe" and will ripen, press the stem end; it will be a little soft. Firm-ripe peaches will ripen at room temperature if you keep them in 1 layer and keep out of direct sunlight.
* To peel peaches, immerse them in boiling water for 10 to 30 seconds, then into cold water. Pinch the skins, then peel them off. Use immediately or brush the peaches with lemon juice to prevent them from turning brown.

* Peaches can be frozen in a dry sugar pack, in a 40% syrup pack or unsweetened. Peel, halve and pit the peaches. Leave in halves or slice. For the sugar pack, add 2/3 c. sugar per qt. of fruit and freeze. For the syrup pack, dissolve 3 c. sugar and 1/2 t. ascorbic acid in 4 c. water and refrigerate. Add 1/2 to 2/3 c. syrup for every pt. of peaches. Freeze.
* For unsweetened, add 1/2 t. ascorbic acid to 1 qt. of water, cover peaches and freeze.

Peanut See also Nuts	1 lb. in shell 1 lb. shelled	2 c. shelled 3 c.					

Cooking and Preparation Hints
* To blanch peanuts, roast them in the oven at 350° for 10 to 20 minutes. Cool and rub off the skins.

Peanut Butter	16 oz. jar	1 3/4 c.	All Recipes	1 c.	1 c. other nut butters (1)		(1) Other nut butters available include almond, cashew, macadamia and pistachio.

Cooking and Preparation Hints
* Before measuring peanut butter, spray the measuring cup or spoon with nonstick cooking spray. The peanut butter will slide out easily.

INGREDIENT	YIELD		SUBSTITUTION			
	Amount Market Form	Yield Equivalent	For Purpose of	Amount	Substitution	Instructions
Pear See also Fruit	1 lb. fresh 1 lb. fresh 1 lb. fresh 1 medium 1 lb. dried 1 lb. dried	3 - 4 medium 2 c. sliced 2 c. cooked 1/2 c. sliced 2 3/4 c. 5 1/2 c. cooked	**Cooking and Preparation Hints** * Pears should be bought when firm and allowed to ripen at home; so buy them 3 to 6 days before you plan to use them. You can hasten ripening by storing them in a paper bag along with an apple. They're ripe when the stem end yields to slight pressure. * The Anjou, Bartlett and Bosc are the best varieties for cooking. The Anjou has a spicy flavor and is ideal for pies, tarts and purees.			The Bartlett is sweet and juicy. The Bosc holds it shape well when it is poached or baked. * Pears can be frozen in a 40% syrup pack although the results are not as good as for other fruits. Dissolve 3 c. sugar and 3/4 t. ascorbic acid in 4 c. water and refrigerate. Add 1/2 to 2/3 c. syrup for each pt. of fruit. Freeze. They will keep for 6 to 8 months.
Pecan See also Nuts	1 lb. in shell 1 lb. shelled	2 c. shelled 4 1/4 c.	**Cooking and Preparation Hints** * If your recipe requires whole nutmeats or large pieces, soak the unshelled pecans in cold water for 2 hours, drain them and let them stand overnight. Crack them gently on the end to remove the nutmeats.			
Pepper See Peppercorn, Bell Pepper, Chili Pepper, Red Pepper						
Pepper Sauce See Hot Pepper Sauce						
Peppercorn See also Herbs/Spices			All Recipes	1 t. ground black 1 t. ground black	1 t. ground white (1) 1 t. dried nasturtium petals (2)	(1) White pepper is a little milder in flavor. (2) This substitution is recommended for ulcer patients.
	Cooking and Preparation Hints * Black, white and green peppercorns all come from the same berries. The differences are in the maturity of the berries when picked. Black peppercorns are harvested when green and		dried until they turn black. Green peppercorns are also picked when unripe but are immediately preserved in brine or freeze-dried. White peppercorns are picked when fully ripe; the outer skins are removed, and only the white core is used.			
Pepperoni			All Recipes	1 oz.	1 oz. salami	

INGREDIENT	YIELD		For Purpose of	SUBSTITUTION		Instructions
	Amount Market Form	Yield Equivalent		Amount	Substitution	
Perch See also Fish/Shellfish			All Recipes	1 lb. freshwater perch 1 lb. freshwater perch 1 lb. freshwater perch 1 lb. ocean perch	1 lb. brim 1 lb. bream 1 lb. crappie 1 lb. rockfish	
	Cooking and Preparation Hints * Perch is complemented by such herbs and spices as tarragon, garlic, pepper, oregano, dill weed, bay leaf and fennel seed.					
Persimmon See also Fruit	9 oz. whole fresh	3/4 c. pulp				* Persimmons can be frozen whole or pureed. For whole persimmons, dry the fruit well and remove the stem. Freeze on a tray until hard, then transfer to individual freezer bags. To thaw them, hold them under cold water.
	Cooking and Preparation Hints * Persimmons can be ripened by placing in the freezer for 2 days. * The pulp of the persimmon can be used much like applesauce and pumpkin and is especially good in pies, quick breads, cookies, cakes and puddings.					
Pfifferlinge See Mushroom						
Pheasant See also Game/Game Birds	3 lb. 1 1/2 lb.	1 average (female) 1 serving				
Pickle	1 oz. whole	2 1/2 T chopped				
	Cooking and Preparation Hints * An unopened jar of pickles will keep in a cupboard for 18 months. Store opened jars in the refrigerator.					
Pickling Spice			Pickling	6 T	2 T mustard seeds + 1 T whole allspice + 2 t. coriander seeds + 2 t. black peppercorns + 2 t. dill seeds + 2 t. cloves + 1 t. ground ginger + 1 t. red pepper flakes + 1 bay leaf crumbled + 2" cinnamon stick crushed	

Ingredient	Amount Market Form	Yield Equivalent	For Purpose of	Amount	Amount	Substitution	Instructions
Pie Crust			All Recipes		16 c. pie crust mix	12 1/2 c. flour + 2 T salt + 5 c. shortening (1)	(1) Combine the flour and salt. Cut in the shortening until the mixture has a corn-meal texture. Store in an airtight container in a cool place for 10 to 12 weeks or in the freezer for up to 12 months. The mixture will make 6 double-crust pies or 12 single-crust pies.

Cooking and Preparation Hints

* For a pie crust that has both flavor and a flaky texture, use equal amounts of solid shortening and unsalted butter. Butter and margarine contain water and, if used alone, will produce a hard, brittle crust.
* Don't overmix or overhandle the dough or it will toughen and not brown well.
* Too much liquid or too little fat will prevent the dough from browning. Too little fat will also result in a thick, doughy crust.
* Cold ingredients and chilling the dough are important for a flaky and tender crust. Chilling also reduces shrinkage and makes it easier to roll out the dough.
* For a pie that requires baking, put it into the oven immediately after filling it or the crust will absorb the wet filling and become soggy.
* For an easier-to-handle pastry dough, add vinegar or lemon juice or juices such as orange or pineapple as part of the liquid used. Their acidity will also promote tenderness.
* For best browning, use a glass pie pan.
* When you're rolling out dough between 2 sheets of waxed paper or parchment paper, the paper sometimes slips on the counter. To prevent slipping, sprinkle the counter top with a little water before putting down the paper.
* To produce a crisp bottom crust and to prevent the crimped edge from burning, bake the pie in the lower third of the oven.
* If the crimped edge begins to brown too much while the pie is baking, cover loosely with aluminum foil.
* When preparing a crumb crust, you will get better results by baking it before filling it rather than by just chilling it. Baking binds the crumbs together and produces a crust that holds together better and cuts more easily. A graham cracker crust should be baked at 375° (or 350° for a glass pie pan) for about 8 minutes; a cookie crust should be baked at the same temperature but for slightly less time.
* Cool your filling before adding to a crumb crust. Otherwise, the heat will melt the butter in the crust, the filling will absorb the crumbs and the crust will become soggy and dissolve.
* Frozen pastry dough will keep a year.

Ingredient	Amount Market Form	Yield Equivalent	For Purpose of	Amount	Amount	Substitution	Instructions
Pie Spice See Apple Pie Spice, Pumpkin Pie Spice							
Pignolo See Pine Nut							
Pike See also Fish/Shellfish			All Recipes		1 lb. 1 lb.	1 lb. pickerel 1 lb. walleye pike	

Cooking and Preparation Hints

* Herbs and spices that complement pike include tar-ragon, garlic, black pepper, red pepper, oregano, dill weed, bay leaf and fennel.
* Pike can be frozen for 4 to 9 months.

INGREDIENT	YIELD			SUBSTITUTION		
	Amount Market Form	Yield Equivalent	For Purpose of	Amount	Substitution	Instructions
Pine Nut (Pignolo, Piñon, Pinhao) See also Nuts	6 oz.	1 1/4 c.	**Cooking and Preparation Hints** * To toast, spread nuts out in a shallow pan and bake at 350° for 5 to 10 minutes until			golden. Shake pan occasionally during baking. Remove from pan and cool.
Pineapple See also Fruit	2 lb. whole fresh 20 oz. can 30 oz. can 8 oz. can chunks 8 oz. can chunks 8 oz. can crushed 8 oz. can crushed	3 c. cubed 10 cored slices 8 large cored slices 2/3 c. chunks, dm'd 1/2 c. liquid 2/3 c. crushed, dm'd 1/3 c. liquid	**Cooking and Preparation Hints** * Gelatin dishes made with fresh pineapple won't gel properly. Use canned pineapple instead. * Fresh pineapple contains an enzyme that breaks down protein. When mixing fresh pineapple with dairy products or protein foods (meat, poultry and fish), add the pineapple just before serving. * Because of the natural enzyme, fresh pineapple can be used to tenderize tougher cuts of meat. You can run a slice over the meat about 15 minutes before cooking. Or			you can add the pineapple to a marinade, but do not marinate for longer than 10 to 15 minutes. * Fresh pineapple pieces or crushed can be frozen unsweetened or in a 30% syrup pack. For the syrup, dissolve 2 c. of sugar in 4 c. water and refrigerate. Add 1/2 to 2/3 c. syrup for each pt. of fruit. * You can remove the canned taste of pineapple slices or chunks by soaking them in cold water for 30 minutes.
Pink Bean See also Beans, Dried	1 lb. dried 1 lb. dried 1 c. dried	2 1/4 c. uncooked 6 c. cooked 2 3/4 c. cooked	All Recipes	1 c. cooked 1 c. cooked 1 c. cooked	1 c. cooked pinto beans 1 c. cooked red beans 1 c. cooked kidney beans (1)	(1) Kidney beans are larger.
Pinto Bean See also Beans, Dried	1 lb. dried 1 lb. dried 1 c. dried 15 oz. can	2 1/4 c. uncooked 6 c. cooked 2 1/2 c. cooked 1 1/2 c.	All Recipes	1 c. cooked 1 c. cooked 1 c. cooked	1 c. cooked pink beans 1 c. cooked red beans 1 c. cooked kidney beans (1)	(1) Kidney beans are larger.
Pistachio See also Nuts	1 lb. in shell 1 lb. shelled 1 oz. in shell 1 c. in shell	2 c. shelled 3 2/3 c. nutmeats About 20 nuts 1/2 c. nutmeats	**Cooking and Preparation Hints** * To restore pistachios that have lost their crispness, toast them in a 200° oven for 10 to 15 minutes. * Red pistachios and natural tan pistachios are the same except that the producers have dyed the red ones to meet the demand of consumers who like the red color. For cooking purposes, use the tan nuts			because the red dye will change the color of the dish you are preparing. * To blanch pistachios, pour boiling water over them and let stand for 5 to 10 minutes. Drain, cool and remove skins. Put them in a single layer on a cookie sheet and dry them for 1 hour in the oven at 200° to 300°. Cool to room temperature.

INGREDIENT	YIELD		For Purpose of	SUBSTITUTION		Instructions
	Amount Market Form	Yield Equivalent		Amount	Substitution	
Plantain (Cooking Banana) See also Fruit	1 1/4 lb. fresh 2 medium	2 medium 2 1/2 c. cook'd slices				**Cooking and Preparation Hints** * Plantains must be cooked to be eaten. * Plantains can be pureed and added to a creamy soup for thickening. * Plantains are best when they are fully ripe, that is when they are deep black in color.
Plum See also Fruit	1 lb. fresh 1 lb. fresh 1 lb. fresh 1 lb. fresh 1 lb. can whole	15 medium 2 c. pitted, quartered 2 c. cooked 3 - 4 servings 10 - 14 plums				syrup pack. Dissolve 3 to 4 3/4 c. sugar and 1/2 t. ascorbic acid in 4 c. water and refrigerate. Add 1/2 to 2/3 c. syrup for each pt. of fruit. **Cooking and Preparation Hints** * To freeze plums you can leave them whole or cut in halves or quarters. Quick-freeze them on trays, then put into freezer bags. You can also freeze plums in a 40% to 50%
Pollock See also Fish/Shellfish			All Recipes	1 lb. 1 lb. 1 lb.	1 lb. cod 1 lb. haddock 1 lb. whiting	**Cooking and Preparation Hints** * Pollock can be frozen for 4 to 6 months.
Pomegranate See also Fruit	1 medium fresh 3 - 4 large	1/2 c. pulp & seeds 1 qt. juice				would an orange; or (2) cut in half, lay cut-side down on your palm, tap the top with a knife handle to release seeds and pulp. * Pomegranate juice will stain your hands and clothes; so wear plastic gloves and an apron when you are removing the pulp and seeds. **Cooking and Preparation Hints** * Avoid using aluminum or carbon steel knives. They will cause the pomegranate juice to turn bitter. * To remove the pulp and seeds: (1) Cut in half and, using an orange juicer, process as you
Pompano See also Fish/Shellfish			All Recipes	1 lb.	1 lb. John Dory	**Cooking and Preparation Hints** * Herbs and spices that complement pompano include tarragon, garlic, black pepper, red pepper, oregano, dill weed, bay leaf and fennel.
Popcorn	1 oz. kernels 1 oz. kernels	2 T 1 qt. popped				**Cooking and Preparation Hints** * Do not add salt to the oil before cooking because the salt will toughen the popcorn. * When popping corn on the stove, make sure the lid to the pan is loose enough to let steam escape. * Popcorn that has lost some of its moisture will not produce fluffy, crunchy kernels. To rejuvenate, put 3 c. of kernels into a qt. jar, add 1 T water and close. Shake the jar every few minutes until all the water is absorbed. Let stand for 2 to 4 days, and the kernels should be ready for popping. * Regular popcorn kernels will keep in the cupboard for 2 years. Microwave popcorn will keep for 18 months. * Popped popcorn freezes well in an airtight container.
Porcini See Mushroom						

INGREDIENT	YIELD			SUBSTITUTION			
	Amount Market Form	Yield Equivalent	For Purpose of	Amount	Substitution	Instructions	

INGREDIENT	Amount Market Form	Yield Equivalent	For Purpose of	Amount	Substitution	Instructions
Porgy See also Fish/Shellfish			All Recipes	1 lb. 1 lb. 1 lb.	1 lb. perch 1 lb. drum 1 lb. scup	
Pork See also Meat	1 lb. raw 4 oz. raw 1 lb. blade chop or steak 1 lb. boneless chop 1 lb. loin or rib chop 1 lb. ham—bone-in 1 lb. ham—boneless 1 lb. blade shoulder-boneless	2 c. ground 3 oz. cooked 2 1/2 - 3 1/2 servings 4 servings 2 1/2 servings 3 servings 4 - 5 servings 3 servings	All Recipes	1 lb. ham 1 lb. ground pork 1 lb. ground pork 1 lb. ground pork 1 lb. ground pork	1 lb. pork butt 1 lb. ground beef 1 lb. ground veal 1 lb. ground lamb 1 lb. ground turkey (1)	(1) When substituting ground turkey, use slightly more seasoning than called for in the recipe to enhance the turkey's milder flavor. Also, the different moisture content of ground turkey can affect recipes; if the ground turkey appears soft, decrease the liquid in the recipe by 1 to 2 T.

Cooking and Preparation Hints
* Boneless chops cook more quickly than bone-in chops.
* Herbs and spices that complement pork include black pepper, basil, dill weed, thyme, oregano, marjoram, sesame seed and garlic.
* The recommended storage time in the refrigerator to insure quality is 2 to 3 days for pork cuts; 1 to 2 days for ground pork; and 3 to 4 days for leftover cooked pork.
* Recommended freezer storage time to insure quality is 6 months for pork cuts; 1 to 3 months for ground pork; and 2 to 3 months for leftover cooked pork.

* Ham, bacon, sausage and other cured meats do not freeze well because their salt content tends to turn the fat in the meat rancid. The optimum time for freezer storage is less than 3 weeks.
* Pork can be cooked frozen by increasing the cooking time. For roasts, increase the time by 1/3 to 1/2.
* Because of improvements in feeding techniques, pork does not have to be cooked to well-done to be free of trichinosis. It is recommended that pork be cooked until it registers 160° on a meat thermometer at which stage it will be tender, juicy and slightly pink.

INGREDIENT	Amount Market Form	Yield Equivalent	For Purpose of	Amount	Substitution	Instructions
	1 lb. blade loin 1 lb. top loin—boneless 1 lb. center loin 1 lb. sirloin—bone-in 1 lb. back ribs 1 lb. spareribs 1 lb. tenderloin	2 servings 3 1/2 servings 3 servings 2 1/2 servings 1 1/2 servings 1 1/4 servings 4 servings				
Pork Fat			All Recipes	1 oz. 1 oz.	1 oz. salt pork (1) 1 oz. unsmoked bacon (1)	(1) Blanch and omit any salt called for in the recipe.
Port Salut Cheese See also Cheese			All Recipes	8 oz. 8 oz. 8 oz.	8 oz. Saint Paulin cheese 8 oz. Tilsit cheese 8 oz. brick cheese	

INGREDIENT	YIELD			SUBSTITUTION		
	Amount Market Form	Yield Equivalent	For Purpose of	Amount	Substitution	Instructions
Pot Cheese See also Cheese			All Recipes	8 oz. 8 oz. 8 oz. 8 oz. 8 oz.	8 oz. hoop cheese 8 oz. baker's cheese 8 oz. farmer cheese (1) 8 oz. creamed cottage cheese, drained 8 oz. dry cottage cheese	(1) Farmer cheese is drier than pot cheese.
Potato See also Sweet Potato, Vegetables	1 lb. fresh 1 lb. fresh 1 lb. fresh 1 lb. fresh 1 lb. fresh 1 1/2 lb. new potatoes	3 medium 3 c. peeled, sliced 2 1/4 c. peeld, diced 4 c. shredded 2 c. mashed 2 c. french fries	All Recipes Mashing	1 lb. 1 lb. 1 lb.	1 lb. sweet potatoes (1) 1 lb. yuca root (2) 1 1/3 c. instant mashed potatoes	(1) Select the pale variety of sweet potato. The taste is not sweet and it will have the cooked consistency of a white baking potato — dry, fluffy and mealy. (2) This root contains more starch than a potato. If you intend to fry it, parboil it first. Then fry it for 3 to 4 minutes until it is crisp but not brown.

Cooking and Preparation Hints

* "Boilers" are waxy-type potatoes that retain their shape when cooked. They are best suited to recipes that require distinct pieces of potato such as salads, soups, stews, scalloped potatoes and boiled or parslied potatoes. They take longer to cook than the mealy-textured "bakers."
* "Bakers" (also known as Idaho or Russet Burbank) have a dry and crumbly texture when cooked. They are best to use when you want them mashed, french fried and, of course, baked. They are the potato of choice for many soufflés, pancakes, gnocchi and dumplings.
* "All purpose" potatoes have characteristics of both boilers and bakers. While they can be used for any recipe, you will get better results by selecting the potato that is most appropriate for your particular cooking method.
* "New" potatoes are not a variety but are potatoes that are freshly dug and shipped directly from the field to market. To prevent the thin skins from bursting when they are boiled, cut a narrow strip of peel from around the middle of each potato before cooking.
* Potatoes lose their moisture as they age. Older potatoes are good for potato dumplings and potato pancakes. They are also good for salads because they absorb more of the salad dressing.
* You can keep peeled or grated potatoes from turning dark for an hour or more by covering them with cold water and adding 2 t. vinegar or lemon juice. Drain well before using. For grated potatoes, dry them in paper towels. Darkening affects the appearance only and has no effect on flavor.
* Adding 1 t. vinegar or lemon juice to the boiling water of potatoes will keep them white.
* Bake potatoes without wrapping in aluminum foil. Otherwise, they will be steamed by the trapped moisture instead of baked.
* A potato will bake faster in the oven if you insert a metal skewer through it lengthwise because the skewer conducts heat to the inside of the potato. You can cook up to 4 potatoes at a time on a long skewer and can remove them from the oven all at once when they're done.
* You can add flavor to boiled potatoes by adding a bouillon cube or granules to the boiling water.
* For the best results when making french fries, use a 2-step frying process. Fry first in oil at 325° until the strips are limp. Remove them and cool to room temperature. Then fry a second time at 375° until brown. The first fry cooks the inside of the potatoes without burning the outside. The strips develop a film of starch on the outside that prevents the further absorption of oil when fried the second time.
* For best results when mashing potatoes, use a hand potato masher, a ricer or medium disk of a food mill. An electric beater on low speed is OK but will not produce as smooth a result. Avoid a food processor or blender because the high speed brings out too much of the starch and turns the potatoes sticky.
* Herbs and spices that complement potatoes include dill weed, paprika, parsley, white pepper, caraway seeds and rosemary.
* Store potatoes in a cool, humid (but not wet), dark and well-ventilated area. Room temperature will suffice, but the potatoes won't keep as long. Warmer temperatures will cause them to sprout and shrivel. Avoid storing potatoes in the refrigerator. The starches are converted to sugar — which produces a sweet taste and causes the potatoes to darken when cooked. Potatoes can keep for months if stored properly.
* Instant mashed potatoes will keep in the cupboard for up to 1 year.

A B C D E F G H I J K L M N O P Q R S T U V W X Y Z

INGREDIENT	YIELD			SUBSTITUTION		Instructions
	Amount Market Form	Yield Equivalent	For Purpose of	Amount	Substitution	

Potato Chip

Cooking and Preparation Hints
* To crisp soggy potato chips, put them under a broiler and remove before they brown.
* Potato chips can be frozen — either in their unopened bags or in airtight freezer containers.

Potato Flour
(Potato Starch)
See Flour

Potato Starch
(Potato Flour)
See Flour

Potherbs
See Greens, Cooking

Poultry
See also individual listings

Cooking and Preparation Hints
* Stuffed poultry takes slightly longer to cook than unstuffed.
* If you are concerned about the stuffing absorbing too much fat from the bird as it cooks, bake the stuffing separately and stuff the bird with vegetables to add flavor to the meat.
* For a meat thermometer to register correctly, it should be inserted so that the bulb is in the center of the inside thigh muscle or in the thickest part of the breast.
* To test for doneness without a meat thermometer, move the drumstick from side to side. When it moves easily, the poultry is done.
* Poultry should stand after roasting and before carving. The length of time depends on the size, but a 20-lb. turkey would require 20 to 25 minutes. The rest period allows the juices to be absorbed back into the tissues. If the bird is carved too soon, the juices will run off and be lost. During the rest period, the flesh becomes firm and makes carving easier.
* Uncooked poultry will keep in the refrigerator for 2 to 3 days and in the freezer for 9 months (pieces) to 1 year (whole). Ground poultry will last 1 to 2 days in the refrigerator and 3 to 4 months in the freezer. Cooked leftovers will keep 3 to 4 days in the refrigerator and 4 months in the freezer.
* If poultry has accidentally thawed but remains cold to the touch, it is safe to cook and refreeze it. Stuffed poultry that has accidentally thawed should be discarded.

Powdered Sugar
(Confectioners' Sugar)
See Sugar

Prawn
See Shrimp

Prickly Pear
See Cactus Pear

INGREDIENT	YIELD		SUBSTITUTION			
	Amount Market Form	Yield Equivalent	For Purpose of	Amount	Substitution	Instructions
Prosciutto			All Recipes	6 oz. 6 oz. 6 oz.	6 oz. unsmoked ham (1) 6 oz. Westphalian ham (1) 6 oz. pancetta (1)	(1) Prosciutto has a more intense flavor.

Cooking and Preparation Hints
* Prosciutto becomes tough when cooked too long. When adding prosciutto to cooked foods such as pasta or vegetables, add it at the last minute to just heat through.

INGREDIENT	YIELD		SUBSTITUTION			
Provolone Cheese See also Cheese			All Recipes	8 oz.	8 oz. Caciocavallo cheese	

Cooking and Preparation Hints
* Provolone can be frozen for up to 6 months. Cut into 1 lb. pieces not more than 1" thick, freezer wrap and store.

INGREDIENT	YIELD		SUBSTITUTION			
Prune See also Fruit	1 lb. dried, pitted 6 oz. dried, pitted 1 c. dried, pitted 1 c. dried, pitted 1 lb. dried, pitted	2 2/3 c. 1 c. 18 - 22 whole 3/4 c. paste 4 3/4 c. cooked				consistency. The prunes may affect the color of the product and will produce a chewy texture. * To plump prunes by a quick cooking method, combine equal amounts of prunes and water, bring to a boil and cover. Simmer pitted prunes 3 to 4 minutes and prunes with pits 10 minutes. * To plump prunes without cooking, cover prunes in a bowl with an equal amount of water or fruit juice (hot or cold) and refrigerate overnight.

Cooking and Preparation Hints
* To prevent prunes from sticking while chopping, you can: (1) Use kitchen scissors dipped occasionally in warm water; (2) Use kitchen scissors wiped with vegetable oil; (3) Add 1 T vegetable oil per lb. of prunes in a food processor; or (4) For baking, toss the prunes with a little flour called for in the recipe, then chop in the food processor.
* Prune paste can substitute for fat in some baked goods. To make paste, put prunes in food processor. Add 1 T water for each oz. of prunes. Process until it reaches a paste

INGREDIENT	YIELD		SUBSTITUTION			
Pumpkin See also Squash	1 lb. fresh 5 lb. fresh 1 lb. can	1 c. cooked, mashed 4 1/2 c. cookd, mashd 2 c.	Savory Recipes	1 lb. fresh 1 lb. fresh 1 lb. fresh	1 lb. acorn squash 1 lb. butternut squash 1 lb. hubbard squash	* Commercially canned pumpkin is finer and more concentrated than that produced at home which is usually pale and watery by comparison. To produce mashed pumpkin that is more like the canned, bake the pumpkin instead of steaming it to reduce any added moisture. Then drain it, mash it and drain it again. The second draining will eliminate more of the excess liquid which will cause a watery pie. * Cooked, pureed pumpkin can be frozen for up to 16 months.

Cooking and Preparation Hints
* Small pumpkins, especially sugar pumpkins, are best suited to cooking. Other varieties good for cooking include New England, Winter Luxury, Connecticut Field and Big Cheese.
* Most traditional recipes require baking pumpkins for an hour or more. A faster method is to peel and cut the pumpkin, then cook the flesh in a steamer or in a little water in a saucepan. The vegetable is tender and cooks quickly.

ABCDEFGHIJKLMNOPQRSTUVWXYZ

| INGREDIENT | YIELD | | | SUBSTITUTION | | |
	Amount Market Form	Yield Equivalent	For Purpose of	Amount	Substitution	Instructions
Pumpkin Pie Spice			Pumpkin Pie	2 t.	1 t. ground cinnamon + 1/2 t. ground ginger + 1/4 t. ground nutmeg + 1/4 t. ground cloves	
Puree See also individual list- ings	1 lb. fruit or vegetable 1 lb. fruit or vegetable with pit or thick skin 1 lb. beans	2 c. puree 1 c. puree 2 1/2 c. puree				

Cooking and Preparation Hints
* Starchy foods (such as carrots, potatoes, peas, parsnips) produce a thicker puree than non-starchy foods (such as tomatoes).
* Most fruits and vegetables puree best when warm. Fruits can be just heated, but vegetables should be cooked until tender.
* Each instrument you use to puree will produce a slightly different texture. A potato masher will produce a coarse texture. Pressing food through a sieve will produce a light, fine texture (how fine depends on the size of the wire mesh). A food mill will produce different tex-

tures according to the plate used. A food processor can eliminate texture altogether if the food is over-processed.
* Foods that are firm textured or fibrous are best pureed with a food mill or ricer. These have the advantage of removing the fibers from the pulp and removing the skin without peeling first.
* For starchy vegetables, avoid using a food processor because the rapid blade movement will make them sticky.
* Purees can be frozen for up to 1 year.

INGREDIENT	YIELD			SUBSTITUTION			
	Amount Market Form	Yield Equivalent	For Purpose of	Amount	Substitution		Instructions
Quail	1 bird 2 - 3 birds	3 - 6 oz. 1 serving					
Quatre Épices (Four Spices)			Seasoning	5 T	3 T white peppercorns + 1 whole nutmeg, crushed + 12 cloves + 1 T ground ginger (1)		(1) Pulverize the peppercorns, nutmeg and cloves and strain through a sieve. Add the ginger and mix well.
Quick Breads			All Recipes/Non Wheat	1 c. baking mix	1 c. wheat-free baking mix		

Cooking and Preparation Hints
* To remove a loaf of quick bread from the pan without sticking, try laying the pan on its side for the initial cooling. During this time the loaf will begin to pull away from the pan on its own.

* If your muffins are already stuck to the pan, put the muffin tin on a wet towel for a few minutes. You should be able to remove the muffins easily.

Cooking and Preparation Hints
* Quince sauces complement ham, duck and chicken.

Quince See also Fruit	1 lb. fresh 1 lb. fresh	3 - 4 medium 4 servings					
Quinoa See also Grains	1 c. uncooked	4 c. cooked					

INGREDIENT	YIELD		SUBSTITUTION			
	Amount Market Form	Yield Equivalent	For Purpose of	Amount	Substitution	Instructions
Rabbit	1 medium 2 lb.	2 lb. 1 1/2 lb. cooked meat				with some liquid or it may turn out dry. * Most chicken recipes can be converted for rabbit. Because rabbit is a more finely textured meat than chicken, you should slightly lower the cooking temperature and increase the amount of cooking time. * Rabbit can be frozen for 6 to 8 months.

Cooking and Preparation Hints
* There is a big difference between hare, the dark-fleshed wild rabbit and the domestic farm-raised, white-fleshed rabbit. The wild rabbit has a very gamy flavor which requires extensive marinating. The farm-raised rabbit (which is sold in most markets) has a mild flavor and very little fat. It should be cooked

INGREDIENT	Amount Market Form	Yield Equivalent	For Purpose of	Amount	Substitution	Instructions
Radish See also Vegetables	1/2 lb.	1 2/3 c. sliced				Then cut "petals" by cutting thin slices around the radish from the root end toward the leaf end — without cutting all the way through. Put in ice water until the petals open.

Cooking and Preparation Hints
* If radishes have become wilted and soft, you can return their crispness by soaking them in ice water for 2 to 3 hours.
* To make a radish rose, cut off the root end.

INGREDIENT	Amount Market Form	Yield Equivalent	For Purpose of	Amount	Substitution	Instructions
Raisin See also Fruit	1 lb. seedless	2 1/2 c.	All Recipes	1 c. 1 c. 1 c. 1 c.	1 c. dried currants (1) 1 c. pitted, chopped dates 1 c. pitted, chopped prunes 1 c. dried cranberries	(1) Dried currants are not true currants but sun-dried tiny Black Corinth grapes.

Cooking and Preparation Hints
* Dark raisins and golden raisins are interchangeable. They come from the same grape and have the same flavor. The difference in color is due to different production methods.
* If raisins become dried out, or when a recipe calls for plumped raisins, just cover them with hot tap water and let them soak for 2 to 5 minutes. Drain and pat dry.
* There are several methods for chopping raisins without having them stick to the knife or food processor blades: (1) Coat the knife with a little oil. (2) Toss each 1 c. raisins with 1 t. oil; (3) Lightly flour the raisins with some of the flour called for in the recipe; (4) Freeze the raisins, then chop in a food processor or blender.
* To insure that raisins are evenly distributed in cakes, chop them first. Reserve 1/4 of the raisins called for in the recipe and sprinkle them on top of the batter that you've poured into the pan.

INGREDIENT	Amount Market Form	Yield Equivalent	For Purpose of	Amount	Substitution	Instructions
Ramp (Wild Leek) See also Vegetables			Flavoring	1 c. sliced 1 c. sliced 1 c. sliced	1 c. sliced scallion (1) 1 c. sliced leek (1) 1 c. chopped onion (1)	(1) Ramp has a slightly stronger flavor.
Raspberry See also Fruit	1 pt. 1 pt. 1 pt.	3/4 lb. 1 3/4 c. 3 servings				* Raspberries can be frozen unsweetened, in a dry sugar pack using 3/4 c. sugar for each 1 qt. of fruit, or in a 40% syrup pack. For the syrup, dissolve 3 c. sugar in 4 c. water and refrigerate. Add 1/2 to 2/3 c. syrup to each 1 pt. of fruit.

Cooking and Preparation Hints
* Raspberries are ripe when picked; so refrigerate them if you don't plan to serve them right away. Do not wash them until just before you use them.

INGREDIENT	YIELD				SUBSTITUTION		
	Amount Market Form	Yield Equivalent	For Purpose of	Amount	Substitution	Instructions	

INGREDIENT	Amount Market Form	Yield Equivalent	For Purpose of	Amount	Substitution	Instructions
Ray See Skate						
Red Bean See also Beans, Dried			All Recipes	1 c. cooked 1 c. cooked 1 c. cooked	1 c. cooked pink beans 1 c. cooked pinto beans 1 c. cooked kidney beans (1)	(1) Kidney beans are larger.
Red Pepper (Cayenne Pepper) See also Herbs/Spices			Seasoning	1 t. crushed (flakes) 3/4 t. ground 1 t. crushed (flakes)	1/2 - 3/4 t. ground 1 - 3 t. hot pepper sauce 1 t. hot chili paste	

Cooking and Preparation Hints
* Storing ground red pepper in the refrigerator will maintain its color and flavor longer than storing it at room temperature.
* Use about 1/8 t. ground red pepper and 1/4 t. crushed red pepper for dishes serving 4 people.

INGREDIENT	Amount Market Form	Yield Equivalent	For Purpose of	Amount	Substitution	Instructions
Red Snapper See also Fish/Shellfish			All Recipes	1 lb. 1 lb.	1 lb. redfish (1) 1 lb. haddock	(1) Redfish is firmer and somewhat fattier.

Cooking and Preparation Hints
* Red snapper tends to break apart when cooked. It's best if you can cook and serve it in the same dish.
* Herbs and spices that complement red snapper include tarragon, garlic, white pepper, black pepper, red pepper, oregano, dill weed, bay leaf and fennel seed.

INGREDIENT	Amount Market Form	Yield Equivalent	For Purpose of	Amount	Substitution	Instructions
Rhubarb See also Fruit	1 lb. fresh 1 lb. fresh 12 oz. frozen	2 c. cooked 4 servings 1 1/2 c. cooked				

Cooking and Preparation Hints
* Be sure to discard any leaves before cooking because they are poisonous.
* To freeze rhubarb, first wash, trim and cut into 1" to 2" pieces. Blanch them for 1 minute, then chill them in cold water for 1 minute. Drain. The pieces can be frozen unsweetened, in a dry sugar pack (1 c. sugar for each 1 qt. of rhubarb pieces) or in a 40% syrup pack. For the syrup, dissolve 3 c. sugar in 4 c. water and refrigerate. Add 1/2 to 2/3 c. syrup for each pt. of rhubarb. The frozen rhubarb will keep for up to 16 months.

INGREDIENT	YIELD			SUBSTITUTION		
	Amount Market Form	Yield Equivalent	For Purpose of	Amount	Substitution	Instructions
Rice See also Wild Rice, Grains	1 c. regular, raw 1 c. parboiled ("converted") 1 c. precooked 1 c. brown	3 c. cooked 4 c. cooked 2 c. cooked 4 c. cooked	All Recipes Soups	1 c. cooked 1 c. cooked 1 c. cooked	1 c. cooked quinoa (1) 1 c. cooked bulgur 1 c. cooked pearl barley	(1) Quinoa cooks like rice but in half the time.

Cooking and Preparation Hints

* White rice is either long-grain, medium-grain or short-grain. When cooked, long-grain rice is light and fluffy, and the grains remain separate. Long-grain is recommended for boiled rice, pilaf and salads. Medium-grain rice is more moist and tender than long-grain and is especially good for rice desserts. Short-grain rice, which is widely used in Oriental and Caribbean cooking, is the most tender but tends to stick together. While differences do exist among these types, they can be used interchangeably in any recipe calling for white rice.

* Parboiled white rice has been cooked before milling by a special steam-pressure process to insure that the grains remain separate when cooked. (The process also improves the nutritive value and storage quality.) Parboiled rice takes a little longer to cook than regular white rice.

* White rice will keep a year or longer if stored in a tightly closed container that keeps out dust and moisture.

* "Enriched" rice has been dusted with vitamins and minerals to replace those that were lost during the milling process. Because the vitamins and minerals are on the surface of the grains and are soluble, do not wash the rice before cooking and don't rinse it afterwards. Also, don't cook it in a large amount of water, then drain it. Enriched rice cooks a little faster than plain rice.

* In general, the more rice you cook, the less water, proportionately, you need. Older rice needs more water. Long-grain rice requires more water than short-grain.

* 1 t. of vinegar or lemon juice in the cooking water will keep white rice white.

* You can check rice for doneness by pressing a grain between your fingers. If you don't feel a hard core, it's done. If the ends of the grain are splayed out, the rice is overcooked; they should stay slightly rounded.

* If your rice is done but there is still water in the pan, you can remove the lid and cook over low heat until the excess water has evaporated. Or if a lot of water remains, you can drain off the water and

return the rice to the heat again until the last of the liquid has evaporated.

* If the water has boiled away but the rice is not completely cooked, sprinkle a little water over the rice, cover and continue cooking.

* The rule-of-thumb for adding rice to soup is 1/2 c. uncooked rice or 1 1/2 c. cooked rice per 2 qt. of soup.

* To make fried rice that is not sticky and soggy, use long-grain rice that has been cooked ahead and refrigerated until firm — preferably overnight. If you are short of time, spread freshly cooked rice on a tray and quick-freeze until it is cold, dry and firm.

* To make rice molds, first rinse the molds with cold water. Fill the molds with hot rice and pack firmly. Bake at 325° for 5 minutes. To unmold, loosen the edges, place a warm serving plate over the mold and then invert.

* Herbs and spices that complement white rice include dill weed, parsley, nutmeg, cinnamon, black pepper, chili powder, saffron, thyme, curry powder and turmeric.

* Brown rice has a limited shelf life due to the oil in the bran layer. It will keep for 2 to 6 months.

* Brown rice requires more water and a longer cooking time than white rice. Use 1 3/4 times as much liquid as rice and cook twice as long as white rice.

* Herbs and spices that complement brown rice include black pepper, parsley, thyme, sage, marjoram, oregano and mint.

* Basmati rice, which is noted for its nutty flavor, should be washed in several changes of cold water and then soaked for 30 minutes before cooking. Washing removes excess starch, and soaking softens the grains.

* In a sealed container, cooked rice will keep in the refrigerator for 1 week and in the freezer for 6 months.

Rice Flour
See Flour

A B C D E F G H I J K L M N O P Q R S T U V W X Y Z

INGREDIENT	YIELD				SUBSTITUTION			
	Amount Market Form	Yield Equivalent	For Purpose of	Amount	Substitution	Instructions	
Rice Wine See Mirin							
Ricotta Cheese See also Cheese	8 oz.	1 c.	All Recipes All Recipes/ Non-Dairy	1 c. 1 c.	1 c. dry cottage cheese 1 c. tofu		
Rock Cornish Hen See Cornish Hen							
Rockfish See Striped Bass							
Rolled Oats See Oats							
Romano Cheese See also Cheese	5 oz.	1 c. finely grated	All Recipes	1 c. grated	1 c. grated Parmesan cheese		
Roquefort Cheese See also Cheese	4 oz.	1 c. crumbled	All Recipes	8 oz. 8 oz. 8 oz.	8 oz. blue cheese 8 oz. Gorgonzola cheese 8 oz. Stilton cheese (1)	(1) Stilton has undertones of cheddar.	
Rosemary See also Herbs/Spices	1/2 oz. fresh 1 t. dried leaves	1/3 c. leaves 3/4 t. crushed					

Cooking and Preparation Hints
* In contrast to other herbs, fresh rosemary has almost the same intense flavor as the dried form. Longer cooking is suggested when you use rosemary.
* Rosemary complements such foods as beef, pork, lamb, veal, poultry, stronger-flavored fish, meat, marinades, vegetable soups, broccoli, cauliflower, potatoes, eggplant, peas, mushrooms and spinach.
* Rosemary can be frozen on its stems or chopped and will keep for 6 months to 1 year.

INGREDIENT	Amount Market Form	YIELD Yield Equivalent	For Purpose of	Amount	SUBSTITUTION Substitution	Instructions
Roux						

Cooking and Preparation Hints

* A roux (a mixture of flour and fat cooked together over very low heat) is used to thicken soups and sauces. It can be either white, blond or brown — depending on the length of time it is cooked. A white roux should be cooked at least 2 minutes to eliminate the raw taste of uncooked flour. It is usually made with butter and is used for white sauces. A blond roux is cooked longer until it becomes a pale gold color. A brown roux, which is used for brown sauces, is cooked even longer until it is lightly browned.
* To prevent lumps from forming when cooking a roux, make sure the heat is very low and use cold liquids instead of hot ones. When a scalded liquid is added to a roux, the mixture thickens immediately and may cause lumps.

INGREDIENT	Amount Market Form	Yield Equivalent	For Purpose of	Amount	Substitution	Instructions
Rum See also Spirits			Flavoring	1 T dark rum 5 T light rum	2 T rum extract (1) 1 T rum extract (1)	(1) Extract is not a good substitute if more than 1/4 c. rum is called for in the recipe.
Rutabaga See also Vegetables	1 lb. fresh 1 1/2 - 2 lb. fresh	2 1/2 c. cubed 4 servings				

Cooking and Preparation Hints

* Rutabagas are best stored at 60° but can be kept at room temperature for about 1 week. Do not refrigerate them; temperatures below 50° may cause chilling injury.
* Herbs and spices that complement rutabaga include black pepper, parsley, mace, bay leaf, allspice, cloves, caraway seeds, cinnamon and dill weed.
* To freeze a rutabaga, first wash, peel and cut into 1/2" cubes. Blanch 2 minutes, chill and pack.

INGREDIENT	Amount Market Form	Yield Equivalent	For Purpose of	Amount	Substitution	Instructions
Rye Flour See Flour						

INGREDIENT	YIELD		SUBSTITUTION			Instructions
	Amount Market Form	Yield Equivalent	For Purpose of	Amount	Substitution	
Saffron See also Herbs/Spices	1/4 t. powdered	4 - 6 crushed threads	Coloring	1/4 t. powdered 1/4 t. powdered	1/4 t. turmeric 3/4 t. dried yellow marigold petals	In liquid to bring out its full color and flavor before it is added in a recipe. For an average recipe, soak 1/4 t. powder or 4 to 6 crushed threads in 2 T water until it turns a bright golden orange color, then add the mixture to the other ingredients. * A rule-of-thumb for adding saffron to rice is 2 to 3 crushed stigmas per 1 c. raw rice. * Saffron complements such foods as poultry, seafood, rice and breads.

Cooking and Preparation Hints
* Saffron is available in 2 forms: stigmas ("threads"), which are the whole form of the spice, and powdered. The threads retain their flavor better than the powdered and should be crushed just before using. When buying whole stigmas, you can judge the quality for yourself. Powdered saffron can be easily adulterated with imitations such as safflower or turmeric. Buying the threads will insure that you get the best quality product.
* Whether whole or powdered, saffron should be partially dissolved

| **Sage** See also Herbs/Spices | 1/2 oz. fresh 1 T fresh, chopp'd | 1/2 c. leaves 1 t. dried | | | | from the stems. Pack leaves loosely into plastic freezer bags or containers. The flavor of sage becomes stronger during freezing. * Sage complements such foods as veal, sausage, poultry, mild white fish, pork, game, poultry stuffings, mushrooms, onions, summer squash, tomatoes, potatoes, beans, eggplant and cheese dishes. |

Cooking and Preparation Hints
* Fresh sage leaves can be stored in oil by layering the leaves in a jar and covering with olive oil or salad oil, and refrigerating. The leaves may discolor, but they will keep for several months. The sage-flavored oil can be used as a base for salad dressings or for sautéing.
* Fresh sage can be frozen for up to 1 year. Wash and pat dry and remove the leaves

| **Sake** See also Spirits | 16 oz. bottle | | | | * Sake removes excess saltiness and strong odors (such as fish smells) from foods. | |

Cooking and Preparation Hints
* Sake (a Japanese alcoholic beverage which is actually a beer rather than a wine) is a good meat tenderizer.

| **Salad Dressing** | 16 oz. bottle 1 oz. - 1.4 oz. dry mix | 2 c. 2 c. prepared | | | | ings from separating, whisk in 1 t. mustard, heavy cream or condensed milk for each 1/2 c. of dressing. Or, add 1 T soy lecithin granules to each 1 c. oil and shake before adding vinegar and herbs. |

Cooking and Preparation Hints
* Unopened bottled dressing will keep in the cupboard for 10 to 12 months. Once opened, it will keep in the refrigerator for 1 to 3 months.
* To prevent your homemade salad dress-

| **Salami** | 1 oz. | | All Recipes | 1 oz. | 1 oz. pepperoni | |

INGREDIENT	YIELD			Amount	SUBSTITUTION	Instructions
	Amount Market Form	Yield Equivalent	For Purpose of		Substitution	
Salmon See also Fish/Shellfish			All Recipes	1 lb.	1 lb. lake trout	

Cooking and Preparation Hints
* In general, the varieties of salmon that have the higher oil content and the deeper red color are the more expensive. Salmon varieties are: chinook or king salmon (very rich in oil, softer in texture than others, available whole and as steaks and filets); sockeye or red or blueback (deep red color, considerable oil, firm texture, mostly available canned and frozen); coho or silver or medium red (lighter in color than sockeye, oil in the medium range, mostly available frozen whole or as steaks or filets, and a good smoking fish); chum or keta (firm texture, light pink color, moderate fat content, available canned, smoked, fresh and frozen); pink salmon (light rose in color, softest in texture, very lit-

Instructions (Salmon):
* tle oil, smallest in size which makes it good for barbecuing, baking or broiling whole).
* The fat content determines how long to cook salmon. The more oil, the longer you have to cook the fish.
* When you're using canned salmon, rinse it with cold water and remove pieces of skin. You do not have to remove the bones; they are edible after the canning process.
* Herbs and spices that complement salmon include tarragon, garlic, white pepper, red pepper, black pepper, oregano, dill weed, bay leaf and fennel seed.
* Salmon can be frozen for 4 to 6 months.

INGREDIENT	YIELD			Amount	SUBSTITUTION	Instructions
Salsify (Oyster Plant, Vegetable Oyster) See also Vegetables						

Cooking and Preparation Hints
* To prevent darkening, cook salsify unpeeled.

INGREDIENT	YIELD			Amount	SUBSTITUTION	Instructions
Salt (Table Salt)	1 lb.	1 1/2 c.	Seasoning	1 t. 1 t. 4 t. seasoned salt	1 t. kosher salt (1) 1 t. sea salt 2 t. salt + 1/2 t. sage + 1/2 t. dried parsley flakes + 1/2 t. onion powder + 1/4 t. marjoram + 1/4 t. paprika	(1) Kosher salt crystals are large and absorb moisture more slowly than table salt crystals. Meats will stay juicier when seasoned with kosher salt.

Instructions (Salt):
* Salt increases the boiling point and lowers the freezing point of water. For boiled foods such as pasta and rice, using salted water can somewhat reduce cooking time. Its chief contribution, however, is that it seasons the starches internally because the pasta and rice absorb the salt water. Because of its effect on the freezing point of water, salt (in particular rock salt) is used to make homemade ice cream. The salt that is mixed with ice surrounding the canister of cream actually lowers the temperature of the ice.
* If you are doubling a recipe, do not double the amount of salt. Taste the final product and add salt if necessary. It is easier to add more than to correct oversalting.

Cooking and Preparation Hints
* Salt draws moisture out of food. It is good for extracting excess liquid from tomatoes, eggplant and cucumbers. However, it will also draw out the juices of meat; so do not add salt to roasts and steaks during the initial cooking.
* Salt promotes coagulation of eggs. If an egg cracks during boiling, add about 1 t. salt to prevent the whites from seeping out into the water. However, while promoting coagulation, salt also toughens eggs; so salt them after, not before, cooking.
* In bread recipes, salt strengthens the gluten in the flour and helps to produce a crisp crust.
* Salt decreases the sourness of acid and increases the sweetness of sugar.

INGREDIENT	YIELD		SUBSTITUTION			
	Amount Market Form	Yield Equivalent	For Purpose of	Amount	Substitution	Instructions
Salt continued	**Cooking and Preparation Hints (continued)** * To keep salt shakers from clogging during humid weather, add 1/2 t. raw rice or a small piece of blotter paper to the salt in the shaker. * If a recipe calls for "coarse" salt, either kosher or coarse sea salt can be used. * If a soup or sauce is too salty, add 1 t. vinegar and 1 t. sugar and reheat. If you oversalt a soup, cut a potato into slices and boil it in the soup to absorb the salt. When the slices are transpar-				ent, discard them. * Use only pickling salt for pickling and canning. Sea salt and iodized table salt contain iodine which can darken the pickles and affect fermentation. Table salt (iodized or not) and kosher salt have been supplemented with anticaking agents which can turn the brine cloudy. * Silver salt shakers should be emptied after each use because the salt will pit the silver, causing permanent damage.	
			Seasoning/Reducing Sodium	1 t.	1 t. Nu-Salt ® 1/2 t. powdered kelp	(2) You can make an herb mixture by combining 2 t. garlic powder, 1 t. dried basil, 1 t. dried oregano and 1 t. grated lemon rind. You can store the mixture in a shaker instead of salt; add rice to prevent caking.
			Soups and Stews	1 t. 1 t. 1 t.	1 t. herb mixture (2) 1 T tamari (3) 2 T miso (3)	(3) This will also add a savory flavor of its own.
Salt Cod (Dried Cod)					at least 2" water and soak for a minimum of 24 hours. For a quick soak method, first rinse the cod under cold running water for 15 minutes. Then put the cod in a pan, cover with water and heat to a boil. Drain and rinse and repeat the heating/rinsing process 2 or 3 more times.	
	Cooking and Preparation Hints * When purchasing salt cod, look for the thickest fish with the lightest color. * Salt cod needs to be soaked before it is used in a recipe to remove excess salt and to rehydrate the fish. Cover salt cod with						
Salt Pork	1/4 lb.	1 c. cracklings	Flavoring	1 oz.	1 oz. bacon (1)	(1) Bacon is less fat and is smoked.
	Cooking and Preparation Hints * Salt pork often needs to be blanched before using to remove excess salt. Drop it into boiling water and simmer for up to 8 minutes. Then drain, cool in cold water and pat dry.					
Sardelle See Anchovy						
Sardine See also Fish/Shellfish		**Cooking and Preparation Hints** * There is really no one fish called "sardine." While cans are labeled that way, the term applies to any tiny fish			with weak bones that can be preserved in oil. The canned fish are usually small herring or pilchards.	

INGREDIENT	YIELD		For Purpose of	SUBSTITUTION		
	Amount Market Form	Yield Equivalent		Amount	Substitution	Instructions
Sauerkraut	16 oz. can	2 c.				
	Cooking and Preparation Hints * Sauerkraut has a high salt content. To remove some of that salt, rinse the sauerkraut in a colander under cold running water and drain well.					
Savory (Summer Savory, Winter Savory) See also Herbs/Spices						veal, pork, poultry, egg dishes, beans, cucumbers, Brussels sprouts, asparagus, carrots, squash and tomatoes. * Savory can be frozen whole for up to 1 year. The tiny leaves come off easily when the herb is frozen.
	Cooking and Preparation Hints * Summer savory and winter savory are similar and can be used interchangeably, but summer savory is more aromatic. * Savory complements such foods as soups, stews, stuffings,					
Scallion (Green Onion, Spring Onion) See also Vegetables	9 fresh with tops 9 fresh with tops	1 c. sliced 1/2 c. chopped	Flavoring	1/4 c. chopped 1/4 c. chopped 1/4 c. chopped 1/4 c. chopped 1/4 c. chopped 1 T chopped	1/4 c. chopped onion 1/4 c. chopped shallots 1/4 c. chopped leeks (1) 1/4 c. chopped ramp (2) 1/4 c. chopped green (fresh) garlic 1 T snipped chives	(1) Leeks have a milder flavor. (2) Ramp has a slightly stronger flavor than scallions.
				become a little tough with a slightly stronger flavor. * To make scallion brushes, first trim both ends. Cut off some of the dark green tops and cut the root end to where the white starts to turn to green. Cut narrow slits from the darker to the lighter green. Put them into cold water (not ice water) until the ends curl — about 15 minutes.		
	Cooking and Preparation Hints * You can chop scallions easily by holding a clean bunch in one hand and snipping them with scissors. * Scallions can be frozen for up to 3 months. They don't need to be blanched; just chop them and put them into a freezer bag or container. They will not be as crisp as fresh scallions and will					
Scallop See also Fish/Shellfish	1 lb. 1 lb.	2 c. 3 servings	**Cooking and Preparation Hints** * While sea scallops are larger than bay scallops and calico scallops, they can all be used interchangeably. Be careful, however, not to overcook the smaller ones. Sauté bay or calico scallops no longer than 3 minutes and sea scallops		no longer than 5 to 7 minutes. * Herbs and spices that complement scallops include dill weed, tarragon, white pepper, chives, dry mustard and paprika.	
Scrod See Cod						

INGREDIENT	YIELD		FOR PURPOSE OF	SUBSTITUTION		INSTRUCTIONS
	Amount Market Form	Yield Equivalent	For Purpose of	Amount	Substitution	Instructions
Sea Bass See also Bass, Freshwater; Striped Bass; Fish/Shellfish			All Recipes	1 lb. 1 lb. 1 lb.	1 lb. grouper 1 lb. jewfish 1 lb. tilefish	
Cooking and Preparation Hints * Herbs and spices that complement sea bass include parsley, bay leaf, tarragon, dill weed, white pepper, black pepper, chives and basil.						
Sea Salt See Salt						
Sea Trout (Weakfish) See also Fish/Shellfish			All Recipes	1 lb. 1 lb. 1 lb. 1 lb.	1 lb. haddock 1 lb. bluefish 1 lb. small drum 1 lb. croaker	
Seafood See Fish/Shellfish						
Seasoned Salt See Salt						
Seasonings See Herbs/Spices						
Seitan (Wheat Meat)	2 c. powdered mix	20 oz. cooked "meat"				
Cooking and Preparation Hints * The flavor will vary depending on the seasonings you use in the cooking broth or added directly to the dough before cooking. * Do not undercook seitan; it will be hard and rubbery. * Once cooked, seitan can be refrigerated in its cooking broth for 1 week. To extend storage beyond that time, cook it in its broth					again for about 5 minutes. Cool it and refrigerate for up to 1 week more. * Seitan freezes well either cooked or uncooked. * Seitan is available pre-cooked, but it may contain salt as a preservative.	
Self-Rising Flour See Flour						

INGREDIENT	YIELD		For Purpose of	Amount	SUBSTITUTION	
	Amount Market Form	Yield Equivalent			Substitution	Instructions
Shad See also Fish/Shellfish			All Recipes	1 oz. shad roe	1 oz. roe of other fresh fish	
	Cooking and Preparation Hints * Herbs and spices that complement shad include basil, thyme, marjoram, garlic, black pepper, red pepper, tarragon, parsley, dill weed, bay leaf, fennel seed, oregano and rosemary.					
Shallot (Eschalot) See also Vegetables	1/4 lb. fresh 1/4 lb. fresh 1/4 lb. fresh	5 medium 1 c. coarsely chop'd 1/2 c. minced	Flavoring	1/4 c. chopped 1/4 c. chopped 1/4 c. chopped	1/4 c. chopped onion 1/4 c. chopped scallion 1/4 c. chopped leek	
	Cooking and Preparation Hints * Do not overcook shallots because they will become bitter. Cook just a few minutes until they are tender.					
Shark See also Fish/Shellfish			All Recipes	1 lb.	1 lb. swordfish	
	Cooking and Preparation Hints * If shark has a strong odor of ammonia, don't buy it or eat it. A very mild smell can be eliminated by soaking the shark in milk or acidulated water.				* A shark's skin is not edible and should be removed in advance to prevent the fish from curling during cooking.	
Shellfish See also Fish/Shellfish						
Sherry See also Spirits, Wine			Flavoring	1/4 c. 1/4 c. 1 T	1/4 c. white wine 1/4 c. Marsala 1 T sherry extract (1)	(1) Use this substitution only when the recipe calls for under 1/4 c. of sherry.
	Cooking and Preparation Hints * Dry sherry is best suited for soups and sauces. Desserts require a sweeter type, such as cream sherry.					
Shortening (Vegetable Shortening) See also Fats	1 lb.	2 1/2 c.	Baking	1 c. 1 c.	1 c. butter (1) 1 c. margarine (1)	(1) Butter and margarine are only 80-85% fat (the rest is water) compared to 100% for shortening. However, when comparing them volume for volume, the air in the shortening compensates for the water in the butter or margarine.
	Cooking and Preparation Hints * Vegetable oil or any liquid shortening is not a good substitute for solid vegetable shortening. Particularly in baking, a liquid shortening will produce a gummy batter. * Use a plastic sandwich bag as a mitten to grease pans and keep it in your can of vegetable shortening for repeated uses.					

INGREDIENT	YIELD		SUBSTITUTION			
	Amount Market Form	Yield Equivalent	For Purpose of	Amount	Substitution	Instructions
Shortening continued			Baking/Reducing Fat	1 c.	16 t. (2 envelopes) Butter Buds ® Mix + 1 c. liquid (2)	(2) Butter Buds ® Mix, liquified, can be used to replace 1/4 to 1/2 of the shortening in cakes; 1/2 of the shortening in pie crusts and muffins; and up to 100% of the shortening in quick breads. For cookies, the dry mix alone can replace 1/4 to 1/2 of the shortening in the recipe. (3) Butter Buds ® Sprinkles can replace 1/4 to 1/2 of the shortening in cakes (decrease the amount of flour slightly); 1/2 to 2/3 of the shortening in brownies (add a little water to the batter); 1/4 to 1/2 of the shortening in cookies (reduce the flour by 25%); 1/2 of the shortening in muffins (increase the liquid by the same amount of shortening that is removed); and up to 3/4 of the shortening in quick breads.
			Greasing Pans	1 c. 1 T 1 T 1 T	1/4 c. Butter Buds ® Sprinkles (3) 1 T butter 1 T margarine 1 second nonstick cooking spray	
			Greasing/Flouring Cake Pans	1 T	Cake pan coating spray as needed	
Shoyu See Soy Sauce						
Shrimp See also Fish/Shellfish	1 lb. colossal, raw in shell	10 - 15				**Cooking and Preparation Hints**
	1 lb. jumbo, raw in shell	21 - 25				* A prawn is actually a different species than a shrimp, but the only real difference is the construction of the shell. However, in popular usage, prawn refers to a large shrimp.
	1 lb. X-large, raw in shell	26 - 30				* Whether to peel a shrimp before or after boiling is a matter of personal preference. Peeling shrimp first is easier. But cooking it in the shell produces a stronger shrimp flavor and prevents curling.
	1 lb. large, raw in shell	31 - 35				* It takes from 3 to 5 minutes to boil or steam 1 lb. of medium-size shrimp in the shell.
	1 lb. medium, raw in shell	43 - 50				* To get rid of the "canned" taste of canned shrimp, soak them for about 15 minutes in a mixture of sherry and vinegar.
	1 lb. small, raw in shell	51 - 60				* Herbs and spices that complement shrimp include bay leaf, thyme, garlic, oregano, fennel seed, black pepper and parsley.
	1 lb. tiny, raw in shell	More than 70				* Raw shrimp can be frozen for 4 to 6 months. Cooked shrimp toughens quickly during freezer storage and should be used as soon as possible; however, it will keep for up to 3 months.
	1 lb. raw in shell	2 - 3 servings				
	1 lb. raw, peeled	2 - 3 servings				
	1 lb. cooked, peeled	3 - 4 servings				
	2 - 2 1/2 lb. raw in shell	1 lb. cooked, peeled				
	6 1/2 oz. can	1 c.				

INGREDIENT	YIELD Amount Market Form	YIELD Equivalent	For Purpose of	Amount	SUBSTITUTION Substitution	Instructions
Silver Hake See Whiting						
Skate (Ray) See also Fish/Shellfish						
Cooking and Preparation Hints * Skate should be soaked in acidulated water to eliminate its natural ammonia odor.						
Snap Bean See Green Bean						
Snow Pea (Chinese Snow Pea, Sugar Pea) See also Vegetables	4 oz. fresh 6 oz. frozen	1 1/2 c. trimmed 1 1/2 c.				
Cooking and Preparation Hints * The tips of both ends of the snow pea should be pinched off before cooking.						
Sodium Bicarbonate See Baking Soda						
Sole See also Flounder, Fish/Shellfish			All Recipes	1 lb. 1 lb. 1 lb.	1 lb. flounder 1 lb. sandab 1 lb. halibut filet * Herbs and spices that complement sole include parsley, peppercorns, bay leaf, tarragon, dill weed, chives and basil.	
Cooking and Preparation Hints * There is no true sole in U.S. waters. What is generally sold as sole is a member of the flounder family. Sole imported from England, Belgium, Denmark or the Netherlands has a different texture than American "sole."						
Sorrel	1/2 oz. fresh	2/3 c.				
Cooking and Preparation Hints * Sorrel can be stored in the refrigerator for up to 2 days. Store it unwashed, wrapped in a dry cloth or paper towels and		placed inside a plastic bag. * Sorrel reacts with iron and should be cut and cooked in stainless steel.				

INGREDIENT	YIELD			SUBSTITUTION		
	Amount Market Form	Yield Equivalent	For Purpose of	Amount	Substitution	Instructions

Soufflé
See also Egg

Cooking and Preparation Hints
* Use eggs that are at least 3 days old. They will produce a fluffier and more stable foam than fresh eggs.
* After buttering the soufflé dish, put it into the refrigerator or freezer. This will help the soufflé to rise straight up.
* To achieve the best volume, let the roux-egg yolk mixture cool to room temperature before adding the beaten whites.
* A soufflé can be prepared, up to a point, in advance. Once you've made the roux-egg yolk base, you can refrigerate it for 2 days. When you're ready to make the soufflé, rewarm the base, beat the egg whites, fold the whites into the base and bake.
* Be sure to preheat the oven before baking a soufflé. Position the oven rack in the lower third of the oven.

Instructions:
* If your soufflé recipe calls for a collar, use baking parchment. Cut the collar so that it extends 3" above the rim of the soufflé dish, and tie it onto the dish with kitchen string. Then butter the inside of the collar and dish and refrigerate. Pour the soufflé batter to the rim of the dish. With a collar you can produce a higher soufflé.
* If you are baking a soufflé without a collar, pour the batter to within 1" of the rim of the soufflé dish. Run your finger around the inside edge of the dish making a groove in the batter. This will cause the soufflé to rise in a top hat shape.
* While it's best to serve a soufflé directly from the oven, it will keep for about 5 minutes standing in the oven with the heat turned off and the door ajar.

Soup
See also Broth

Amount Market Form	Substitution
3/4 t. soup base	1 c. prepared liquid
1 T soup base	1 qt. prepared liquid

Cooking and Preparation Hints
* If your soup is too salty, add a raw, peeled and quartered potato to and cook for about 15 minutes. Then discard the potato. The potato will absorb some of the excess salt. If your soup contains other vegetables that might become overcooked with the extra simmering, remove them while the potato is cooking.
* A quick method for rescuing salty soup is to add 1 t. vinegar and 1 t. sugar and reheat.
* A variety of ingredients can be used for thickening soups—depending on the kind of soup you are preparing: (1) flour; (2) quick-cooking tapioca; (3) egg yolks; (4) pureed vegetables; (5) grated raw potato or instant mashed potatoes; (6) okra; (7) oatmeal; (8) cornmeal; (9) cooked and pureed rice; (10) bread; (11) miso; (12) kasha.
* When adding noodles to soup, allow 1 c. uncooked noodles or 2 c. cooked noodles for 2 qt. soup.
* When adding rice to soup, allow 1/2 c. uncooked rice or 1 1/2 c. cooked rice for 2 qt. soup.
* When adding barley to soup, allow 1 1/2 c. cooked barley for 2 qt. soup.
* A rule-of-thumb for adding wine to soup is 1/4 to 1/2 c. wine for each 1 qt. of soup. Be careful not to oversalt the soup because the wine will accentuate the saltiness.
* Curdling is an inherent problem when you make a cream soup

where milk or cream is added to an acid food such as tomatoes. One way to overcome the problem is to first make a white sauce from the milk or cream, then slowly add the tomatoes over moderate heat. Another preventive measure is to substitute evaporated milk for the whole milk or cream. Also, avoid excess salt, too high a heat and overcooking.
* To remove fat from soup, try any of the following methods: (1) Drop ice cubes into the soup and remove immediately. The grease will stick to the cubes. (2) Wrap paper towels around the ice cubes and skim the surface. (3) Refrigerate the soup until the fat solidifies on the surface. It is then easily removed.
* Dry soup mixes will keep in the cupboard for 6 to 9 months.
* Cooked soups will keep for 3 to 4 days in the refrigerator and for 2 to 3 months in the freezer. Cream soups may separate after freezing but will usually become smooth if you stir them as you reheat them.
* To economize on freezer space when freezing soup, eliminate half of the liquid in the recipe. Add the liquid when you reheat the soup.
* Vegetables should be undercooked in soups that are to be frozen because they will continue to cook during the reheating process.

INGREDIENT	YIELD			SUBSTITUTION		
	Amount Market Form	Yield Equivalent	For Purpose of	Amount	Substitution	Instructions
Sour Cream	8 oz. carton 1 c.	1 c. 1 3/4 - 2 1/2 c. whipped	Baking	1 c. 1 c. 1 c. 1 c.	1 c. yogurt + 1 t. baking soda 3/4 c. sour milk + 1/3 c. butter 3/4 c. buttermilk + 1/3 c. butter 3/4 c. yogurt + 1/3 c. butter	

Cooking and Preparation Hints

* While sour cream can be whipped, it will form soft peaks — not stiff like whipping cream. Start with very cold sour cream and whip it for about 5 minutes. It will seem to thin out at first but will thicken. If it takes longer than 5 minutes, chill the sour cream and whip it again. It can be whipped several times without curdling.

* In cooking, sour cream should not be boiled but should be heated over low heat and stirred gently. Overstirring may cause the cream to thin and curdle.
* Sour cream does not freeze well. It tends to separate and lose its smooth texture.

			For Purpose of	Amount	Substitution	Instructions
			Cooked Sauces	1 c. 1 c.	1 c. yogurt + 1 T flour + 2 T water (1) 1 c. evaporated milk + 1 T vinegar or lemon juice (2)	(1) Yogurt is thinner than sour cream. In cooking, yogurt tends to thin even more. The addition of flour or cornstarch or arrowroot dissolved in cold water will thicken and stabilize the sauce. Do not heat yogurt for too long or at very high heat. Also, do not beat it too vigorously or the texture will break down. (2) Let the mixture stand for 5 minutes or so until it thickens. (3) Yogurt is more tart and thinner than sour cream. If the yogurt is too thin, it can be thickened by letting it drain in a fine sieve set over a bowl in the refrigerator for 20-30 minutes. (4) Puree in food processor or blender.
			Dips/Dressings	1 c. 1 c.	1 c. yogurt (3) 1 c. cottage cheese + 1/4 c. yogurt or buttermilk (4)	
				1 c.	6 oz. cream cheese + 3 T milk (4)	
			Dips/Reducing Fat and Calories	1 c. 1 c. 1 c. 1 c.	1 c. low- or no-fat sour cream substitute 1 c. low calorie imitation sour cream 1 c. nonfat yogurt 1 c. mashed potatoes (5)	(5) To produce 1 c. mashed potatoes of the consistency of sour cream, cook a 12 oz. potato and mash with 8 T of liquid such as chicken broth.
			Dessert Toppings	1 c.	1 c. cottage cheese + 1/4 t. vanilla + sweetener to taste (4)	

Soy Flour
See Flour

INGREDIENT	YIELD			SUBSTITUTION			
	Amount Market Form	Yield Equivalent	For Purpose of	Amount	Substitution		Instructions

INGREDIENT	Amount Market Form	Yield Equivalent	For Purpose of	Amount	Substitution	Instructions
Soy Milk See Milk						
Soy Sauce			All Recipes	1/4 c. 1/4 c.	1/4 c. shoyu (1) 3 T Worcestershire sauce + 1 T water	(1) Shoyu is Japanese soy sauce and is comparable to light Chinese soy. It uses a higher proportion of wheat and is slightly different in taste.
			All Recipes/Non-Wheat	1/4 c.	1/4 c. tamari	
			All Recipes/ Reducing Sodium	1/4 c.	1/4 c. low sodium soy sauce	

Cooking and Preparation Hints
* Soy sauce will keep 3 years unopened in the cupboard. It is best to refrigerate soy sauce after opening, but it can keep up to 9 months unrefrigerated.

INGREDIENT	Amount Market Form	Yield Equivalent	For Purpose of	Amount	Substitution	Instructions
Soybean See also Beans, Dried	1 lb. dried 1 c. dried	2 c. 3 c. cooked			* To freeze fresh soybeans, first blanch them in their pods for 5 minutes. Chill them in ice water. Shell and pack.	

Cooking and Preparation Hints
* Don't salt the beans before they're done because they will get tough.

INGREDIENT	Amount Market Form	Yield Equivalent	For Purpose of	Amount	Substitution	Instructions
Soybean Curd See Tofu						
Spaghetti See Pasta						
Spaghetti Squash (Vegetable Spaghetti) See Squash						
Speculaas Spices			All Recipes	2 t.	1/2 t. cinnamon + 1/2 t. ground ginger or nutmeg + 1/2 t. coriander + 1/4 t. ground cloves + 1/4 t. cardamom or white pepper	

INGREDIENT	YIELD		For Purpose of	SUBSTITUTION		
	Amount Market Form	Yield Equivalent		Amount	Substitution	Instructions
Spices See Herbs/Spices						
Spinach See also Greens, Cooking; Vegetables	1 lb. fresh 1 lb. fresh 1 lb. fresh 15 oz. can 10 oz. frozen	10 - 12 c. 1 1/2 - 2 c. cooked 1/2 c. cooked/squeezed 2 c. 1 1/2 c.	Cooked Recipes	1 lb. fresh	1 lb. fresh Swiss chard (1)	(1) The flavor of Swiss chard is similar to that of spinach, but it should be cooked longer. The stems should be cooked separately or started earlier so that the leaves are not overcooked.

Cooking and Preparation Hints
* Wash spinach in tepid water, rather than cold water, to remove dirt and grit more easily.
* Chop spinach with a knife rather than in a food processor which may turn the spinach into puree. Use a stainless steel knife; plain steel will leave a metallic taste.
* Herbs and spices that complement spinach include nutmeg, mace, basil, marjoram, oregano, mint and grated lemon peel.
* Spinach can be frozen for up to 12 months. Blanch 1 1/2 to 2 minutes, then chill and pack.

INGREDIENT	YIELD		For Purpose of	SUBSTITUTION		
Spirits See also Wine, Individual listings			All Recipes Desserts Flavoring	1/4 c. liqueur 1/4 c. eaux-de-vie 1/4 c. liqueur 1/4 c.	1/4 c. fruit-flavored brandy (1) 1/4 c. liqueur or flavored brandy (2) 1/4 c. fruit juice or nectar 1/4 t. extract	(1) They both consist of an alcohol base that has been flavored and sweetened. They both are fairly low in alcohol content. They can be used interchangeably as long as the basic flavors agree. (2) Eaux-de-vie are pure fruit brandies that have not been colored or sweetened (such as kirsch or framboise). They are dry, clear and have a high alcohol content. Because liqueurs are sweet, they are not good substitutes for savory dishes but may do well in sweet dishes.

Cooking and Preparation Hints
* In general, when a recipe calls for only 1 to 2 T of a spirit, it can be left out entirely.
* The amount of alcohol that is left after cooking varies dramatically (from 4% to 85%) and depends on cooking temperature, length of cooking time, cooking method and the type of cooking equipment used. Long cooking times and large surface areas of pans lead to greater losses.

* When your recipe calls for igniting a spirit for flambéing, first warm it in a saucepan or ladle over low heat. To ignite it, touch a lighted match to the fumes just above the surface. For the sake of safety, use a long matchstick; and do not use high flames on the stove or chafing dish which can ignite the fumes before you are prepared.

INGREDIENT	YIELD		For Purpose of	SUBSTITUTION		
Spring Onion See Scallion						
Sprouts	16 oz. can bean sprouts	2 c. drained				taste slightly like pea pods. Adzuki bean sprouts have a flavor reminiscent of peanuts. Fenugreek sprouts taste spicy.

Cooking and Preparation Hints
* Fresh sprouts will keep in the refrigerator for up to 4 days.
* Sprouts have differing flavors. Mung bean sprouts

INGREDIENT	YIELD		SUBSTITUTION			
	Amount Market Form	Yield Equivalent	For Purpose of	Amount	Substitution	Instructions
Squab See also Poultry	1 bird 1 bird	3/4 - 1 lb. 1 serving	**Cooking and Preparation Hints** * Squab is a young pigeon. It can be frozen for 8 to 12 months.			
Squash See also Pumpkin, Zucchini, Vegetables	1 lb. winter squash 1 lb. winter squash 12 oz. frozen winter squash 2 lb. spaghetti squash 1 lb. summer squash 1 lb. summer squash 1 lb. summer squash 10 oz. frozen summer squash	1 c. cooked, mashed 2 - 3 servings 1 1/2 c. 4 c. "spaghetti" 3 medium 2 1/2 c. sliced 3 - 4 servings 1 1/2 c.	**Cooking and Preparation Hints** * "Winter" squash refers to the hard-shelled varieties such as acorn, buttercup, butternut, hubbard, pumpkin, spaghetti and turban. They should be stored in a cool, dry place and will keep for 3 months or more. Butternut and acorn varieties keep the longest. Do not refrigerate them because they will lose their sweetness and texture. The winter varieties can be used interchangeably. * To make cutting a hard-shelled squash easier, try (1) heating the squash in a microwave on high for 2 minutes and then letting it rest for 2 minutes or (2) scoring the squash where you want it cut, then inserting a knife 1/4" into the squash and tapping the knife handle lightly with a hammer or meat mallet. * "Summer" squash refers to the tender-skinned varieties such as crookneck, patty-pan (or scallop), straightneck and zucchini. Their skins and soft seeds are edible. * Summer squash has a high water content. Don't salt squash before cooking or too much of the water will be lost. On the other hand, if you plan to cook the squash in the		microwave, cover it with wax paper. Wax paper keeps in some of the water but not so much of it that the vegetable gets soggy. * Once spaghetti squash is cooked, use 2 forks to scrape and pull out the flesh in spaghetti-like strands. * Herbs and spices that complement winter squash include cinnamon, nutmeg, pumpkin pie spice, thyme, marjoram, allspice, basil, cloves, ginger, mint, mustard seed and rosemary. * Herbs and spices that complement summer squash include basil, oregano, parsley, dill weed, paprika, chives and black pepper. * To freeze winter squash, first cook until tender — about 20 to 25 minutes. Then mash or puree, cool and pack. It will keep for up to 12 months. * To freeze summer squash, cut into slices 1/2" thick. Blanch the slices for 3 minutes, then chill and pack. They will keep for 8 to 12 months.
Squid See also Fish/Shellfish	12 oz. whole 6 oz. cleaned	1 serving 1 serving	All Recipes	8 oz. 8 oz.	8 oz. conch (1) 8 oz. abalone (1)	(1) The taste and texture are similar.

Cooking and Preparation Hints
* Squid need not be rubbery. To insure tenderness when sautéing or frying, cook the squid less than a minute over high heat. To insure tenderness when stewing, cook the squid slowly over low heat for at least 30 minutes.

INGREDIENT	YIELD				SUBSTITUTION		
	Amount Market Form	Yield Equivalent	For Purpose of	Amount	Substitution		Instructions

Stilton Cheese
See also Cheese

Cooking and Preparation Hints
* Stilton has a somewhat crumbly texture. To keep it from crumbling while cutting, try using a heavy thread, dental floss or wire.

Instructions: * Refrigerating Stilton will cause it to dry out. To store a leftover piece, wrap it in a cloth that has been moistened with salt water and place it in a cool area.

Stock
See also Broth

For Purpose of: All Recipes

Amount	Substitution
1 c. beef stock	2 t. beef stock base + 1 c. water
1 3/4 c. beef stock	14 1/2 oz. can beef bouillon (1)
1 3/4 c. beef stock	14 1/2 oz. can beef consommé (1)
2 t. beef stock base	1 beef bouillon cube
1 t. beef stock base	1 t. beef extract
1 c. chicken stock	1 T chicken stock base + 1 c. water

Instructions: (1) For double strength canned bouillon or consommé, you can dilute them with equal parts water or less to suit your taste.

Cooking and Preparation Hints
* For meat stocks, cut the meat in small pieces to expose as much surface as possible. This will extract the most flavor. When adding bones, have the butcher crack large pieces, such as knuckles. These bones will add flavor and gelatinize the stock.
* A rule-of-thumb for meat stocks is to use about 1 lb. of bones for each qt. of water. For a richer stock, add meat and about 1 c. cut-up vegetables.
* To reduce the strength of a strong-tasting stock, just add water. To increase the strength, remove the solid food and reduce the liquid to the desired strength. Or you can add a bouillon substitute to taste.
* For vegetable stock, cut the vegetables in large pieces so they won't disintegrate during cooking and cloud the liquid.

* For vegetable stock, begin with cold water. Hot water can seal the flavors in instead of releasing them.
* Water is the liquid usually used for stocks. However, to add flavor and nutrients you can also use vegetable juice, leftover liquid from cooked vegetables or the liquid from canned vegetables.
* For convenience, pour strained stock into ice cube trays and freeze. Store the frozen cubes in plastic freezer bags for future use. Allow about 4 cubes for 1 c. stock.
* Consommé is clarified stock and is made by heating the stock with egg whites and egg shells. The whites and shells will collect the impurities and rise to the top. Simply strain the stock, and you'll have a clear consommé.

For Purpose of: All Recipes

Amount	Substitution
1 3/4 c. chicken stock	14 1/2 oz. can chicken broth (1)
1 1/2 t. chicken stock base	1 chicken bouillon cube
1 c. fish stock	1 c. clam juice (2)
1 c. fish stock	1 c. diluted chicken stock
1 c. fish stock	1 fish stock cube + 1 c. water
1 c. vegetable stock	1 vegetable stock cube + 1 c. water

Instructions: (1) (2) Clam juice has an intense salty taste; so do not add salt until you have tasted the dish.

INGREDIENT	YIELD		SUBSTITUTION			
	Amount Market Form	Yield Equivalent	For Purpose of	Amount	Substitution	Instructions
Strawberry See also Fruit	1 pt. fresh	12 large - 36 small				**Cooking and Preparation Hints** * Strawberries should be refrigerated, unwashed, in a single layer or shallow container until ready to use. To extend their storage life, put a wet paper towel on top of the strawberries before closing the container. They will keep this way for up to 2 weeks. * Strawberries can be frozen for up to 6 months. For whole strawberries, quick-freeze on trays for about 2 hours, then pack in plastic freezer bags. Whole or sliced berries can be frozen in natural fruit juice. In a dry sugar pack with 3/4 c. sugar for each 1 qt. of fruit or in a 50% syrup pack. For the syrup, dissolve 4 3/4 c. sugar in 4 c. water and refrigerate. Add 1/2 to 2/3 c. syrup per 1 pt. of fruit and freeze.
	1 pt. fresh	3 1/4 c. whole				
	1 pt. fresh	2 1/4 c. slices				
	1 pt. fresh	1 2/3 c. pureed				
	4 oz. fresh	1 c. whole				
	1 c. whole	1/2 c. puree				
	20 oz. frozen whole	4 c. whole				
	20 oz. frozen whole	2 1/2 c. sliced				
	20 oz. frozen whole	2 1/4 c. pureed				
	10 oz. frozen sliced	1 1/4 c. with syrup				
String Bean See Green Bean						
Striped Bass (Rockfish) See also Sea Bass; Bass, Freshwater; Fish/Shellfish			All Recipes	1 lb.	1 lb. sea bass	**Cooking and Preparation Hints** * Herbs and spices that complement striped bass include tarragon, garlic, white pepper, black pepper, red pepper, oregano, dill weed, bay leaf and fennel seed. * Striped bass can be frozen for 7 to 9 months.
				1 lb.	1 lb. grouper	
Stuffing Mix	8 oz. bag	4 c.	All Recipes	1 c.	1 c. croutons	
	1 c. dry mix	1 1/3 c. cooked		1 c.	1 c. toasted bread cubes	
Suckling Pig See also Pork	1 1/4 lb.	1 serving				
Sugar	1 lb. granulated	2 c.	Baking	1 c. granulated	1 c. superfine (caster) (1)	(1) Brown sugar is a fine substitute for any recipe that won't be harmed by a slight molasses flavor. (2) To compensate for honey's liquid state, reduce the amount of liquid in the recipe by 1/4 c. for every 1 c. of honey used. You can neutralize the acidity of honey by adding 1/4 t. baking soda per 1 c. honey — although this is not necessary if sour cream or sour milk is called for. Honey caramelizes at a lower temperature than sugar; so to prevent burning, lower the oven temperature by 25°. Honey will give baked products a browner color and a honey flavor and will produce a soft and moist product that will stay fresh longer.
	1 lb. confectioners'	3 3/4 c. unsifted		1 c. granulated	1 c. light brown sugar (1)	
	1 lb. confectioners'	4 1/2 c. sifted		1 c. granulated	1/2 c. honey + 1/2 c. granulated sugar (2)	
	1 lb. brown	2 1/3 c. firmly packed		1 c. granulated	3/4 c. honey (2)	
				2 c. granulated	1 1/4 c. molasses + 1 c. granulated sugar (3)	
				2 c. granulated	3/4 c. maple syrup + 1 c. granulated sugar (4)	

INGREDIENT	YIELD			SUBSTITUTION		
	Amount Market Form	Yield Equivalent	For Purpose of	Amount	Substitution	Instructions

Sugar
continued

Cooking and Preparation Hints

* For convenience in dusting baked goods with confectioners' sugar, fill an empty and clean shaker-top spice jar with the sugar.
* Brown sugar is moist because of the film of molasses that coats each grain. When brown sugar loses its moisture, it becomes hard and lumpy. You can prevent moisture loss by storing brown sugar in an airtight container in the refrigerator or in the freezer. You can also add a piece of slightly stale bread to the container. When the bread turns hard, replace it with another piece.
* Once brown sugar has hardened, you can soften it in several ways: (1) Put some aluminum foil or plastic wrap on top of the sugar in an airtight container. Add either a dampened paper towel or a wedge of apple and close the container. The sugar will soften in 1 to 2 days when it has absorbed the moisture of the towel or apple. (2) For quick softening, heat the sugar in a slow oven (250° to 300°) until soft. Measure the sugar immediately because it will harden again when it cools. (3) Put a wedge of apple into a bag or box of brown sugar and microwave it on high power for 20 seconds per 1 c. of sugar. (4) Put the sugar in a food processor or blender and whirl until it has no more lumps.
* The amount of sugar should be reduced when baking at high altitudes. At 3,000 ft. reduce the sugar by 1 T for every 1 c. called for in the recipe. At 5,000 ft. reduce the sugar by 2 T for each 1 c. At 7,000 ft. reduce sugar by 3 T for each 1 c. in the recipe.

For Purpose of	Amount	Substitution	Instructions
Baking	1 c. granulated	1 c. corn syrup + 1/2 c. granulated sugar (5)	(3) For each 1 c. of molasses used, reduce the amount of liquid in the recipe by 1/4 c. and add 1/2 t. baking soda. There will be a molasses flavor in the final product.
	1 c. superfine (caster)	1 c. granulated sugar (6)	(4) Reduce the amount of liquid in the recipe by 1/4 c. for every 1 c. maple syrup used. The final product will have a maple flavor.
	1 c. light brown	1/2 c. dark brown sugar + 1/2 c. granulated sugar	
	1 c. light brown	1 c. demerara sugar (7)	(5) Reduce the amount of liquid called for in the recipe by 1/4 c. for every 1 c. corn syrup used.
			(6) Put the regular granulated sugar in a blender and process until fine. Superfine sugar is popular in baking because the small grains dissolve quickly in batters and meringues.
			(7) Demerara has larger crystals that are less moist than brown sugar crystals.
Stove-Top or Uncooked Recipes	1 t. granulated	1 t. superfine sugar	(8) Confectioners' sugar contains cornstarch to prevent caking. Because of this there will be some cloudiness when added to beverages.
	1 t. granulated	1 3/4 t. confectioners' sugar (8)	(9) Date sugar is not really a sugar. It's made from dried dates and ground to the consistency of coarse sugar. It does not dissolve completely and is not a good sweetener for beverages.
	1 t. granulated	1 t. light brown sugar (1)	(10) Depending on the recipe, you may need to reduce the amount of liquid called for.
	1 t. granulated	1 t. maple sugar	
	1 t. granulated	2 t. date sugar (9)	
	1 t. granulated	3/4 t. honey (10)	(11) Turbinado (raw) sugar retains some of the light golden color and flavor from the molasses in the sugar cane.
	1 t. granulated	1 1/4 t. molasses (10)	(12) If the very fine grains are important to the recipe, whirl the granulated sugar in a blender until fine.
	1 t. granulated	3/4 t. maple syrup (10)	(13) Dark brown sugar will impart a stronger molasses taste.
	1 t. granulated	2 t. corn syrup (10)	
	1 t. granulated	1 t. turbinado Sugar in the Raw ® (11)	
	1 t. superfine	1 t. granulated sugar (12)	
	1 t. light brown	1/2 t. liquid brown sugar	
	1 t. light brown	1/2 t. dark brown sugar + 1/2 t. granulated sugar	
	1 t. light brown	1 t. dark brown sugar (13)	
	1 t. light brown	1 t. demerara sugar (7)	

INGREDIENT	YIELD		SUBSTITUTION		
	Amount Market Form	Yield Equivalent	For Purpose of	Amount	Substitution	Instructions

INGREDIENT	Amount Market Form	Yield Equivalent	For Purpose of	Amount	Substitution	Instructions
Sugar continued			Stove-Top or Uncooked Recipes Jam, Jelly, Marmalade, Preserves	1 t. maple sugar	2 t. maple syrup (10)	(14) For making jelly, this substitution is good when no pectin is used. When pectin is added, you can substitute honey for sugar on a one-to-one basis up to 2 c.
				1 c. granulated	1/2 c. granulated sugar + 1/2 c. honey (14)	(15) Invert sugar (a liquid sugar made by heating a mixture of sugar syrup and an acid such as cream of tartar) slows the development of sugar crystals. Corn syrup and honey do the same thing.
			Candy	1 T invert sugar(fondant)	1 T corn syrup (15)	
				1 T invert sugar(fondant)	1 T honey (15)	
			Sweetening/Reducing Calories	2 t. granulated	1/3 t. (1 packet) Sweet'N Low ®	
			Cakes/Reducing Calories	1 c. granulated	2 t. (6 packets) Sweet'N Low ® + 1/2 c. sugar (16)	(16) As a general rule, retain 1/2 c. sugar in cake recipes and substitute an equivalent amount of Sweet'N Low ® for the remaining sugar — that is 1 t. (3 packets) per 1/4 c. sugar. When removing 1/2 c. sugar or less, you can compensate for the lost bulk and moisture by (1) adding 1 egg or 2 egg whites or (2) increasing liquid by 1/4 c. When removing more than 1/2 c. sugar, you can (1) decrease dry ingredients by 25% and add 1 egg or 2 egg whites or (2) increase liquid by 1/4 c. Use slightly smaller pans than called for and reduce baking time — 10 minutes for layer cakes and 20 minutes for loaf or bundt cakes. The finished cakes will not rise as high as with the original recipe.
				1 c. brown	2 t. Sweet'N Low ® Brown Sugar + 1/2 c. brown sugar (16)	
			Cookies/Reducing Calories	1 c. granulated	2 t. (6 packets) Sweet'N Low ® + 1/2 c. sugar (17)	(17) As a general rule, retain 1/2 c. sugar in cookie recipes and substitute an equivalent amount of Sweet'N Low ® for the remaining sugar — that is 1 t. (3 packets) per 1/4 c. sugar. To compensate for the loss of moisture and bulk, you should (1) reduce dry ingredients by 25% and, if the batter is stiff, add 1 egg white or (2) increase liquid by 1/4 c. Cookies will require less baking time and should be placed no lower than the middle rack of the oven. The finished cookies may be softer than with the original recipe.
				1 c. brown	2 t. Sweet'N Low ® Brown Sugar + 1/2 c. brown sugar (17)	
Sugar Pea See Snow Pea						

INGREDIENT	YIELD		SUBSTITUTION			Instructions
	Amount Market Form	Yield Equivalent	For Purpose of	Amount	Substitution	
Sugar Syrup See Syrups						
Summer Savory See Savory						
Sunchoke See Jerusalem Artichoke						
Superfine Sugar (Caster Sugar) See Sugar						
Sweet Marjoram See Marjoram						
Sweet Pepper See Bell Pepper						
Sweet Potato See also Potato, Vegetables	1 lb. 1 lb. 1 lb. 16 oz. can	3 medium 3 c. sliced 1 3/4 c. mashed 2 c.	All Recipes	1 lb.	1 lb. yam (1)	(1) They are different vegetables but can be used interchangeably.
Sweetbreads See also Meat	1 lb. beef	5 servings				
Swiss Chard See also Greens, Cooking	1 lb. fresh	4 c. cooked	Cooked Recipes	1 c. fresh leaves	1 c. fresh spinach (1)	(1) Spinach cooks more quickly than Swiss chard.

Cooking and Preparation Hints
* There are 2 main varieties of sweet potatoes that you will find in the market. One is pale-skinned and firm-fleshed. It has a mealy, dry texture when cooked and does not have a sweet taste. The other variety has a darker, copper-color skin and is often, but mistakenly, labeled "yam." Its flesh is bright, soft, moist and sweet.
* The pale variety of sweet potato can be baked, boiled, fried or mashed and can substitute for regular potatoes in most recipes.
* The darker-skinned variety can be used, when cooked and mashed, as a substitute for fats in baked goods. See Fats.
* Sweet potatoes do not keep well at home. Store them in a cool, dark area and use them within a week.
* Herbs and spices that complement sweet potatoes include cinnamon, nutmeg, allspice, mace, cardamom, cloves, lemon peel and orange peel.
* Before freezing sweet potatoes, cook, peel and slice or mash them. To prevent darkening, dip slices into lemon water for a few seconds. For mashed, add 1 T lemon juice to each 2 c. mashed potatoes.

INGREDIENT	YIELD			SUBSTITUTION		
	Amount Market Form	Yield Equivalent	For Purpose of	Amount	Substitution	Instructions
Swiss Chard continued	**Cooking and Preparation Hints** * The stalks require longer cooking than the leaves. Either cook them separately or begin cooking the stalks 5 minutes ahead of the leaves. * In their raw state, Swiss chard leaves taste like beet greens; cooked, they taste like spinach. The stalks taste similar to celery.				* Swiss chard will discolor when cooked in aluminum or iron pans. * Herbs and spices that complement Swiss chard include basil, nutmeg and oregano. * Swiss chard should be blanched before freezing; 2 minutes for the leaves and 3 to 4 minutes for the stalks. They will keep up to 12 months.	
Swiss Cheese See also Cheese	4 oz.	1 c. shredded	All Recipes	8 oz. 8 oz.	8 oz. Gruyère (1) 8 oz. Emmenthal	(1) Gruyère is firmer, creamier and more pungent than Swiss.
Swordfish See also Fish/Shellfish	**Cooking and Preparation Hints** * Herbs and spices that complement swordfish include basil, thyme, marjoram, garlic, black pepper, tarragon, parsley, dill weed, bay leaf, fennel seed, red pepper, oregano and rosemary.		All Recipes	1 lb.	1 lb. shark	
Syrups	**Cooking and Preparation Hints** * To make sugar syrup, or simple syrup, combine 1 part water and 2 parts sugar and boil for 5 minutes or until it becomes a heavy syrup. Sugar syrup is handy for mixing cocktails and prevents undissolved sugar granules from sticking to the glass. * When moistening cake with a syrup, heat the syrup first. Hot				syrup is more readily absorbed. The syrup should be drizzled gradually over the cake because it is absorbed slowly and can cause the cake to become soggy if added too quickly. * Unopened containers of syrup can be stored at room temperature. Once opened, they should be refrigerated to prevent mold. If crystals form, place the container in hot water.	

INGREDIENT	YIELD		For Purpose of	SUBSTITUTION		Instructions
	Amount Market Form	**Yield Equivalent**		**Amount**	**Substitution**	

INGREDIENT	Amount Market Form	Yield Equivalent	For Purpose of	Amount	Substitution	Instructions
Table Salt See Salt						
Taco Seasoning	1.25 oz. pkg.	4 T	Seasoning	1 T	1 t. instant minced onion + 1/2 t. chili powder + 1/2 t. salt + 1/4 t. garlic powder + 1/4 t. cornstarch + 1/4 t. ground cumin + 1/4 t. ground red pepper	
Tamari See Soy Sauce						
Tangerine See also Fruit	2 medium	1 c. sections	All Recipes	1 c. sections	1 c. orange sections	

Cooking and Preparation Hints
* While most citrus fruits are stored uncovered in the refrigerator, tangerines should be refrigerated in a plastic bag.

INGREDIENT	Amount Market Form	Yield Equivalent	For Purpose of	Amount	Substitution	Instructions
Tapioca	8 oz. quick-cooking	1 1/2 c.	Thickening	1 T quick-cooking 1 T quick-cooking 1 T quick-cooking	2 T pearl tapioca (1) 1 1/2 t. cornstarch (2) 1 T all purpose flour	(1) Soak for at least an hour before using. (2) Like tapioca, cornstarch is good for thickening very acid fruits because it doesn't lose its thickening power in the presence of acid as quickly as flour does. However, cornstarch produces a more rubbery quality than tapioca.

Cooking and Preparation Hints
* When a recipe calls for tapioca, it usually refers to quick-cooking tapioca.
* Pearl tapioca requires several hours of soaking before it can be used. If all of the water is not absorbed, the pearls are too old to use.
* A rule-of-thumb is to use 1 1/2 to 3 T quick-cooking tapioca per 2 c. liquid for thickening soup; 3 T tapioca per 2 c. liquid for puddings; and 1 1/2 to 3 T tapioca for the pie filling for an 8" to 9" pie.
* Stir tapioca while it is cooking, but be careful not to overstir when it's cooling because it will cause a sticky, gelatinous mixture. Tapioca continues to thicken as it cools.

INGREDIENT	Amount Market Form	Yield Equivalent	For Purpose of	Amount	Substitution	Instructions
Tarragon See also Herbs/Spices	1/2 oz. fresh 1 T fresh, chopped	1/3 c. 1 t. dried	All Recipes	1/2 c.		area packed in a container with distilled white vinegar. Rinse and pat dry before using. * Fresh tarragon can be frozen for up to 1 year. Wash and pat dry. Freeze on their stems in plastic freezer bags or containers.

Cooking and Preparation Hints
* Tarragon complements such foods as veal, lamb, chicken, mild white fish, crab, shrimp, egg dishes, soups, carrots, squash, onions, artichokes, beans, potatoes and beets.
* To extend its storage time, fresh tarragon can be kept in the refrigerator or in a cool

INGREDIENT	Amount Market Form	Yield Equivalent	For Purpose of	Amount	Substitution	Instructions
Tartar Sauce	8 oz. jar	1 c.	All Recipes	1/2 c.	6 T mayonnaise + 2 T chopped pickles or pickle relish	

A B C D E F G H I J K L M N O P Q R S T U V W X Y Z

INGREDIENT	YIELD			SUBSTITUTION			
	Amount Market Form	Yield Equivalent	For Purpose of	Amount	Substitution	Instructions	

INGREDIENT	Amount Market Form	Yield Equivalent	For Purpose of	Amount	Substitution	Instructions
Tautog (Blackfish) See also Fish/Shellfish	1 medium	2 - 4 lb.	All Recipes	1 lb.	1 lb. striped bass	
Tea	1 lb. leaves 1 lb. leaves 1 t. leaves 1 T leaves 1 1/2 oz. instant	6 1/3 c. 300 c. brewed 1 c. brewed 2 tea bags 64 c. brewed	**Cooking and Preparation Hints** * The rule-of-thumb for brewing tea is 1 t. leaves per c. of water. If you're making more than 4 c. and want a little stronger tea, add an extra 1 t. leaves "for the pot." * To insure the best flavor, start with cold water and heat it only until it begins to boil. Meanwhile rinse a teapot with hot water and add your tea leaves or tea bags. Pour the hot water into the pot and let the tea steep for 3 to 5 minutes. The metal extracts the bitter tannic acid from the tea.		* Tea that has been refrigerated for iced tea may become cloudy. You can remove the cloudiness by adding a small amount of boiling water to the tea. You can also make cloudless iced tea by using the cold water method. Put 8 to 10 tea bags in 1 qt. cold water and let it stand at room temperature or in the refrigerator for at least 6 hours. Remove the tea bags and serve over ice. * Tisane is the general term for herb teas. Tisanes are brewed the same way as tea. Herbs commonly used include camomile, tansy, mint, balm and hyssop. * Leftover tea can be frozen in ice cube trays for later use in iced tea.	
			* Use a glass or ceramic teapot for brewing instead of a metal one.			
Teff See also Grains	1 c.	3 1/2 c. cooked				
Thyme See also Herbs/Spices	1/2 oz. fresh 1 T fresh, chopped	1/3 c. leaves 1 t. dried	**Cooking and Preparation Hints** * Thyme complements such foods as beef, pork, veal, poultry, game, mild white fish, vegetable soups, tomato-based soups and sauces, eggs, cottage cheese, carrots, green beans, mushrooms, beets, onions, tomatoes, zucchini, eggplant,		peppers, potatoes, peas, squash, spinach and turnips. * Thyme sprigs can be frozen whole for up to 1 year in a plastic freezer bag or container. The tiny leaves come off easily while the sprigs are frozen.	
Tilapia See also Fish/Shellfish			All Recipes	1 lb.	1 lb. orange roughy	
Tilefish (Tile Bass) See Sea Bass						

INGREDIENT	Amount Market Form	Yield Equivalent	For Purpose of	Amount	Substitution	Instructions
Tisane (Herb Tea) See Tea						
Tofu (Bean Curd, Soybean Curd)	1 lb. firm tofu in liquid	2 c.				
Tomato See also Vegetables	1 lb. fresh 1 lb. fresh 16 oz. can 1 oz. sun-dried (dry pack)	3 medium 1 1/2 c. chopped 2 c. 10 tomatoes	All Recipes	16 oz. can 16 oz. can	2 1/2 c. chopped (1) 16 oz. can stewed tomatoes	(1) Simmer for 10 minutes.

Cooking and Preparation Hints
* Tofu is generally available in 3 forms based on firmness. Soft tofu is smooth and is good for use in dips, sauces, salad dressings, cream soups and puddings because it produces a creamy texture. Regular (or medium-firm) tofu has had its excess liquid removed and is formed in a block. It is especially suited for mashing or crumbling for sandwich fillings and salads. Firm (or hard) has been drained and compressed even further than the regular. It is the best choice for recipes that require slices, cubes or strips because it holds its shape better than the others.
* Fresh tofu comes packed in water and will keep in the refrigerator about a week. The water should be changed daily to maintain its freshness. Pasteurized tofu has a longer shelf life and does not require this special treatment.
* The easiest way to measure tofu is by the water displacement method. To measure 1 c. tofu, pour 3 c. cold water into a 4 c. measuring cup. Add enough tofu pieces to raise the water level to the 4 c. mark. Drain the tofu and proceed according to your recipe.
* If a recipe calls for marinating tofu for more than 1/2 hour, do so in the refrigerator to prevent bacterial growth.
* Freezing will give tofu a chewier, meaty texture.

Cooking and Preparation Hints
* Store tomatoes at room temperature but out of direct sunlight with the stem ends down.
* Putting tomatoes in a brown paper bag will promote the release of ethylene gas which will help ripen the tomatoes and intensify their flavor.
* To peel tomatoes easily, use 1 of the following methods: (1) Blanch the tomatoes in boiling water for 10 to 30 seconds, then plunge into cold water. The skins will slip off easily with a knife. You can blanch tomatoes several hours in advance and peel them later. (2) Hold the tomatoes on a fork over an open flame or high heat until the skin splits. Plunge into cold water, then peel. (3) To skin tomatoes without heating them, run the dull edge of a knife over their surface, using moderate pressure, until the skin is wrinkled. Then peel.
* The flesh under the peel will remain firm and fresh.
* To seed and juice a tomato, cut it in half — not through the core. Hold each half over a sieve set in a bowl and squeeze. Without too much pressure the juice and the gelatinous substance containing the seeds should be removed. If any remains, you can get it out with your fingers.
* The best tomatoes for cooking purposes are those with the most flesh, the least juice and the fewest seeds. The seeds can turn bitter when heated and affect the taste of your sauce or soup. Plum tomatoes are a good choice for cooked dishes.
* The longer tomatoes are cooked, the more acidic they can become. To counteract the acid taste, you can add sweet vegetables such as carrots and onions or a small amount of sugar, honey or cinnamon. If you plan to use canned tomatoes and are concerned about acidity, make sure that citric acid has not been added as a preservative.
* When substituting reconstituted sun-dried tomatoes for fresh, you will not need as many because the drying process concentrates flavor. You may have to add more liquid to the recipe.
* To stuff cherry tomatoes, put the filling into a plastic storage bag, cut off a corner of the bag and squeeze the filling into the tomatoes.
* Herbs and spices that complement tomatoes include basil, oregano, marjoram, black pepper, dill weed, thyme, garlic, bay leaf, celery seed, sesame seed, tarragon, chives and parsley.
* Tomatoes cannot be frozen raw and whole. They are best frozen as cooked sauce, puree or paste.

INGREDIENT	YIELD		SUBSTITUTION			
	Amount Market Form	Yield Equivalent	For Purpose of	Amount	Substitution	Instructions
Tomato Juice			All Recipes	1 c.	2 medium fresh tomatoes (1)	(1) Peel the tomatoes, then liquify them in a food processor.
			Cooked Recipes	1 c.	1/2 c. tomato sauce + 1/2 c. water	
				1 c.	1/4 c. tomato paste + 3/4 c. water + dash salt + dash sugar	
			Cooking and Preparation Hints * Tomato juice can be frozen for up to 10 months.			
Tomato Paste	6 oz. can 4 1/2 oz. tube	2/3 c. 7 1/2 T	All Recipes	1 T 1/2 c. 1/2 c.	1 T ketchup 1 c. tomato sauce (1) 1 c. tomato puree (1)	(1) Simmer until reduced to 1/2 c.
	Cooking and Preparation Hints * You can freeze leftover tomato paste in handy individual portions. Drop the paste in T quantities on a baking sheet lined with wax paper. Freeze. Peel off the wax paper and store the tomato paste balls in a plastic freezer bag.					
Tomato Puree	16 oz. can	2 c.	All Recipes	1 c. 1 c.	1 c. tomato sauce 1/2 c. tomato paste + 1/2 c. water	
Tomato Sauce	16 oz. can	2 c.	All Recipes	1 c. 1 c.	1 c. tomato puree (1) 1/2 c. tomato paste + 1/2 c. water (1)	(1) Tomato puree and paste are not seasoned. You may want to add some salt, pepper and spices.
	Cooking and Preparation Hints * An opened can of tomato sauce will keep for 5 days in the refrigerator.					
Tomato Soup			All Recipes	10 3/4 oz. can	1 c. tomato sauce + 1/4 c. water	
Tongue See also Meat	1 beef tongue 1 veal tongue 1 pork tongue 1 lamb tongue 1 lb. tongue	2 - 5 lb. 1/2 - 2 lb. 1 lb. 1/4 lb. 5 servings	**Cooking and Preparation Hints** * To facilitate peeling tongue, add 2 T vinegar to the cooking water and add 10 minutes to the cooking time. Peel the tongue while it is still hot.			
Treacle			All Recipes	1 c. dark (regular) 1 c. light (golden syrup)	1 c. light molasses 1 c. corn syrup	

INGREDIENT	YIELD		For Purpose of	Amount	SUBSTITUTION	Instructions
	Amount Market Form	Yield Equivalent			Substitution	
Triple Sec See also Spirits			All Recipes	1 c. 1 c.	1 c. curaçao 1 c. Cointreau	
Trout See also Fish/Shellfish	1 - 3 whole	1 serving				* Sea trout can be frozen for up to 3 months; lake trout and rainbow trout can be frozen for 4 to 6 months.
			Cooking and Preparation Hints * Herbs and spices that complement trout include parsley, peppercorns, bay leaf, tarragon, dill weed, chives and basil.			
Truffle			All Recipes	1 oz.	1 oz. shiitake mushrooms	
Tuna See also Fish/Shellfish	6 oz. can	1 c. drained				
			Cooking and Preparation Hints * Fresh tuna can be frozen for 4 to 6 months.			
Turbot See also Fish/Shellfish			All Recipes	1 lb. 1 lb. 1 lb.	1 lb. flounder 1 lb. sole 1 lb. halibut	
		Cooking and Preparation Hints * Herbs and spices that complement turbot include parsley, black pepper, white pepper, bay leaf, tarragon, dill weed, chives and basil.				
Turkey See also Poultry	1/2 - 1 lb. whole 1 1/4 lb. whole (prestuffed) 1 lb. boneless roast 1 lb. breast 1 lb. whole leg	1 serving 1 serving 3 - 4 servings 2 - 3 servings 2 - 3 servings	**Cooking and Preparation Hints** * When thawing a frozen turkey, it's important to keep it cold to prevent bacterial growth. To thaw in the refrigerator, simply place the turkey in its original wrap in a pan or tray. The rule-of-thumb for thawing time using this method is 5 hours per lb. That translates into 1 to 2 days for an 8 to 12 lb. turkey; 2 to 3 days for a 12 to 16 lb. turkey; 3 to 4 days for a 16 to 20 lb. turkey; and 4 to 5 days for a 20 to 24 lb. turkey. * A quick method for thawing a frozen turkey is in cold water. Immerse the turkey in its unopened wrapping in cold water, and change the water every 30 minutes. (If the original wrapping is torn, place the turkey in another plastic bag closed tightly and continue.) The thawing time using this method is 4 to 6 hours for an 8 to 12 lb. turkey; 6 to			9 hours for a 12 to 16 lb. turkey; 9 to 11 hours for a 16 to 20 lb. turkey; and 11 to 12 hours for a 20 to 24 lb. turkey. * Prestuffed turkeys should not be thawed before cooking. * A rule-of-thumb for stuffing a turkey is 3/4 c. stuffing for each 1 lb. of turkey. * If you use ground turkey as a replacement for other ground meats, use slightly more seasoning to compensate for the turkey's milder flavor. Also, the ground turkey may contain more moisture; if the turkey seems soft, decrease the liquid in the recipe by 1 to 2 T. * Herbs and spices that complement turkey include poultry seasoning, black pepper, paprika, garlic, sage and oregano.

INGREDIENT	YIELD			SUBSTITUTION			
	Amount Market Form	Yield Equivalent	For Purpose of	Amount	Substitution	Instructions	

Turmeric
See also Herbs/Spices

| | | | All Recipes | 1 t. | 1 t. dry mustard | * Turmeric complements such foods as chicken, duck, turkey, curried dishes, pickles, relishes and salad dressings. |

Cooking and Preparation Hints
* Turmeric is a powerful dye; so avoid contact with clothing.

Turnip
See also Vegetables

1 lb. fresh — 3 medium
1 lb. fresh — 2 c. cooked

Cooking and Preparation Hints
* Turnips can keep for months when stored in a cool, well-ventilated area, or they can be kept in the refrigerator tightly wrapped 2 to 4 weeks.
* To improve the taste of old turnips, blanch them for 5 minutes before cooking.

* You can reduce the smell of cooking turnips by adding 1 t. sugar to the cooking water.
* Herbs and spices that complement turnips include black pepper, red pepper, dry mustard, basil and caraway seeds.
* To freeze turnips, remove tops, wash and peel. Slice or cut into 1/2" cubes. Blanch for 2 minutes, chill and pack.

Turnip Greens
See also Greens,
Cooking

1 lb. fresh — 3 c. cooked
16 oz. can — 2 c.
10 oz. frozen — 1 1/2 c. cooked

Cooking and Preparation Hints
* Cut the greens from the turnips and store separately. Greens should be placed in a tightly sealed plastic bag and refrigerated. They will keep for up to 1 week.
* Turnip greens are too bitter and chewy to be used raw. To prepare them for

cooking, remove the tough stem and ribs.
* Turnip greens will discolor if cooked in aluminum or iron pans.
* Before freezing them, blanch turnip greens for 2 minutes. They will keep for up to 12 months.

Turtle Bean
See Black Bean

Tuscan Bean
See Cannellini Bean

INGREDIENT	YIELD		SUBSTITUTION			
	Amount / Market Form	Yield Equivalent	For Purpose of	Amount	Substitution	Instructions

A B C D E F G H I J K L M N O P Q R S T U V W X Y Z

INGREDIENT	YIELD		SUBSTITUTION			
	Amount Market Form	Yield Equivalent	For Purpose of	Amount	Substitution	Instructions
Vanilla	1" bean, scraped	1 t. extract	Flavoring	1 t. extract	1 t. imitation vanilla extract (1)	(1) Imitation vanilla can leave a bitter aftertaste and will become decidedly bitter when used in foods that are frozen. While pure vanilla extract loses strength when cooked at high temperatures, imitation vanilla retains its flavor. The term "fold" on a label of imitation vanilla refers to its strength compared to pure vanilla; a label that says the contents are 4 fold or 8 fold means that the imitation vanilla is 4 times and 8 times, respectively, the strength of pure vanilla. Adjust the substitution accordingly.
	1 t. extract	1/2 t. powdered				

Cooking and Preparation Hints
* A vanilla bean can be slit lengthwise and used whole or cut into pieces. If the bean is being added to a mixture that will be heated, add the bean as the mixture is cooling. Let it steep for several minutes, then remove. For a stronger flavor, you can scrape the small black seeds from the pod and add directly to the mixture.
* A vanilla bean can be reused several times — as long as it retains its aroma. After using the bean, wash it in cold water. Store it in a container of

* granulated or confectioners' sugar to prevent the bean from drying out. This also flavors the sugar which can then be used for any dish that would benefit from a vanilla flavor.
* Because vanilla extract can lose its flavor when cooked, add it to a cooked mixture after the mixture has been removed from the heat.
* You can make your own vanilla extract. Add 4 to 5 split vanilla beans to 2 c. brandy, bourbon or vodka and cover tightly. Let stand for at least 2 weeks.

INGREDIENT	Amount Market Form	Yield Equivalent	For Purpose of	Amount	Substitution	Instructions
Veal See also Meat	1 lb. chops	2 servings	All Recipes	4 oz. veal scallops	4 oz. chicken breast meat, pounded thin	* Veal will keep in the refrigerator 1 to 2 days for cuts of veal; 1 to 2 days for ground; and 3 to 4 days for leftover cooked veal.
	1 lb. round steak	3 1/2 servings		4 oz. veal scallops	4 oz. turkey scallops	
	1 lb. shoulder steak	2 1/2 servings				
	1 lb. boneless cutlet	4 servings				* Veal can be stored in the freezer 6 to 9 months for veal cuts; 3 to 4 months for ground; and 2 to 3 months for leftover cooked veal.
	1 lb. leg roast	3 servings				
	1 lb. boneless shoulder roast	3 servings				
	1 lb. rib roast	2 servings				
	1 lb. riblets	1 1/2 servings				
	1 lb. ground	4 servings				

Cooking and Preparation Hints
* The secret to preparing veal scallops without overcooking them is to sauté the slices very quickly at a high temperature. The high temperature seals the outer layer without overcooking the inside.
* Herbs and spices that complement veal include parsley, dill weed, basil, paprika, tarragon, chives and celery seed.

INGREDIENT	Amount Market Form	Yield Equivalent	For Purpose of	Amount	Substitution	Instructions
Vegetable Oil See Oil						
Vegetable Spaghetti See Squash						
Vegetables See also individual listings	1/2 lb. fresh	1 serving/main dish				
	1/3 lb. fresh	1 serving/side dish				
	1 lb. 13 oz. can	3 1/4 - 3 1/2 c.				
	1 lb. 4 oz. can	2 1/4 - 2 1/2 c.				
	16 - 17 oz. can	2 c.				
	12 oz. can	1 1/2 - 1 3/4 c.				
	8 - 8 1/2 oz. can	1 c.				
	10 oz. frozen	1 1/4 c.				

Cooking and Preparation Hints
* To maintain the bright color of green vegetables: (1) Do not overcook them. The acid that is the natural component of the vegetables will, upon lengthy cooking, turn the vegetable gray. (2) Never add acid ingredients such as wine, tomatoes, vinegar or lemon juice to green vegetables during cooking. (3) Cook green vegetables without a lid on the pan — at least for the first 3 minutes. Otherwise, the acids will condense on the underside of the lid and fall back onto the vegetables. (4) You can sprinkle a little salt over the vegetables at the beginning of cooking.

INGREDIENT	YIELD			SUBSTITUTION		
	Amount Market Form	Yield Equivalent	For Purpose of	Amount	Substitution	Instructions

Vegetables
continued

Cooking and Preparation Hints (continued)

(5) You can blanch the vegetables first, then "freeze" the color by immersing the vegetables in ice water. (6) Do not add baking soda to the cooking water. Besides destroying the nutritive value of the vegetables, it will make them mushy.

* To maintain the color of red and white vegetables, add about 1 t. acid such as vinegar or lemon juice for each 1 c. cooking water.
* Do not soak vegetables in water because they will lose their sugars and vitamins and minerals.
* Some general rules for cooking vegetables in the microwave: (1) Add 2 T liquid for every 2 c. sliced or chopped vegetables. Exceptions to this rule are to add 1/2 c. liquid per 1 lb. green beans; 1/4 c. liquid per 1 1/2 lb. potatoes; no additional liquid after washing cooking greens; and no liquid and no lid on the cooking dish for mushrooms, eggplant and tomatoes. (2) If you plan to add salt to the vegetables during cooking, add it to the cooking liquid instead of directly on the vegetables. Salt attracts more microwave energy than the vegetables do and can cause toughness. (3) Stir the vegetables once or twice during cooking. Otherwise, the vegetables on the outside of the dish will cook more quickly than the ones in the middle.

Instructions column:

* If you've oversalted your vegetables, try adding a little sugar and lemon juice.
* Canned vegetables can be stored for up to 2 years.
* With few exceptions, vegetables should be blanched before freezing. Blanching stops the maturation process, maintains the fresh taste of the vegetable, retains the nutritive value and heightens the color. Pay attention to blanching times. Underblanching stimulates enzyme activity and is worse than no blanching at all. Overblanching destroys color, nutritive value and flavor. After blanching, immerse vegetables in ice water to stop the cooking process. Drain vegetables well before freezing; excess moisture will develop into ice crystals and soften the texture of the vegetables. In general, vegetables can be frozen for up to 8 months.
* Frozen vegetables can be cooked without thawing. They will cook in 1/2 to 2/3 of the time required for fresh vegetables because they have been partially cooked during blanching.
* When canning vegetables, wipe the outside of the jar with white vinegar after it is sealed to prevent mold from forming due to a damp storage area.

Venison
See also
Game/Game
Birds

Cooking and Preparation Hints
* Trim all of the fat from venison before cooking because it has an unpleasant taste.
* A good seasoning for venison stew is 1 bay leaf, 3 juniper berries and 1 t. thyme leaves. Tie them up in cheesecloth and drop them into the liquid for cooking.
* Venison can be frozen for 6 to 12 months.

Vinegar

	Amount	Substitution
Acidulation Salad Dressing	1 t.	1 t. lemon or lime juice
	4 T	4 T lemon juice
	4 T red wine vinegar	3 T cider vinegar + 1 T red wine
Marinade	1 t.	1 t. lemon juice
	1 t.	1 t. wine

Cooking and Preparation Hints
* For general cooking purposes, you can use either wine or cider vinegar — although cider vinegar is preferable for baking. For salad dressings, you can use almost any kind of vinegar. For pickling, distilled white vinegar is the best; it's more acid and sour than cider vinegar and benefits both the color and taste of the foods being pickled.
* Vinegar and salt can be used to balance each other. The sourness of a sauce made with vinegar can be diminished with the addition of salt. And vinegar and salt can be added to a dish that has been oversalted to reduce the salty taste. For this purpose, use rice vinegar if you have it; it's half as acid as cider vinegar.

| INGREDIENT | YIELD | | | SUBSTITUTION | | | |
| | Amount Market Form | Yield Equivalent | For Purpose of | Amount | Substitution | | Instructions |

INGREDIENT	Amount Market Form / Yield Equivalent	For Purpose of / Amount	Substitution	Instructions
Vinegar continued	**Cooking and Preparation Hints cont.** * Vinegar can be used to reduce the odor when cooking strong foods such as cabbage and onions. * Fruit vinegars lose their aroma when heated; so use a wine vinegar instead and add some fruit or puree to your sauce at the end of cooking.		Another thing to remember when using fruit vinegars is that they don't go well with olive oil in salad dressings; use milder nut oils instead. * Unopened vinegar will keep indefinitely; once opened it will keep in a cool cupboard for about 6 months. Vinegar can be refrigerated for longer storage.	
Vitamin C See Ascorbic Acid				

INGREDIENT	YIELD		For Purpose of	SUBSTITUTION		
	Amount Market Form	Yield Equivalent		Amount	Substitution	Instructions

INGREDIENT	Amount Market Form	Yield Equivalent	For Purpose of	Amount	Substitution	Instructions
Walnut See also Nuts	2 lb. in shell 1 lb. in shell 1 lb. shelled 4 oz. shelled	1 lb. shelled 2 c. shelled 4 c. 1 c.			can then remove the whole nut intact. * The process of blanching and toasting walnuts has 2 positive effects. It removes the slightly bitter taste of the skins, and it protects the crispness of the nuts when they will be used in moist mixtures such as salad dressings, sauces or gelatins. Add walnuts to boiling water, remove from the heat and let stand for 2 minutes. Drain. Spread the nuts on a baking sheet and toast them at 375° for 10 minutes.	

Cooking and Preparation Hints
* To prevent shelled walnuts from becoming stale too quickly, store them in the refrigerator for up to 6 months or in the freezer for up to 1 year. Do not toast or salt them until you're ready to use them.
* If your recipe calls for whole walnuts instead of pieces, use the following method to shell them. Add 1 T salt to 2 qt. water. Add the walnuts and let them soak overnight. Drain them, pat them dry, and carefully separate the shell halves with a small screwdriver. You

INGREDIENT	Amount Market Form	Yield Equivalent	For Purpose of	Amount	Substitution	Instructions
Water					tion of ingredients. Add 2 T per 1/2 c. dressing. * At high altitudes water boils at a lower temperature than at sea level. When foods prepared in water are being cooked at a lower temperature, they require longer cooking times. When cooking at high altitudes, keep this in mind when preparing vegetables, eggs and braised meats.	

Cooking and Preparation Hints
* Water can be used as a substitute for milk in a variety of recipes, including cakes and scrambled eggs. In cakes it produces a delicate, moist texture. In scrambled eggs it produces a light and soft texture, in contrast to the coarse texture when made with milk. Add 2 to 5 t. water per egg.
* Water can be added to salad dressing to prevent the separa-

INGREDIENT	Amount Market Form	Yield Equivalent	For Purpose of	Amount	Substitution	Instructions
Water Chestnut See also Vegetables	8 oz. can	1 c. sliced	All Recipes	6 oz.	6 oz. jicama	

Cooking and Preparation Hints
* Water chestnuts can be eaten raw or cooked. To eat them raw, remove the brown skin with a potato peeler. For cooked water chestnuts, peel them after cooking.

INGREDIENT	Amount Market Form	Yield Equivalent	For Purpose of	Amount	Substitution	Instructions
Watercress			All Recipes	1 c. leaves	1 c. nasturtium leaves	

Cooking and Preparation Hints
* Watercress can be stored in the refrigerator for up to 5 days. It is best stored with the stems standing in a glass of cold water and covered with a plastic bag.

INGREDIENT	Amount Market Form	Yield Equivalent	For Purpose of	Amount	Substitution	Instructions
Watermelon See also Melon, Fruit	14 lb. whole	24 c. cubes				

Cooking and Preparation Hints
* There is no sure way to determine the ripeness of an uncut watermelon. The best way to insure you get ripe watermelon is to buy it in sections, looking for firm, red flesh.

Wax Bean See Green Bean

INGREDIENT	YIELD		SUBSTITUTION			
	Amount Market Form	Yield Equivalent	For Purpose of	Amount	Substitution	Instructions
Weakfish See Sea Trout						
Wheat Germ See also Grains	4 oz.	1 c.				**Cooking and Preparation Hints** * Wheat germ should be stored in the freezer in a sealed container to prevent it from turning rancid.
Wheat Meat See Seitan						
Wheat, Cracked See also Grains	1 c.	2 3/4 c. cooked	All Recipes	1 c.	1 c. bulgur (1)	(1) Bulgur is steamed before being cracked and has more of a toasted flavor than cracked wheat. **Cooking and Preparation Hints** * Store cracked wheat in a sealed container in the freezer to keep it from turning rancid.
White Bean See also Beans, Dried	1 lb. dried 1 c. dried	2 c. 3 c. cooked	All Recipes	1 c. cooked 1 c. cooked 1 c. cooked 1 c. cooked 1 c. cooked 1 c. cooked	1 c. cooked great nothern beans 1 c. cooked white kidney beans 1 c. cooked navy beans 1 c. cooked cannellini beans 1 c. cooked marrow beans 1 c. cooked pea beans	
White Flour (All Purpose Flour) See Flour						
Whitefish See also Fish/Shellfish			All Recipes	1 lb.	1 lb. salmon (1)	(1) Salmon has the same moist, fatty texture. **Cooking and Preparation Hints** * Whitefish can be frozen for 7 to 9 months.
Whiting (Silver Hake) See also Fish/Shellfish			All Recipes	1 lb. 1 lb. 1 lb.	1 lb. cod 1 lb. haddock 1 lb. pollock	**Cooking and Preparation Hints** * Herbs and spices that complement whiting include tarragon, garlic, black pepper, white pepper, red pepper, oregano, dill weed, bay leaf and fennel seed. * Whiting can be frozen for up to 4 months.
Whole Wheat Flour (Graham Flour) See Flour						

INGREDIENT	YIELD		SUBSTITUTION			
	Amount Market Form	Yield Equivalent	For Purpose of	Amount	Substitution	Instructions
Wild Leek See Ramp						
Wild Rice See also Grains	1 lb. 1 c.	3 c. 4 c. cooked			rice include marjoram, thyme, oregano, black pepper and chives. * Wild rice can be stored for up to 6 months.	
			Cooking and Preparation Hints * Wild rice should be cleaned by rinsing or soaking for a few minutes before using. * Herbs and spices that complement wild			
Wine See also Spirits			All Recipes	1 c. 1/2 c. rice wine(min) 1 T rice wine (min)	1 c. dealcoholized wine 1/2 c. sherry 1 T sake	(1) Cook until syrupy. (2) The vermouth will produce a sauce that is a little sweeter.
			Marinades	1/2 c.	+ 1 t. sugar (1) 1/4 c. vinegar + 1/4 c. water + 1 T sugar	
			Savory Recipes	1/2 c. dry white wine	1/2 c. dry vermouth (2)	
	Cooking and Preparation Hints * Cook only with wines that you would drink. The better tasting the wine, the better the cooked dish will taste. Avoid cooking wines, which are usually inferior wines and sometimes have additives such as salt. * 1 c. wine will reduce to 1/4 c. when cooked uncovered for about			10 minutes.	* A rule-of-thumb for adding wine to soup is 1/4 to 1/2 c. wine to 1 qt. soup. Wine intensifies the salty flavor of the soup; so be careful not to oversalt. * To prevent curdling, add the wine first to recipes that also call for milk, cream, eggs or butter.	
				1/2 c. dry white wine 1/2 c. dry white wine 1/2 c. red wine 1 c. champagne 1/2 c. fortefied wine	1/2 c. chicken broth 1/2 c. veal broth 1/2 c. beef broth 1 c. white wine 1/4 c. unsweetened fruit juice	
			Cooked Recipes Sweet Recipes	1/2 c. red wine 1/2 c. white wine	+ sugar to taste 1/2 c. unsweetened grape juice 1/2 c. apple juice	
Winter Savory See Savory						
Witloof See Belgian Endive						
Worcestershire Sauce			Flavoring	1 T	1 T soy sauce + 1/8 t. hot pepper sauce + 1/8 t. lemon juice + pinch sugar	**Cooking and Preparation Hints** * Worcestershire sauce will keep in the cupboard for up to 30 months either opened or unopened.

INGREDIENT	YIELD		SUBSTITUTION			
	Amount Market Form	Yield Equivalent	For Purpose of	Amount	Substitution	Instructions

A B C D E F G H I J K L M N O P Q R S T U V W **X** Y Z

INGREDIENT	YIELD			SUBSTITUTION			
	Amount Market Form	Yield Equivalent	For Purpose of	Amount	Substitution	Instructions	

INGREDIENT	Amount Market Form	Yield Equivalent	For Purpose of	Amount	Substitution	Instructions
Yam See also Vegetables			All Recipes	1 lb.	1 lb. sweet potatoes	many stores label the dark, orange-color variety of sweet potatoes as "yams." * Herbs and spices that complement yams include cinnamon, nutmeg, allspice, mace, cardamom, grated lemon peel, grated orange peel and ginger.

Cooking and Preparation Hints
* Although yams and sweet potatoes have some similarities and can be used interchangeably in cooking, they are entirely different vegetables. Yams grow on a tropical vine and can range in size from under 1 lb. to over 100 lb. To confuse matters further,

INGREDIENT	Amount Market Form	Yield Equivalent	For Purpose of	Amount	Substitution	Instructions
Yam Bean See Jicama						
Yeast	.6 oz. cake fresh 2 oz. cake fresh 1/4 oz. package dry	1/4 oz. package dry 3 (1/4 oz.) packages dry 2 1/2 t.	Baking	1 package active dry 1 package active dry	1 package quick-rising yeast 2 c. yeast starter mixture	(1) Quick-rising yeast is more finely ground and acts faster than regular dry yeast. It cuts rising time by about 50% and is ideal for use in food processors. The mixing process is different, however. The quick-rising yeast is combined directly with the dry ingredients in the recipe and is not first dissolved in warm water.

Cooking and Preparation Hints
* Compressed fresh yeast and active dry yeast can be used interchangeably. However, when dissolving compressed yeast, the water should be between 80° and 90°, and the water for the active dry should be between 105° and 115°.
* Compressed yeast should be moist, smooth and crumbly. It will keep in the refrigerator for 2 to 3 weeks and should be brought to room temperature before using.
* Dry yeast has a shelf life of 1 to 2 years. To test for freshness (to

"proof"), dissolve 1 T yeast in 1/4 c. warm water with 1 t. sugar. Let sit for 5 minutes. If the mixture becomes frothy and increases in volume, it is active.
* A rule-of-thumb for breadmaking is to add 1 package of active dry yeast for every 1 lb. (or 3 1/2 to 4 c.) of flour.
* When a recipe for yeast dough requires letting it rise until it has doubled in bulk, here is a test to determine if it has. Press 2 fingers into the center of the dough. If the indentations remain, the dough has doubled.

INGREDIENT	YIELD		SUBSTITUTION			Instructions
	Amount Market Form	Yield Equivalent	For Purpose of	Amount	Substitution	
Yogurt	8 oz.	1 c.	All Recipes	1 c. cow's milk yogurt	1 c. unflavored soy yogurt	
	3 c. nonfat	1 c. yogurt "cheese"	All Recipes/ Reducing Fat	1 c. plain	1 c. nonfat plain	
			Salad Dressings/Dips	1 c.	1 c. sour cream	

Cooking and Preparation Hints

* Beating will break down the texture of yogurt. When adding it to other ingredients, gently fold it in.
* Generally speaking, yogurt and heat don't mix. However, there are some steps you can take to achieve the results you want: (1) Have yogurt at room temperature before adding it to a hot mixture, then heat the mixture at a low temperature just until the yogurt is warm. (2) You can stabilize yogurt to withstand heat by adding a little cornstarch, arrowroot or flour dissolved in cold water.

* Yogurt cheese can be used as a substitute for cream cheese. To make it, line a colander with a double thickness of cheese cloth and set the colander over a bowl. Pour nonfat yogurt into the colander, cover with plastic wrap and refrigerate it overnight. The yogurt cheese will remain after the liquid has drained into the bowl. It will keep covered in the refrigerator for up to 1 week.
* Fruit-flavored yogurt can be frozen in its original container for up to 6 weeks. Thaw it in the refrigerator before using.

INGREDIENT	YIELD		SUBSTITUTION			Instructions
Youngberry See also Fruit			All Recipes	1 c.	1 c. blackberries	
				1 c.	1 c. boysenberries	
				1 c.	1 c. loganberries	
				1 c.	1 c. dewberries	

Cooking and Preparation Hints

* Youngberries can be frozen unsweetened, in a dry sugar pack using 3/4 c. sugar for each qt. of berries, or in a 40% to 50% syrup pack. For the syrup, dissolve 3 to 4 3/4 c. sugar in 4 c. water and refrigerate. Add 1/2 to 2/3 c. syrup to each pt. of fruit. Unsweetened young-berries can be frozen for 6 months; frozen in syrup, the berries will keep for up to 16 months.

Ingredient	Amount Market Form	Yield Equivalent	For Purpose of	Amount	Substitution	Instructions
Zucchini See also Squash, Vegetables	1 lb. fresh 1 medium	3 medium 1 c. sliced	All Recipes	1 c. sliced	1 c. sliced yellow summer squash	

Cooking and Preparation Hints
* A zucchini about 5" to 7" in length will have the best taste and texture.
* Zucchini can be refrigerated in a plastic bag for 5 to 7 days.
* Don't rinse them until you're ready to use them.
* Herbs and spices that complement zucchini include oregano, black pepper, basil and marjoram.

A B C D E F G H I J K L M N O P Q R S T U V W X Y Z

✄ ∞ ✗

COMMON EQUIVALENT MEASURES

As a general rule, use metal measuring cups for dry ingredients and glass measuring cups for liquids. To measure most dry and solid ingredients, spoon them into the cup rather than packing them down. Two notable exceptions are brown sugar and shortening, both of which should be packed.

Teaspoons

10 drops	=	1 dash
60 drops	=	1 t.
6 dashes	=	1 t.
1 pinch	=	1/8 t.
3 t.	=	1 T

Tablespoons

1 T	=	3 t.
1 T	=	1/2 fluid oz.
2 T	=	1 fluid oz.
4 T	=	1/4 c. or 2 oz.
16 T	=	1 c. or 8 oz.

Cups

1/8 c.	=	1 oz.
1/8 c.	=	2 T
3/8 c.	=	6 T
1/3 c.	=	5 T + 1 t.
1/2 c.	=	8 T or 4 oz.
1 c.	=	1/2 pt.
2 c.	=	1 pt. or 16 oz.
4 c.	=	1 qt.

Dry Volumes

2 c.	=	1 pt.
2 pt.	=	1 qt.
4 qt.	=	1 gallon
2 gallons	=	1 peck
4 pecks	=	1 bushel

Liquid Measures

1 oz.	=	2 T
1 oz.	=	1 pony
1 1/2 oz.	=	1 jigger
8 oz.	=	1 c.
2 c.	=	1 pt.
1 pt.	=	16 oz.
1 fifth	=	25.6 oz.
1 qt.	=	32 oz.
1 qt.	=	64 T
1 liter	=	33.8 oz.
1 liter	=	~4 1/4 c.
1 liter	=	67 T + 2 t.

Tab-1

OVEN TEMPERATURE EQUIVALENTS

Very Slow	=	250ºF - 300ºF
Slow	=	300ºF - 325ºF
Moderate	=	350ºF - 375ºF
Very Hot	=	450ºF - 475ºF
Extremely Hot	=	500ºF - 525ºF

300º F	=	149º C
325º F	=	163º C
350º F	=	177º C
375º F	=	191º C
400º F	=	205º C
425º F	=	218º C
450º F	=	232º C
500º F	=	260º C

The equations for converting Fahrenheit and Celsius (centigrade) temperatures are:

* Fahrenheit temperature minus 32 divided by 9 multiplied by 5 equals the Celsius temperature.

* Celsius temperature divided by 5 multiplied by 9 plus 32 equals the Fahrenheit temperature.

Tab-2

⚶⚶✄
BAKING PAN SUBSTITUTIONS

The size pan a recipe calls for is based on the amount of batter that is produced. Substituting a different size pan can cause problems with texture, rising and browning; but if changing the pan size is necessary, select a pan that is closest in area measurement and volume. You may need to adjust baking time and temperature. In general, larger, more shallow pans need a higher temperature; smaller, deeper pans need a lower temperature. If you use a cake recipe to make cupcakes, cut the baking time in half.

Pan Sizes	Approximate Volume
Square and Rectangular:	
8" x 8" x 1 1/2"	6 c.
8" x 8" x 2"	8 c.
9" x 9" x 1 1/2"	8 c.
9" x 9" x 2"	10 c.
11" x 7" x 2"	6 c.
13" x 9" x 2"	15 c.
8" x 4" x 2 1/2" loaf pan	4 c.
8 1/2" x 4 1/2" x 2 1/2" loaf pan	6 c.
9" x 5" x 3" loaf pan	8 c.
Round:	
8" x 1 1/2"	4 c.
8" x 2"	5 1/2 c.
9" x 1 1/2"	6 c.
9" x 2"	8 1/2 c.
10" x 2"	10 3/4 c.
9" x 3" bundt pan	9 c.
10" x 3 1/2" bundt pan	12 c.
9" x 3" tube pan	9 c.
9" x 3" springform pan	10 c.
1 3/4" x 3/4" mini muffin cup	1/8 c.
2 3/4" x 1 1/8" muffin cup	1/4 c.
2 3/4" x 1 3/8" muffin cup	1/2 c.
3" x 1 1/4" giant muffin cup	5/8 c.
8" x 1 1/4" pie plate	3 c. level or 4 1/2 c. mounded
9" x 1 1/2" pie plate	4 c. level or 6 c. mounded
9" x 2" deep dish pie plate	6 c.

Tab-3

༄ ∞ ✖

BIBLIOGRAPHY

BOOKS

Bellerson, Karen J. The Complete & Up-To-Date Fat Book. Avery Publishing Group, 1991.

American Home Economics Association. Handbook of Food Preparation. American Home Economics Association, 1980.

Bailey, Adrian, Elisabeth Lambert Ortiz, and Helena Radecka. The Book of Ingredients. Mermaid Books, 1980.

Bear, Marina, and John Bear. How To Repair Food. Ten Speed Press, 1987.

Beard, James A. James Beard's Fish Cookery. Little, Brown and Company, 1954.

Bloch, Barbara. If It Doesn't Pan Out: How To Cope With Cooking Disasters. Dembner Books, 1981.

Bray, Elizabeth H., Anne T. Buttrick, Mary H. Thomsen, and the New England Aquarium Council. A Feast of Fishes. The Globe Pequot Press, 1988.

Brown, Sarah, ed. Vegetarian Cooking. The Reader's Digest Association, Inc., 1991.

Byrne, Jane and Michelle Duggan, eds. The Complete Family Cookbook. Curtin Publications, Inc., 1970.

Child, Julia. The Way To Cook. Alfred A. Knopf, 1989.

Claiborne, Craig. The New York Times Food Encyclopedia. New York Times Co., 1985.

Eliason, Karine, Nevada Harward, and Madeline Westover. Complete Make-A-Mix Cookbook. HP Books, 1991.

Ellis, Merle. Cutting-Up In The Kitchen. Chronicle Books, 1975.

Epstein, Becky Sue and Hilary Dole Klein. Substituting Ingredients: A Cooking Reference Book. The East Woods Press, 1986.

Good Cook's Handbook. Lane Publishing Co., 1986.

Hagman, Bette. The Gluten-Free Gourmet: Living Well Without Wheat. Henry Holt and Company, 1990.

Herbst, Sharon Tyler. Food Lover's Companion. Barron's Educational Series, Inc., 1990.

Jones, Bridget. Does It Freeze? Wardlock Ltd., 1991.

Khoee, Debbie. 1,000 Cooking Substitutions. Global Trade Co., 1990.

Leggatt, Jenny. Cooking With Flowers. Ballantine Books, 1987.

Marquis, Vivienne and Patricia Haskell. The Cheese Book. Simon and Schuster, 1964.

McCully, Helen. Nobody Ever Tells You These Things. Holt, Rinehart & Winston, 1967.

McGee, Harold. On Food and Cooking: The Science and Lore Of The Kitchen. Charles Scribner's Sons, 1984.

McGruter, Patricia Gaddis. The Great American Tofu Cookbook. Autumn Press, Inc., 1979.

Moore, Marilyn M. The Wooden Spoon Bread Book. Atlantic Monthly Press, 1987.

Nelson, Meryl. This For That: A Treasury of Savvy Substitutions For The Creative Cook. R&E Publishers, 1991.

Null, Gary. The New Vegetarian Cookbook. Collier Books, 1980.

Rehberg, Linda and Lois Conway. Bread Machine Magic. St. Martin's Press, 1992.

Rombauer, Irma S. and Marion Rombauer Becker. Joy Of Cooking. The Bobbs-Merrill Company, Inc., 1975.

Romweber, Marilyn. Under The Mushroom. Evergreen Press, 1977.

Rose, Gloria. Enjoying Good Health. Herm Barr Publishing Company, 1987.

Schneider, Elizabeth. Uncommon Fruits and Vegetables: A Common Sense Guide. Harper & Row, 1986.

Smith, Leona Woodring. The Forgotten Art of Flower Cookery. Pelican Publishing Company, 1985.

Thorne-Thomsen, Kathleen and Linda Brownridge. Why The Cake Won't Rise And The Jelly Won't Set: A Complete Guide To Avoiding Kitchen Failures. A&W Publishers, Inc., 1979.

Worth, Helen. Cooking Without Recipes. The Bobbs-Merrill Company, Inc., 1959.

MAGAZINES AND NEWSPAPERS

Better Homes and Gardens. August 1993, 132.

Belsinger, Susan and Carolyn Dille. "Peppercorns." The Herb Companion, December 1992/January 1993, 42.

Bon Appetit. February 1977 - July 1993.

Cooking Light. August 1991 - July 1993.

Cook's Illustrated. Charter Issue - September/October 1993.

Gourmet. February 1975 - July 1993.

Greene, Ellen R. "101 Terrific Kitchen Tips and Timesavers." Woman's Day, February 1, 1992, 88.

Kourebanas, Maria. "Baker's Choice." Eating Well, December 1992, 16.

Kummer, Corby. "Tomatoes." Martha Stewart Living. June and July 1992.

Los Angeles Daily News. October 24, 1991 - November 19, 1992.

Los Angeles Times. October 6, 1977 - June 17, 1993.

Vegetarian Gourmet. Spring 1992 - Winter 1992.

FOOD PRODUCERS, MANUFACTURERS AND ASSOCIATIONS

Almond Board of California
American Egg Board
American Home Food Products, Inc.
American Institute of Baking
American Lamb Council
American Pop Corn Company
American Spice Trade Association
Arrowhead Mills, Inc.
Baker's/Kraft General Foods
Beatrice/Hunt-Wesson, Inc.
Benckiser Consumer Products
Best Foods/CPC International Inc.
The Birkett Mills
Blue Diamond Growers
Calavo Growers of California
California Apricot Advisory Board
California Artichoke Advisory Board
California Avocado Commission
California Beef Council
California Pistachio Commission
California Prune Board
California Raisin Advisory Board
California Strawberry Advisory Board
Calorie Control Council
Carnation Company
Carrageenan Marketing Corp.
Cherry Marketing Institute, Inc.
Culinary Arts Institute
Cumberland Packing Corporation
Del Monte Foods
The Dutch Dairy Bureau
Florida Department of Citrus
Food Marketing Institute
Fresh Garlic Association
Frieda's Finest/Produce Specialties, Inc.
General Mills, Inc.
Goody's Manufacturing Corporation
Handy Soft Shell Crabs
Heinz Consumer Test Kitchens
Hershey Foods Corporation

Ingro, Inc.
International Apple Institute
Knudsen
McCormick & Company, Inc. McCormick/Schilling Division
McIlhenny Company
Nabisco Brands Inc.
National Fisheries Institute
National Livestock and Meat Board
National Pecan Marketing Council
National Pork Producers Council/National Pork Board
National Turkey Federation
Nestle USA Inc./Nestle Chocolate & Confection Company
North American Blueberry Council
The NutraSweet Company
Pel-Freez Rabbit Meat, Inc.
PET Incorporated
The Pillsbury Company
The Pineapple Growers Association of Hawaii
The Popcorn Institute
The Potato Board
The Quaker Oats Company
Shields Date Gardens
Specialty Brands Inc.
Sun-Diamond Growers of California
TAD Enterprises
Try-Foods International, Inc.
United States Department of Agriculture
University of Illinois at Urbana-Champaign/The Illinois Cooperative Extension Service
U.S. Mills
The Vegetarian Resource Group
The Vinegar Institute
Walnut Marketing Board
Washington Apple Commission
Washington State Fruit Commission
White Consolidated Industries, Inc.
Wilton Enterprises, Inc.

INDEX

SAVE 25¢
ON YOUR NEXT PURCHASE OF SWEET 'N LOW®
GRANULATED SUGAR SUBSTITUTE
(EXCEPT 50 COUNT)

Retailer: This coupon will be redeemed for face value plus 8¢ handling charges towards your purchase of Sweet 'N Low® Brand Granulated Sugar Substitute (bulk or packets) provided terms of offer have been complied with. Any other application of this coupon constitutes fraud. Invoices proving sufficient stock to cover coupons must be made available upon request. This offer void in any state or locality prohibiting licensing or regulating these coupons. Mail coupons to: Cumberland Packing Corp., Lee's Marketing Services, Dept 1750, 11500 Rojas, El Paso, TX 79936. Cash value 1/20th of 1¢.

5 44800 50125 6

44800 410 026

SAVE 25¢
ON YOUR NEXT PURCHASE OF BUTTER BUDS®
BUTTER FLAVORED MIX
SPRINKLES OR POWDERED MIX

Retailer: This coupon will be redeemed for face value plus 8¢ handling charges towards your purchase of Butter Buds® Sprinkles or Powdered Mix provided terms of offer have been complied with. Any other application of this coupon constitutes fraud. Invoices proving sufficient stock to cover coupons must be made available upon request. This offer void in any state or locality prohibiting licensing or regulating these coupons. Mail coupons to: Cumberland Packing Corp., Lee's Marketing Services, Dept 1750, 11500 Rojas, El Paso, TX 79936. Cash value 1/20th of 1¢.

5 44800 51125 5

44800 420 028

SAVE 25¢
ON YOUR NEXT PURCHASE OF NU-SALT®
SALT SUBSTITUTE

Retailer: This coupon will be redeemed for face value plus 8¢ handling charges towards your purchase of Nu-Salt® Salt Substitute provided terms of offer have been complied with. Any other application of this coupon constitutes fraud. Invoices proving sufficient stock to cover coupons must be made available upon request. This offer void in any state or locality prohibiting licensing or regulating these coupons. Mail coupons to: Cumberland Packing Corp., Lee's Marketing Services, Dept 1750, 11500 Rojas, El Paso, TX 79936. Cash value 1/20th of 1¢.

5 44800 50225 3

44800 450 027

VISA

MasterCard

ORDER FORM
COOK IT RIGHT!

POSTAL ORDERS: Sandcastle Publishing, Customer Service—Order Dept.
P.O. Box 3070, South Pasadena, CA 91031-6070 U.S.A.

PHONE/FAX MASTERCARD/VISA ORDERS: PH: (800) 891-4204 (213) 255-3616
Please fill out form and have your card # and expiration date available.

DISTRIBUTION TO THE BOOKTRADE: PH: (800) 891-4204 (213) 255-3616
Competitive discount schedule, terms & conditions. Will work from official
store purchase orders. STOP orders OK. If CA business, resale number must
accompany order.

**Please send the following books. I understand that I may return any books
in unmarked and resalable condition for a full refund—for any reason, no
questions asked within 7 days of receipt of the book.**

Number of Books Ordered: _____

Cost of Books: $22.95 x   _____   =   _____

Sales Tax: =   _____
Please add 8.25% sales tax if you live in California or Tennessee.
($1.89 for one book, $3.78 for two, etc.)

Packaging/Shipping: $4.25 for first book plus $1.38/add'l book =   _____

TOTAL   =   _____

Please send my order to:

_____
Name

_____
Address

_____
City   State   Zip Code

_____
Daytime Phone Number with area code first

Thank you